Cyber-Risk and Youth

Cyber-risks are moving targets and societal responses to combat cyber-victimization are often met by the distrust of young people. Drawing on original research, this book explores how young people define, perceive, and experience cyber-risks, how they respond to both the messages they are receiving from society regarding their safety online, and the various strategies and practices employed by society in regulating their online access and activities. This book complements existing quantitative examinations of cyberbullying assessing its extent and frequency, but also aims to critique and extend knowledge of how cyber-risks such as cyberbullying are perceived and responded to.

Following a discussion of their methodology and their experiences of conducting research with teens, the authors discuss the social network services that teens are using and what they find appealing about them, and address teens' experiences with and views towards parental and school-based surveillance. The authors then turn directly to areas of concern expressed by their participants, such as relational aggression, cyber-hacking, privacy, and privacy management, as well as sexting. The authors conclude by making recommendations for policy makers, educators and teens – not only by drawing from their own theoretical and sociological interpretations of their findings, but also from the responses and recommendations given by their participants about going online and tackling cyber-risk.

One of the first texts to explore how young people respond to attempts to regulate online activity, this book will be key reading for those involved in research and study surrounding youth crime, cybercrime, youth culture, media and crime, and victimology – and will inform those interested in addressing youth safety online how to best approach what is often perceived as a sensitive and volatile social problem.

Michael Adorjan is an Associate Professor in the Department of Sociology at the University of Calgary, Canada, and a Fellow with the Centre for Criminology, University of Hong Kong, China.

Rosemary Ricciardelli is a Professor and the Coordinator of Criminology in the Department of Sociology at Memorial University, Newfoundland, Canada. She is an Associate Director of the Canadian Institute for Public Safety Research and Treatment (CIPSRT), where she leads the community and institutional corrections research sector, and a Senior Research Fellow with Correctional Services Canada.

Routledge Studies in Crime and Society

For more information about this series, please visit: www.routledge.com/
Routledge-Studies-in-Crime-and-Society/book-series/RSCS

Cyber-Risk and Youth

Digital Citizenship, Privacy, and
Surveillance

Michael Adorjan and
Rosemary Ricciardelli

Routledge
Taylor & Francis Group

LONDON AND NEW YORK

First published 2019
by Routledge
2 Park Square, Milton Park, Abingdon, Oxon OX14 4RN

and by Routledge
52 Vanderbilt Avenue, New York, NY 10017, USA

First issued in paperback 2020

Routledge is an imprint of the Taylor & Francis Group, an informa business

British Library Cataloguing-in-Publication Data
A catalogue record for this book is available from the British Library

Library of Congress Cataloging-in-Publication Data
Names: Adorjan, Michael, author. | Ricciardelli, Rosemary, author.
Title: Cyber-risk and youth : digital citizenship, privacy and
surveillance / Michael Adorjan and Rosemary Ricciardelli.
Description: Abingdon, Oxon ; New York, NY : Routledge, 2019. |
Includes bibliographical references and index.
Identifiers: LCCN 2018022494| ISBN 9781138067387 (hardback) |
ISBN 9781315158686 (ebook)
Subjects: LCSH: Internet and youth. | Privacy, Right of. |
Computer crimes–Prevention.
Classification: LCC HQ799.9.I58 A296 2019 | DDC
004.67/8083–dc23
LC record available at https://lccn.loc.gov/2018022494

ISBN 13: 978-0-367-66320-9 (pbk)
ISBN 13: 978-1-138-06738-7 (hbk)

Typeset in Bembo
by Wearset Ltd, Boldon, Tyne and Wear

For April, Ashima, and Logan – M. Adorjan
For Paige, Johnathan, Nathaniel, Sadie, and Stephen – R. Ricciardelli

Contents

About the authors

Michael Adorjan is an Associate Professor in the Department of Sociology at the University of Calgary, Canada, and a Fellow with the Centre for Criminology, University of Hong Kong, China. His research and teaching focus on youth crime and cyber-risk, fear of crime, and perceptions of police. With co-author Wing Hong (Eric) Chui, he published *Responding to Youth Crime in Hong Kong: Penal Elitism, Legitimacy and Citizenship (2014, Routledge)*, and with Rose Ricciardelli he published *Engaging with Ethics in International Criminological Research (2016, Routledge)*. His research also appears in *British Journal of Criminology, Theoretical Criminology, The Sociological Quarterly, Journal of Contemporary Ethnography*, and *The Prison Journal*.

Rosemary Ricciardelli is a Professor and the Coordinator of Criminology in the Department of Sociology at Memorial University, Newfoundland, Canada. She is an Associate Director of the Canadian Institute for Public Safety Research and Treatment (CIPSRT), where she leads the community and institutional corrections research sector, and a Senior Research Fellow with Correctional Services Canada. She has published over 65 journal articles, 25 chapters, and over 150 presentations and invited talks, all in a range of academic journals including *British Journal of Criminology, Sex Roles* and *Theoretical Criminology*. She has published four books, her first entitled *Surviving Incarceration: Inside Canadian Prisons* (2014, Wilfrid Laurier University Press), explores the realities of penal living for federally incarcerated men in Canada. Other books include *Violence, Sex Offenders, and Corrections*(with Dale Spencer (2017, Routledge). She has also published three edited collections, including *Engaging with Ethics in International Criminological Research* with Michael Adorjan (2016, Routledge). Her primary research interests include evolving conceptualizations of masculinity, and experiences and issues within different facets of the criminal justice system both on and offline.

Acknowledgments

The original research in this book, conducted by Adorjan and Ricciardelli, was funded by a grant from the Social Sciences and Humanities Research Council of Canada, grant no. 430–2015–00157.

Sections of this book draw from original research articles:

Michael Adorjan and Rosemary Ricciardelli. "A new privacy paradox? Youth agentic practices of privacy management despite 'nothing to hide' online," forthcoming in *Canadian Review of Sociology*, published by Wiley. Content from this article is reproduced in Chapter 6, "Privacy mindsets," pp. 91, 92, 94, 95, 97, 98, 102-106.

Michael Adorjan and Rosemary Ricciardelli. "Youth responses to the surveillance school: The bifurcation of antagonism and confidence in surveillance among teenaged students," forthcoming in *Young*, published by Sage. Content from this article is reproduced in Chapter 4, "Youth attitudes and experiences towards parental and school surveillance," pp. 50–53, 59–61, 63–65.

Rosemary Ricciardelli and Michael Adorjan. "If a girl's photo gets sent around, that's a way bigger deal than if a guy's photo gets sent around: Gender, sexting, and the teenage years," forthcoming in *Journal of Gender Studies*, published by Taylor & Francis. Content from this article is reproduced in Chapter 7, "Gender, sexting, and the teenaged years," pp. 111–128.

Chapter 1

Introduction

The internet and advances in communications technology over the last ten years, specifically in terms of broadband connections coupled with the rise of social network sites (SNS) and social media, has amplified not only opportunities for youth regarding expressions of identity, intimacy, and sociability, but also risks related to privacy, abuse, and misunderstandings in their lived experiences (Livingstone, 2008). Youth are bombarded by messages from parents, peers, law enforcement, teachers, the media, and the government regarding how to manage web-based risks when online. Often encouraged to self-monitor, youth are to be responsible (and are often held accountable) for their online actions, with the directive of teaching youth to avoid harm from cyberbullying, sending nudes, or "sexting," and other forms of risk (including from online sexual predators) (boyd, 2014; Karaian, 2013). This is especially true for female adolescents, whose risk potential is often thought to be higher than that of their male peers (Bailey & Steeves, 2015). Cyberspace itself presents a virtually "limitless victimization risk" (Hinduja & Patchin, 2009: 24).

The internet has engendered an electronic panopticon (Haggerty, 2006; see below for details regarding the theoretical frameworks of this book) – an omnipresent yet often invisible sense of surveillance online to which people orient themselves to (cf. Foucault, 1977). Calvert (2000: 94), reflecting on the online world, posits that "we want to be watched, we expect to be watched, and concomitantly, we expect to be able to watch others." Calvert's words are undeniably reflected in the societal messages directed to young digital natives (Livingstone, 2003: 148; Prensky, 2001), which place great emphasis on young peoples' self-responsibilization. Here self-responsibilization refers to the ways youth receive and react to warnings about potential harms online, and their moral steering. Although these messages come from many sources, scholars recognize that governance, beyond the purview of centralized states, is distributed across civil society, including NGOs, families, and schools (Chhotray & Stoker, 2009; Yar, 2013). Governments have minimal ability to govern online worlds that are often decentralized, crossing boundaries and borders beyond direct control of governments (Crawford, 2006;

Rose, 1996a). As such, responsibility for the management of populations is downloaded to particular communities and organizations. Schools and parents (similarly challenged as big government) are themselves responsibilized for the ongoing moral training of youth by, for example, patterns of monitoring and surveillance that align with state interests (Kelly & Caputo, 2011).

A number of governmental initiatives in Canada, for instance, have targeted youth with messages about online risk and potential harm – some in response to tragedies such as the death by suicide of both Rehtaeh Parsons in Nova Scotia and Amanda Todd in British Columbia. Researchers have highlighted how female youth in Canada, largely exclusively, are encouraged to self-regulate their use of the internet, especially regarding the distribution of sexual self-images, through governmentally approved, yet controversial, campaigns (e.g., Karaian, 2013). Comparable campaigns and media discourses are found in the United States and the United Kingdom, which also aim to responsibilize mainly female adolescents regarding their production and distribution of sexual images online (Marker, 2011; Pedersen, 2013). Apart from governmental sources, adolescents receive many messages from parents, teachers, police, and media about how to retain privacy, manage online risks, and about the negative potential of anonymity. However, scholars have revealed a disjunction between what teens define as risk and "safety."

Specifically, some adolescents define privacy online in terms that are not related to their visibility to strangers (i.e., their safety) but instead to "inappropriate others," including parents, teachers and those in "direct authority to them" (i.e., the risk of "getting in trouble"; Pedersen, 2013: 407). Further, students often express doubts over the ability for school officials (and even the police, see Adorjan, Ricciardelli, & Spencer, 2017) to help in situations of cyberbullying, and some are also reluctant to inform parents for fear of losing their online privileges (Agatston, Kowalski, & Limber, 2007: S60; Q. Li, 2010: 382). Students use texting, multiple Facebook accounts, and other techniques to hide their activities online from distrusted teachers and parents, making cyber-risk more difficult to detect by school officials, parents, and other members of the community, and masking potential signs of mental health problems that may contribute to depression or suicidal ideations (Allen, 2012; boyd, 2014; see also Chapter 5 for a more detailed discussion of relational aggression among teens).

Exacerbating this maligned view of the wider community, the advice given to students to mitigate the risk of harm online is often a variant of "don't talk to strangers": they are told they are responsible for protecting their private information and passwords and never to disclose this information to anyone on or offline (boyd, 2014; Hinduja & Patchin, 2009: 151). This self-responsibilization ethos, culled from broader late modern ideology and state governance (Rose, 1996b), is revealed by some interview-based research on cyberbullying, where students have expressed that "no one cares" about cyber-victims, and that the message from communities remains "deal with it

yourself" (Q. Li, 2010: 384). Here, self-responsibilization is tethered to resig-
nation and distrust, further isolating youth who may be dealing with complex
emotional violations in a very public space. The result being a form of victim
blaming that penetrates in youths' public and private lives because of the
online sphere in which it begins. Said another way, the messages youth
receive regarding online risks, when internalized, result in the perpetuation of
inequalities related especially to gender. For example, recent research indicates that teen and young adult females are more likely than males to apply
privacy features (e.g., restricting access to their profiles) on SNS (Hoy &
Milne, 2010; Patchin & Hinduja, 2010; Sheehan, 1999). This likely reflects
the internalization of cyber-safety messages that subtly imply online realities
are thought to be more disparaging for females in comparison to males and,
perhaps as an unintentional consequence, reinforce gender stereotypes about
expected male versus female qualities and persons (see Connell, 2005). Nonetheless, governmental resources to address problems like cyberstalking and
cyberbullying, including websites that provide resources and services, may
ironically be viewed with distrust by youth because they are provided
through the same medium through which victimization is experienced (Spitzberg & Hoobler, 2002: 87). Little is currently known about how such initiatives, as well as parental and school-based efforts at monitoring and managing
cyber-risk, are being perceived and responded to by youth.

Exploring the experiences of youth and cyber-risk in Canada

This book seeks to contribute to emerging knowledge regarding how youth
experience cyber-risks in their own words. It complements existing quantitative examinations of cyberbullying assessing its extent and frequency, but
also aims to critique and extend knowledge of how cyber-risks such as cyberbullying are perceived and responded to. This is particularly important since,
as we examine in Chapter 5 regarding relational aggression, cyberbullying as a
concept promoted through media, cyber-safety programs, and so forth may
not gel with how youth are perceiving interpersonal conflict (see also Walton,
2005). In Canada, research has yet to explore how youth are interpreting per-
petually evolving cyber-risks (though see Bailey & Steeves, 2015), and how
they are receiving and potentially resisting societal messages about risk management. Youth are not passive consumers nor receivers of content and ideology; they have agency (i.e., the ability to make decisions on their own
accord) and as such are active digital citizens who are "much more active and
social with their use of media," especially online (Cassidy, Faucher, &
Jackson, 2013: 594; see also Chu, 2010). Echoing Haggerty's (2006) observation that models of contemporary surveillance, often presuming top–down
forms of governance, exclude the "actual experiences of people being subjected to different governmental regimes," and that "modestly realist projects"

are required "that analyze the politics of surveillance on the experiences of the subjects of surveillance" (42), we examine Canadian youth perceptions towards cyber-risk as well as strategies to govern youth conduct online. Our study responds to those who suggest that scholarship on governance and "governmentality" – the examination of the efforts by various sectors of society to govern conduct – would greatly benefit from grounded empirical research (Haggerty, 2006; T. Li, 2007; Nadesan, 2008).

Researchers looking at the risks facing youth today usually center on particular areas, such as cyberbullying (including "flaming" or hostile and aggressive interactions, harassment and cyberstalking; Hinduja & Patchin, 2009; Q. Li, 2010), sexting (i.e., sending or receiving sexual messages online; Karaian, 2013), or radicalization through "narrowcasting" (targeted messaging) of extremist ideological content to youth (Lombard, 2007). Yet, recognizing that cyber-risks are moving targets, we seek to ask youth what is most significant to them, if anything, regarding online risk, rather than explore specific areas of risk and crime per se. Thus, our focus is on the areas and forms of cyber-risk that youth report as most pertinent to them, expressed in their own words. The book largely centers on teens' experiences within networked publics, defined as spaces "restructured by network technologies" (boyd, 2014: 8). Specifically, we are referring to spaces that are simultaneously "constructed through networked technologies and … the imagined community that emerges as a result of the intersection of people, technology and practice" (boyd, 2014: 8). An example of such a space is any social media or network site, which, throughout this book, we refer to as a social network site. Today, SNS such as Facebook, Twitter, and Instagram are accessed by teens using a variety of devices, primarily their (smart) cell phones, iPads, and other handheld technologies, and not just through their respective websites (the likely etymological origin of the term social network site). Despite the different ways SNS can be accessed, boyd and Ellison's (2007) prescient definition of SNS (originally capturing all "web-based services") remains applicable and relevant today. They argue that SNS enable users to:

> (1) construct a public or semi-public profile within a bounded system, (2) articulate a list of other users with whom they share a connection, and (3) view and traverse their list of connections and those made by others within the system.
>
> (boyd & Ellison, 2007: 211)

boyd (2014) further describes four properties of SNS highly relevant to how teens use these platforms as well as the warnings they usually receive about inherent risks: persistence (i.e., the durability of online content); visibility (i.e.., one's "digital footprint" which becomes visible to the projected audience); spreadability (i.e., the ease through which content is easily shared); and searchability (i.e., the accessibility of content through internet searches, which are relatively easy to find given the other three components). boyd argues that, taken together, these features enable users to articulate and make visible their social networks which, acting together, engender both the risks and opportunities discussed in this book.

Within SNS spaces, existing research, especially in the Canadian context, has generated significant and crucial knowledge on select areas such as cyberbullying (e.g., the extent and severity in schools; see Q. Li, 2010), yet insufficiently captures what online risks are most salient to youth from their own perspectives and in their own words, or how youth respond to these risks. Moreover, the ways in which youth appropriate and have agency to actively resist directives from parents, police, educators, and the wider community to manage online risks and ameliorate harm is an under-explored area of cyber-risk research. Accordingly, we examine the perceptions and responses youth hold towards cyber-risks as a function of "the interaction among its components," including peers, teachers, administrators, and police, "rather than simply focusing on any group in isolation" (Q. Li, 2010: 376). Through focus group discussions with teens aged 13–19 (see Chapter 2 for methodological details), we look to fulfil three interrelated objectives in this book. We ask (1) How youth define, perceive, and experience cyber-risks and which cyber-risks are most salient in their lived experiences (Chapters 3, 5, and 7); (2) How youth are responding to these cyber-risks (especially the strategies they employ to safeguard their privacy; Chapters 3 and 6); and (3) How youth are responding to the various messages, strategies, and practices they receive from society regarding their safety online. Here our focus is on messages from parents and educators, as well as responses to parental and school-based monitoring and surveillance (Chapters 4 and 8).

Chapter overview

This book is structured in the following way. Following this introduction, in Chapter 2 we detail the methodology for the research described in this book, including details of our sample as well as the processes involved in recruitment, focus group facilitation, and data analysis. We also discuss our experiences conducting research with teens and address issues related to positionality, power, and the importance of applying an "ethical imagination" (Adorjan, 2016) regarding research with youth broaching topics such as cyberbullying, sexting, and having participants who may have survived such attacks.

Chapter 3 sets the groundwork for the "whats" and "whys" of teen online sociality. That is, we discuss what SNS teens are using and what they find appealing about them. We begin here because for teens the emotional medium of connection and identification is online; it is where they seek and establish their visibility, project an evolving self, and receive feedback from their peers. The cyber-risks and more deleterious experiences that are highlighted in the chapters that follow exist alongside and, moreover, are enmeshed within the positive and enticing features of going online (Livingstone, 2008). In Chapter 3 we underscore the value of SNS for the role they play in *social connection* – the most important positive feature of going online identified by the teens with whom we spoke. Chapter 3 also highlights the question of teen internet addiction. We asked our participants how often they logged onto social media, and if they felt themselves to be "addicted." The overwhelming response, interestingly, embraced the discourse of addiction (often with shared laughter among the group), though our participants stressed the importance and multifaceted use of technology, not only for socializing but school work and accessing information. Despite the opportunities for social connection online, this is also accompanied by a persistent search for social acceptance driven by a fear of missing out (FOMO), and often, social comparison which, we argue, indicates a festering paranoia that lies at the heart of growing up with such communications technology.

Chapter 4 addresses teenagers' experiences with and views towards parental and school-based surveillance. First, we delineate between "monitoring" which is often accepted (sometimes begrudgingly) by adolescents as justified based on parental concerns for their safety online, and "surveillance," which is perceived as more coercive and often performed without consent. While our participants evidence active resistance to surveillance, especially in relation to parental surveillance, it is often tempered most directly in relation to school-based surveillance. Participant acquiescence to surveillance reflects a wider context of *panoptic hegemony*, referring not only to the omnipresence of surveillance technologies, but the wider expectation of their deterrent efficacy and embedding within society as "the way things are," so as to stymie critical responses of the current system. We show how the internalization of this argument – in effect neutralizing the impetus for resistance – is facilitated through the attitude (first introduced in Chapter 6) that youth have "nothing to hide" online, and "don't do anything wrong." This signals neither a rejection nor resistance to panoptic surveillance but, instead, an acquiescence to and internalization of a wider neoliberal ethos which suggests that for this generation of teens the debasement of privacy has become hegemonic (i.e., a pragmatic adjustment to common sense and the way things are).

Chapter 5 turns more directly to areas of concern expressed by our participants. We argue that the best concept to capture these concerns is that of "relational aggression," which is a more nuanced and inclusive concept not linked to narrower (and less relevant, from some teens' perspectives) conceptualizations of cyberbullying. While cyberbullying is a topic broached in our discussions, our participants made more specific reference to forms of relational aggression linked to gender norms, such as dealing with "drama" (especially among female teens). We also explore an emerging area of research involving "digital self-harm," a variant of cyberbullying engaged in through anonymous messaging platforms such as Formspring and, more recently, Ask. fm. We explain this phenomenon as it is linked to attention-seeking behaviors and a search for validation as discussed in Chapter 3. Another significant area of concern is hacking, which we discuss also with reference to the theme of relational aggression. The connection between concerns over cyberbullying and hacking becomes clearer when considering how significant *offline peer groups* are to teens; i.e., the more serious issues and emotional investment with others online relates to those in one's own peer groups offline, most frequently in school. The sort of messages about strangers hacking into private accounts is therefore brushed off among our participants, as well as concerns over hacktivist groups. Simply put, teens see themselves as "small fish" compared with the corporate and governmental targets of hacktivist groups. That said, breaches of privacy and losing control over one's actions online based on hackers *is* a concern when it relates to peers where the consequences of stigma and ostracization are much more salient.

Chapter 6 addresses a consistent theme running through our discussions of cyber-risk with teens: privacy and privacy management. It begins with a reminder that research has actively challenged media-perpetuated stereotypes of teens disregard for privacy online. Alongside others, we highlight the most prominent strategies such as password management, blocking users, untagging photos, and creating multiple profiles. While similar strategies have been noted in extant research in the United States (boyd, 2014), the United Kingdom (Livingstone, 2008), and Canada (Heath, 2015), we go beyond documenting these strategies to explore how teens manage identity and privacy *across* SNS. We highlight how perceived audiences drives differing approaches to posting content. For instance, most teens' parents and even grandparents are now active Facebook users. While some teens create multiple Facebook accounts in an attempt to carve out more authentic and private spaces away from parental monitoring, our participants also spoke of gravitating towards newer and more popular platforms, such as Instagram and Snapchat, where they felt less likely to be watched, and therefore more free to present authentic selves, or else explore identities relatively free of judgement. This is also because of a greater sense of control and privacy management on these sites: teens project to smaller, more intimate audiences here rather than on the "big" sites such as Facebook. Interestingly, our participants frequently complained about Facebook becoming over-commercialized, replete with pop-up advertisements, and in general too broad. As ever, the widespread gravitation towards Instagram (which some participants also felt less homophobic) and Snapchat (which is associated, besides sexting, with open sharing of mundane, everyday activities with close friends) is strongly related to privacy management and the online presentation of self. That said, some participants challenged the idea that blocking other users is effective (a message often received from parents and cyber-safety programs). This is due to the disconnection that occurs with offline peers who, if blocked, undermine teens' ability to know what is being said about them and respond in turn. In this chapter, we also situate findings with broader theories of privacy mindsets (i.e., attitudes towards privacy that influence behavior), highlighting several salient approaches including "social" versions, but also indicating a gravitation towards an individualistic conception that holds up the dictum that the individual is personally responsible to keep their online activities private. We show that this mindset is most salient among females living in our urban location, Cyber City. Finally, we underscore a trend in our discussions indicating that as teens mature, especially approaching graduation from high school, while privacy management remains on the radar it becomes less relevant to teens given the frequent refrain that they have "nothing to hide" online. Implications of this mindset are discussed.

Chapter 7 centers on digital sexual expression, i.e., sending and receiving nudes online or "sexting," most frequently associated with the app Snapchat by our participants. While most of our participants did not admit to sending sexual images of themselves to others, they did speak of instances of friends sending or receiving sexts, and in some cases school-based incidents and school responses to sexting scandals. We highlight the gendered dimensions of sexting, with a majority of the female participants in our sample at some point receiving a graphic image of a penis (often referred to as "dick pics") from a male peer, friend, or partner. Likewise, female participants described feeling pressured by male peers to respond to requests to send sexts (e.g., flashing their breasts). The pressure that female teens are under to send nudes are situated within the wider pressures to gain popularity and social acceptance (see Chapter 3). Our discussions thus evidence a normalization of the experience of sexting among our female participants. Theories related to gender, specifically masculinities, frame our findings. For instance, our participants' reflections on sexting suggest not new norms regarding gender online, but rather well-established sociological archetypes such as the double standard associated with free expression of sexuality: girls are labelled and stigmatized as "sluts" while boys are emboldened and rewarded as "studs." Here too the female teens we spoke with repeatedly referred to the responsibility lying with themselves to regulate their sexual expressions online; for which a form of cyber-abstinence was often advocated. Here too this discourse resonates with broader societal messages directed at female teens to abstain from sexting or, more generally, posting anything that could brand them a "slut" or deviant (Hasinoff, 2012; Karaian, 2012, 2013). Our participants' remarks reinforce sexual and gender norms disincentivizing any sexual expression among girls and young women. Advancing existing studies of female teenagers' experiences of sexting, we include the voices of young males and explore their responses to sexting, its gendered nature, and their own ostensible culpability in perpetuating the victimization of their female peers. We also suggest such gendered patterning is reinforced through messages of cyber-safety received in school).

We conclude the book with Chapter 8, in which we offer a cogent summary of our results and theoretical implications before shifting on focus to policy recommendations based on our findings. Several key findings are summarized towards a discussion of recommendations for educators and teens themselves. During our focus group discussions we asked our participants if they had any advice to offer other youth their age, as well as schools and parents, about going online and tackling cyber-risk. We draw from their responses, as well as our own theoretical and sociological interpretation of our findings, to inform those interested in addressing youth safety online how to best approach what is often perceived as a sensitive and volatile social problem. We address areas such as parental surveillance of children (especially the use of "spyware" technologies), school-based policies towards technology in the classroom, and school-based surveillance of students, as well as cyber-safety programs and presentations. We explore implications according to trends related to a young person's age, gender, and urban versus rural residence. One of our aims in this chapter is to set aside academic debates and bring to the fore the practical outcomes of our study that can help foster trusting relationships and open lines of communication between teens and concerned adults, before suggesting areas for future research.

Overall, in many respects, the Canadian teens we spoke to reflected experiences and attitudes germane to teens in general, comparable to findings in the United States, the United Kingdom, and elsewhere. One of our major goals in this book is to dispel concerns, often amplified through sensationalistic media coverage, that a substantial proportion of teens are being negatively impacted from their activities online, with serious incidents of criminal harassment, stalking, breaches of privacy and identity fraud, and so forth leading some teens to significant levels of distress, even self-harm and suicide. Serious incidents do occur. During the course of conducting this research, some of the participating schools shared with us incidents of students engaging in non-consensual distribution of nudes and uttering serious threats to other students and teachers. Despite these incidents, it is imperative that societal reactions are informed by research evidence. What we do know is that youth who are most at risk online are most frequently those who are also at risk offline, due to factors wholly removed from technological impacts. At the same time, we suggest several areas where how we react as a society matters.

Growing up today *is* different because of information communications technologies. Fights among previous generations of students that often petered out are immortalized online. The importance of chasing "likes" on Facebook and feeling left out, if not ostracized, through subtle tactics such as not being "tagged" in a group photo; these things hold a high emotional valence for teens and need to be acknowledged by parents and educators, discussed openly and frequently. That older teens seem to shrug aside concerns for privacy, seeing privacy as irrelevant given a view that they are not doing anything wrong indicates a dangerous societal trajectory where the only reason one should have something to hide is if they are engaged in illicit and/ or immoral activities. Even if some of these teens *are* in fact engaging in such activities despite declaring that they have nothing to hide, the internalization of this logic indicates the debasement of social conceptualizations of privacy, reinforcing to teens the messages they have been receiving since they were children – that they are on their own; that there is no one to help them through all this; that they are solely responsible when they fail to live up to the high, neoliberal expectations placed upon their projects of self.

References

Adorjan, M. (2016). The ethical imagination: Reflections on conducting research in Hong Kong. In M. Adorjan & R. Ricciardelli (Eds.), *Engaging with Ethics in International Criminological Research* (pp. 36–51). New York: Routledge.

Adorjan, M., Ricciardelli, R., & Spencer, D. (2017). Youth perceptions of police in rural Atlantic Canada. *Police Practice and Research, Online First.*

Agatston, P., Kowalski, R., & Limber, S. (2007). Students' perspectives on cyber bullying. *Journal of Adolescent Health, 41*(6), S59–S60.

Allen, K. (2012). Off the radar and ubiquitous: Text messaging and its relationship to 'drama' and cyberbullying in an affluent, academically rigorous US high school. *Journal of Youth Studies, 15*(1), 99–117.

Bailey, J., & Steeves, V. (Eds.). (2015). *eGirls, eCitizens.* Ottawa: University of Ottawa Press.

boyd, d. (2014). *It's Complicated: The Social Lives of Networked Teens.* London: Yale University Press.

boyd, d., & Ellison, N. (2007). Social network sites: Definition, history, and scholarship. *Journal of Computer-Mediated Communication, 13*(1), 210–230.

Calvert, C. (2000). *Voyeur Nation: Media, Privacy, and Peering in Modern Culture.* Boulder: Westview Press.

Cassidy, W., Faucher, C., & Jackson, M. (2013). Cyberbullying among youth: A comprehensive review of current international research and its implications and application to policy and practice. *School Psychology International, 34*(6), 575–612.

Chhotray, V., & Stoker, G. (2009). *Governance Theory and Practice: A Cross-Disciplinary Approach.* London: Palgrave Macmillan.

Chu, D. (2010). In search of prosumption: Youth and the new media in Hong Kong. *First Monday, 15*(2–1), np. http://firstmonday.org/ojs/index.php/fm/article/view/2772/2451 (accessed May 2014).

Connell, R. (2005). *Masculinities (2nd Ed.).* Berkeley, CA: University of California Press.

Crawford, A. (2006). Networked governance and the post-regulatory state? Steering, rowing and anchoring the provision of policing and security. *Theoretical Criminology, 10*(4), 449–479.

Foucault, M. (1977). *Discipline & Punish: The Birth of the Prison* (A. Sheridan, Trans.). New York: Pantheon.

Haggerty, K. (2006). Tear down the walls: on demolishing the panopticon. In D. Lyon (Ed.), *Theorizing Surveillance: The Panopticon and Beyond* (pp. 23–45). Mill Street, Uffculme: Willan Publishing.

Hasinoff, A. (2012). Sexting as media production: Rethinking social media and sexuality. *New Media & Society, 15*(4), 449–465.

Heath, S. (2015). Security and insecurity online: Perspectives from girls and young women. In J. Bailey & V. Steeves (Eds.), *eGirls, eCitizens* (pp. 361–383). Ottawa: University of Ottawa Press.

Hinduja, S., & Patchin, J. (2009). *Bullying Beyond the Schoolyard: Preventing and Responding to Cyberbullying.* Thousand Oaks, CA: Corwin Press (Sage).

Hoy, M. G., & Milne, G. (2010). Gender differences in privacy-related measures for young adult Facebook users. *Journal of Interactive Advertising, 10*(2), 28–45.

Karaian, L. (2012). Lolita speaks: "Sexting," teenage girls and the law. *Crime Media Culture, 8*(1), 57–73.

Karaian, L. (2013). Policing "sexting": Responsibilization, respectability and sexual subjectivity in child protection/crime prevention responses to teenagers' digital sexual expression. *Theoretical Criminology* (available online http://tcr.sagepub.com/content/early/2013/09/26/1362480613504331).

Kelly, K., & Caputo, T. (2011). *Community: A Contemporary Analysis of Policies, Programs, and Practices.* Toronto: University of Toronto Press.

Li, Q. (2010). Cyberbullying in high schools: A study of students' behaviors and beliefs about this new phenomenon. *Journal of Aggression, Maltreatment & Trauma, 19*(4), 372–392.

Li, T. (2007). Governmentality. *Anthropologica, 49*(2), 275–281.

Livingstone, S. (2003). Children's use of the internet: Reflections on the emerging research agenda. *New Media & Society, 5*(2), 147–166.

Livingstone, S. (2008). Taking risky opportunities in youthful content creation: Teenagers' use of social networking sites for intimacy, privacy and self-expression. *New Media & Society, 10*(3), 393–411.

Lombard, K.-J. (2007). Gen E (Generation Extremist): The significance of youth culture and new media in youth extremism. In P. Mendis, J. Lai, E. Dawson, & H. Abbass (Eds.), *Recent Advances in Security Technology* (pp. 168–178). Melbourne: Proceedings of the 2007 RNSA Security Technology Conference.

Marker, B. (2011). *Sexting as Moral Panic: An Exploratory Study into the Media's Construction of Sexting.* (Masters of Science), Eastern Kentucky University, Richmond, Kentucky.

Nadesan, M. (2008). *Governmentality, Biopower, and Everyday Life.* New York: Routledge.

Patchin, J., & Hinduja, S. (2010). Trends in online social networking: Adolescent use of MySpace over time. *New Media and Society, 12*(2), 197–216.

Pedersen, S. (2013). UK young adults' safety awareness online – is it a "girl thing"? *Journal of Youth Studies, 16*(3), 404–419.

Prensky, M. (2001). Digital natives, digital immigrants Part 1. *On the Horizon, 9*(5), 1–6. http://dx.doi.org/10.1108/10748120110424816 (accessed May 2018).

Rose, N. (1996a). The death of the social? Re-figuring the territory of government. *Economy and Society, 25*(3), 327–356.

Rose, N. (1996b). Governing "advanced" liberal democracies. In A. Barry, T. Osborne, & N. Rose (Eds.), *Foucault and Political Reason: Liberalism, Neo-Liberalism and Rationalities of Government* (pp. 37–64). London: UCL Press.

Sheehan, K. B. (1999). An investigation of gender differences in on-line privacy concerns and resultant behavior. *Journal of Interactive Marketing, 13*(4), 24–38.

Spitzberg, B., & Hoobler, G. (2002). Cyberstalking and the technologies of interpersonal terrorism. *New Media & Society, 4*(1), 71–92.

Walton, G. (2005). The notion of bullying through the lens of foucault and critical theory. *The Journal of Educational Thought, 39*(1), 55–73.

Yar, M. (2013). *Cybercrime and Society (2nd Ed.).* Los Angeles: Sage.

Chapter 2

Research focus and methodology

Research on cyberbullying, understandably given the prominence of being online, has proliferated since the turn of the century. Concerns that the affordances of the internet, including anonymity and permanence, would morph bullying in schools into more insidious forms have largely treaded this growing body of scholarship. Much of the extant research on bullying comes from wide-scale, representative samples of youth, surveyed about both the extent and severity of cyberbullying, often within the context of school (Hinduja & Patchin, 2014; Li, 2010; Vandebosch & Cleemput, 2009). These projects are crucial in assessing not only the scope of the problem, but fostering appropriate responses (Paul, Smith, & Blumberg, 2012). A sizable number of articles are psychological examinations, exploring questions of motive, emotion, and cognition (for a meta-analysis see Kowalski, Giumetti, Schroeder, & Lattanner, 2014). Various studies have pinpointed particular areas of concern, such as sexting (Englander, 2012; Lenhart, 2009; Marker, 2011; see also Chapter 7).

Moreover there is an emphasis, coming from psychological studies that draw from behaviorist assumptions, on the negative effects of new media and information communications technologies (ICT) on youth (Buckingham, 2002, cited in Mcmillan & Morrison, 2006: 74). There is thus good reason to move beyond such studies – informative though they may be – and focus attention on "listen[ing] to young people's own experiences with new media technologies" (Mcmillan & Morrison, 2006: 74). To this end, researchers have started to study cyberbullying and related areas of cyber-risk through qualitative approaches, such as interviewing youth or engaging in "cyber" ethnographies or "netnographies" (Kozinets, 2010; Livingstone, 2008; Maher, 2008). In the United States, dana boyd and her collaborator's work over the last decade illuminates a wide range of issues and experiences through both interviews with teens and "hanging out" with them during their regular routines (boyd, 2008; boyd & Hargittai, 2010; Marwick & boyd, 2011, 2014). In Canada, recent interview-based research by Valerie Steeves, Jane Bailey, and their colleagues, that focused exclusively on female teens, addressed important gaps in knowledge regarding the lived experiences of Canadian teens online and the interrelated offline impacts (Bailey & Steeves, 2013, 2015; Bailey, Steeves, Burkell, & Regan, 2013). This prescient body of recent research serves as a direct inspiration for our current project.

First, we acknowledge the suggested need for further qualitative research designs geared toward unpacking the contexts within which cyber-risk is experienced. For example, European studies reveal about 15–20% of teens feel threatened or distressed online (Hasebrink, Livingstone, Haddon, & Olafsson, 2009). However, what this means in the context of young person's lives is "methodologically tricky" to untangle (Livingstone, 2009: 160). Qualitative research, in response, is geared toward exploring important nuances that add detail and context to existing quantitative surveys, and in so doing complements said findings. To this end, we support Vandebosch and Cleemput's (2009) argument that

> measuring respondents' experiences with a range of activities presumed to represent forms of cyberbullying, without taking into account the context in which these activities take place and the interpretations of those involved (as sender or receiver), is not an adequate method to investigate cyberbullying.
>
> (1367)

As such, our aim is to explore the contexts and lived experiences of teens towards cyber-risk from the perspective of teens themselves. Reflecting on Vandebosch and Cleemput (2009), we adopt this qualitative design as it is geared to generating "thick description" (Geertz, 1973) through dialogue. Our intention is to capture interpretive details and nuances which we mine for depth and meaning, and that can complement the breadth of current survey-based research.

Research design: focus groups

To explore these issues, rather than one-to-one individual interviews, we opted to conduct focus groups. Focus groups are useful for unpacking the "situated character" of experience within the "practical and mundane contexts" of people's everyday lives (Sparks, Girling, & Loader, 2001: 888; see also Madriz, 1997, 2000; Stewart, Shamdasani, & Rook, 2007), because the dynamic group interactions and discussions generate knowledge that extends beyond attitudes and opinions (Morgan, 1997). Researchers increasingly draw on systematic focus group designs to examine cyber-risk issues, like cyberbullying and sexting (Agatston, Kowalski, & Limber, 2007; Allen, 2012; Lenhart, 2009; Pelfrey & Weber, 2014; Vandebosch & Cleemput, 2008), because such group discussions among peers can provide a space that accounts for the illumination of salient social contexts and personal interpretations which are largely left out of survey-based methods. Vandebosch and

Cleemput (2008), for instance, chose to examine cyberbullying using focus groups as they

> expected that the interaction among youngsters about a conversation topic that is part of their everyday (social) life – namely, ICT – would reveal detailed information about their concrete Internet and mobile phone practices and their individual and group norms and values with regard to electronic communication.
>
> (500)

In the context of schools there may be a risk that students in a group discussion may "obfuscate views or opinions in order to enhance their status in the group" (Pelfrey & Weber, 2014: 402; see also Heary & Hennessy, 2002), we aimed to mitigate such risks by keeping groups relatively small and providing a semi-structured interview schedule to keep discussions focused (see below), while leaving room to explore novel directions and emergent themes (Pelfrey & Weber, 2014). Since going online and socializing on SNS is, at root, a social activity experienced by peers, having discussions within a group context can help participants feel a sense of shared experience and connection. While moderators aimed to keep discussions on track, the advantage of focus groups is that discussions progress in directions controlled by participants more than moderators (Madriz, 1997), and as such garner a "certain ecological validity" illuminating the lived experiences of participants (Stewart et al., 2007: 39). This is especially important for groups involving youth, who often are challenged to find a platform for their voice (cyberspace being one such platform).

Our participants: the sample

Comparable studies to those discussed above, drawing on focus group research on youth and cyber-risk, are lacking in Canada. In addition, we strived to include enough participants to make comparisons by age, gender, and residence location. We employed a purposive, snowball sampling design, whereby initial contacts in various sectors such as schools and universities helped provide references to additional participants. In total, we conducted 35 focus groups with 115 participants aged 13–19 (average age of 15), with an average number of 3.3 participants per group (a minimum of two and maximum of five). Although we aimed for groups with no less than four participants, sometimes not all participants scheduled for a group showed up, reducing the size of some groups to two participants (akin more to small group discussions than focus groups). We chose to include these groups as their conversations generated significant knowledge, and as we are not in this study interested in examining the interactional dynamics of larger groups of teens per se. Groups of four to six have been found to be optimal to ameliorate the effects of "over sharing" or domineering participants, as well as participants who may feel intimidated and become silent within larger groups (Morgan, 1997; Twinn, 1998). Each discussion lasted between 30 to 120 minutes and were conducted by both authors as well as select trained research assistants. Participants were referred through participating schools in both Western and Eastern Canada, specifically urban Western and rural Atlantic regions. Both public and private schools participated in the project. Other participants were either university undergraduate students or the children of parents attending classes in university.

Throughout this book we will refer to the Western, urban locations as Cyber City, and the rural, Atlantic locations as Cyberville (the collapse of multiple locations into these two pseudo-regions ensure the anonymity of participants while facilitating thematic comparisons of the data). Fifteen groups were conducted in Cyber City; the remaining 20 groups were conducted in Cyberville. A total of 67 females and 48 males participated in our study. Most groups were held with youth of the same gender and age/grade levels, a sampling stratification strategy designed to help ensure participants interacted with others that they would not perceive as threatening and with whom their experience may also resonate (Madriz, 1997; Morgan, 1997). Our examination thus touches upon trends based on age, area of residence (i.e., urban vs. rural), and gender (i.e., male or female; only a single participant identified as "gender fluid" (see section on "positionality" below). While there is much value in focusing research on female teens in relation to cyber-risk (e.g., Bailey & Steeves, 2015), we include both males and females because of the importance tied to considering how significant a role gender (i.e., norms governing expectations related to how males and females are "supposed" to behave) plays (Connell, 2005; West & Zimmerman, 1987). Acquiring male perspectives here adds crucial knowledge to how cyber-risks are responded to and experienced. Indeed, those in our sample can be described as mainly "skilled risk takers" from middle-class backgrounds that have learned to take advantage of many of the opportunities offered online. Of course, in so doing they also encounter "a range of risks" (Livingstone, 2009: 172). Our interest here is what these risks are, how they are defined, understood, responded to, and how youth are responding to the messages that they receive about how to mitigate these risks. As we highlight throughout the book, gender bears a strong impact in how issues of privacy, surveillance, and relational aggression are perceived and responded to.

In addition to gender, we contribute to research on youth and the internet which explores similarities and differences across urban and rural regions (see Burkell & Saginur, 2015). Our sample of youth from Cyberville, similar to students from rural regions in Europe and elsewhere, often lacked or were less likely to have high-speed internet access in comparison to urban residents, with a select few opting not to go online much at all (e.g., Fisk, 2016). It should be noted that internet access at home is increasing in both urban and rural areas (Burkell & Saginur, 2015). Surveys conducted in 2009 and 2010 found that almost 70% of rural households in Canada had home internet access, versus just under 80% for urban households (Burkell & Saginur, 2015). Burkell and Saginur (2015) proceed to argue that this lack of difference "may be explained by the relative independence of online social networks from geographic constraint, and the 'friend of friend' linking that tends to characterize online social networks" (134). This argument by Burkell and Saginur draws from an arguably latent cyber-optimism that suggests the emancipating and "leveling" effects of cyberspace. While we also found more similarities than differences in terms of which SNS teens are using and the reasons why, there are marked differences in our findings based on our focus group discussions; e.g., in relation to privacy and surveillance.

Process

We opted, with permission, to audio record each focus group in order to preserve the accuracy of dialogue, and to enable us to give the participants our full attention during discussions (we did not need to take notes, which would have led to sacrificing eye contact and keeping track of the discussion in progress). Transcripts of the focus groups were produced that preserve the idiosyncrasies of speech, including pauses, "um," "ah," "so," and "you know" (the word "like" was also preserved as a modifier and was found to be the most frequently used word across all groups).

Following the approach of Vandebosch and Cleemput (2008), our discussions began on general, open ground. We asked participants about everyday experiences with technology, leaving room for both positive and negative remarks. These were followed up with questions about the most popular SNS, how frequently each was used, interpretation of SNS addiction or any concern that was raised by a participant during the introductory conversation (this was usually privacy or sexting). Next, questions explicating experiences and attitudes towards these concerns were explored. Unlike other research specifically centered on risks such as cyberbullying (e.g., Vandebosch & Cleemput, 2008), in our focus groups, we sought to go beyond capturing general experiences online and perceptions towards cyber-risk by asking teens about how they are responding to societal messages they are receiving about online safety and risk, especially from parents and educators. This often led to discussions about parental and school-based regulation of technology, including monitoring and surveillance of children and students. Some groups opted to discuss schools before parents and vice versa in others. All groups were asked about both parents and schools. Thus, in cases where discussion voluntarily gravitated towards parental policies regarding technology but schools were not raised, participants were asked explicitly about school-based policies (and vice versa). In addition, participants were asked what advice they have for parents and schools regarding how they approach cyber-safety and the various cyber-risks discussed. Responses to these questions are very useful as they inform not only participant perspectives but bear policy implications. Before the discussions were completed, participants were also asked whether they had anything in addition to contribute that was not addressed in the discussion up to that point in time. In the majority of cases all participants agreed that they did not have anything further to contribute, but in a few cases some would elaborate on previous remarks (usually incidents related to relational aggression).

Data analysis

The transcribed focus group data was analyzed using an inductive, comparative approach without initially arriving at any definitive substantive or theoretical conclusions about what the data reflected sociologically (Berg, 2004; Strauss & Corbin, 1990). Concepts and theories emerged naturally through the dynamic interaction of participants. NVivo qualitative analysis software, specifically the parent and child node functions, was used to conduct analyses of the data. The initial stages of "widely open inquiry" involved "open coding" of the data (Berg, 2004: 278) following Anselm Strauss' advice to "believe in everything and believe nothing" about what was being analyzed (Strauss, 1987: 28). To this end, initially, all mentions of a particular topic/theme within a session were noted (i.e., captured as "nodes" and reported as "references" in NVivo), allowing for comparison across sessions (Morgan, 1997). Coding schemes were developed through first-level coding (i.e., parent nodes), involving close readings of the data. Using NVivo, prominent themes emerged through the tracking of coding "nodes" both across and within groups. Appropriate for focus group discussions, often references included a range of dialogue between participants. This usually began with a particular question from the facilitator, followed by a series of exchanges. The reference would normally end once participants discussing a particular topic finished their exchange and a new question was asked. Our conversations, as expected, often led in a number of unanticipated yet interrelated directions, and coding decisions were made where one coding sequence ended and where another began. Regular research meetings between the investigators ensured that thematic development emerged in a consistent and reliable manner, and helped to ensure a hermeneutically attuned validity of the data (cf. Twinn, 1998). While Adorjan took initial responsibility for coding all data, both Adorjan, Ricciardelli, and research assistants (RAs) worked with the coded data to collectively vet the final results in terms of validity and thematic accuracy. In this book we report on theme saliency in this paper by reference to both the number of focus groups where a theme was discussed (N), as well as the number of references made across these groups (R): (N, R). For example, if 25 of the 35 groups expressed concern for anonymity online, and if 100 references were made to anonymity across all 35 focus groups, this is indicated as (25N, 100R). At other times we simply refer to the number of groups and/or references made to a particular theme. Primarily, our focus is to the "thick description" of our focus group discussions. However, thematic saliency is relevant in order to highlight wider trends in the data as they relate to age, gender, and residence location.

Positionality, reflexivity, and an ethical imagination

Both authors of this book are academics with male and female children under ten, and consider themselves aware, yet not active (nor inactive) users of social media. Entering into this research, as parents especially, we sometimes had to pause and reflect upon our discussions with teens, how their concerns may impact our own parenting practices and concerns for our children. Both of us have also become more attuned to the perceptions of parents and teachers at our children's school regarding technology, cyber-risk, and especially in relation to surveillance and monitoring. We became more aware of the concerns some parents have over particular websites and applications (apps) their children access, issues of appropriate age of access, as well as the various policies and practices of schools geared to instill safety and security for students. These "awareness contexts" (Glaser & Strauss, 1964) helped inform how we conducted our research, influencing the questions we asked about parents and schools in particular. This was therefore a major challenge writing this book: the blending of the personal with the need to engage in academic research which, we felt with the utmost of importance, must remain agnostic to the veracity of the social problems being discussed (Gubrium & Holstein, 2011; Spector & Kitsuse, 1977).

This agnosticism did not preclude our own (often strong) opinions – one way or another – of the things being told to us. Take as an example the declaration, among some of the older teens in our sample, that they no longer expect privacy online nor care much about privacy because they have nothing to hide online and do nothing wrong (see Chapter 6). We aimed to probe this remark, suspicious that teens may well be saying one thing (especially in groups of their peers) while conducting themselves online differently. One of the limitations of our research is that we did not complement our discussions with participant observation in the home, in school, or in public (cf. boyd, 2014; Livingstone & Sefton-Green, 2016). However, our agnostic stance to this led us away from trying to tease out the objective truth of such remarks, and instead pushed us toward understanding how such remarks fit the wider logic teens projected regarding socialization under the neoliberal emphasis of self-responsibilization and moral self-regulation. While both of us use and have used various SNS, including Facebook and Twitter, we do not currently use Instagram, Snapchat, or other popular SNS often used by teens today. Sometimes references were made in our discussions that we were simply naïve to, such as the relatively new Snapchat "Snapstreak" feature (see Chapter 3). We of course asked our teen participants what such things are, and more importantly, why these things matter and what it means to them. Rather than seeing our relative "outsider" status in relation to teen's lives as a disadvantage, this helped us remain non-judgmental and foster trust through an ethical process which informed the way we conducted our research (Adorjan, 2016).

Our discussions centered on difficult topics to broach. While our research is not focused on cyberbullying victimization per se, discussions among our groups sometimes did address prior experiences teens had dealing with relational aggression or current circumstances involving parents and schools. Participants were informed of counseling resources and other help they could receive if they experienced distress. They were also informed of their right to decline to answer any or all questions, and stop their participation at any time (ethics approvals were obtained both from university and school research ethics boards). Our approach entailed asking our participants if issues such as cyberbullying, relational aggression, sexting, and so forth were problems they found among their peers, in their schools or wider community. This helped deflect any pressure upon individuals to disclose personal experiences of victimization. Where personal experiences were recalled disclosure was strictly voluntary.

A particularly salient theme across all our groups is digital sexual expression (see Chapter 7). To help participants feel secure in the confidentiality of what is discussed and to facilitate honest disclosures, most groups were held with youth of the same gender and age/grade levels. The gender and age sampling stratification was designed to help ensure participants interacted with others they were likely to perceive as not threatening (Madriz, 1997; Morgan, 1997). We did not ask our participants about their gender or sexual identification. This choice was made deliberately – we simply felt such questions may be too intrusive and stymie the trust we sought to establish with our participants, or at least augment the direction of our conversations. Sexting, and especially messages directed to teens about sexting, often contain heteronormative presumptions of who are victims and victimizers. By *not* asking questions about gender and sexual identification, we let participants discuss topics like sexting in their own words, raising issues such as homophobia and transphobia where and when relevant to them. Broaching such topics as sexting and the issue of sending and receiving nudes and "dick pics" required a careful approach if we were to elicit responses that were not unduly influenced by prejudicial questions. If groups answered questions on such topics differently based on whether the facilitator asking the question was a male or female, we saw no evidence of it. That said, Adorjan, being the only male facilitator of focus groups in our research, took extra care in asking groups about this topic. For male groups, the ethical process involved raising the issue without implying that males are often pressuring girls to do so (which many of our female participants expressed), nor that such a phenomenon is ubiquitous among teens (which, we argue based on our discussions, is very much the case). The *question* needed a delicate phrasing, often posed by asking if sexting or sending and receiving "dick picks" is a problem among their friends or at school. For all groups, we did not raise this topic until the discussion was in "full swing" and some degree of rapport and trust was established. This also helped Adorjan feel when the topic could be approached ethically in all female and co-ed groups. Even for a female researcher speaking to a group of female youth, talking about sexting could be awkward and thus it was important to establish trust and to approach the subject with care and caution. Here too participants were often asked about the saliency of such online activity in their school or among their friends, rather than about their direct engagement in such action, as either the sender or the recipient. The power of our "ethical imagination" (Adorjan, 2016) and agnostic approach to our research helped ensure that seemingly existential gaps in age and gender between facilitators and participants had, to our best knowledge, minimal impact on fostering a climate of trust and mutual empathy.

Our sample of teens purposefully excludes other direct "stakeholders" in the debates over youth and cyber-risk, including parents and educators. We justify this simply on the basis of our research questions, centered on teen perceptions. The answers we received, and detail in this book, are considered less along lines of what is "correct" and "incorrect," versus how teens illuminate (in some cases internalizing, in other cases resisting) discourses projected to them regarding staying safe and secure online. There are sometimes statements regarding parenting and teaching that beg the question of whether parents and educators would have different "takes" on what is said. For instance, some of our participants expressed with assurance that their schools are capable of using sophisticated surveillance technologies to track their activities online, e.g., through the use of "Wi-Fi perimeters" (see Chapter 4). School teachers and counselors, however, during some of our research dissemination activities, were skeptical of this. We also did not follow up with parents to gather their perspectives in response to our participants' expressions of distrust towards parental use of "spyware" technologies to surveille their actions online. We proceed, then, with this limitation noted here, arguing that what follows is not to suggest what is said reflects what parents *are* doing, or schools *are* doing – or even what is possible to do (i.e., we did not verify the narratives reported by youth). Rather, what follows is simply reversing the usual direction of communication; not talking 'at' youth about cyber-risk, but listening to what they have to say. Doing so offers new opportunities to reflect on possibly different ways to approach the social issues affecting their routine activities online.

References

Adorjan, M. (2016). The ethical imagination: Reflections on conducting research in Hong Kong. In M. Adorjan & R. Ricciardelli (Eds.), *Engaging with Ethics in International Criminological Research* (pp. 36–51). New York: Routledge.

Agatston, P., Kowalski, R., & Limber, S. (2007). Students' perspectives on cyber bullying. *Journal of Adolescent Health, 41*(6), S59–S60.

Allen, K. (2012). Off the radar and ubiquitous: Text messaging and its relationship to "drama" and cyberbullying in an affluent, academically rigorous US high school. *Journal of Youth Studies, 15*(1), 99–117.

Bailey, J., & Steeves, V. (2013). Will the real digital girl please stand up?: Examining the gap between policy dialogue and girls' accounts of their digital existence. In J. M. Wise & H. Koskela (Eds.), *New Visualities, New Technologies: The New Ecstasy of Communication* (pp. 41–66). Farnham, Surrey: Ashgate.

Bailey, J., & Steeves, V. (Eds.). (2015). *eGirls, eCitizens.* Ottawa: University of Ottawa Press.

Bailey, J., Steeves, V., Burkell, J., & Regan, P. (2013). Negotiating with gender stereotypes on social networking sites: From "bicycle face" to Facebook. *Journal of Communication Inquiry, 37*(2), 91–112.

Berg, B. (2004). *Qualitative Research Methods for the Social Sciences* (5th Ed.). Long Beach: Pearson.

boyd, d. (2008). *Taken Out of Context: American Teen Sociality in Networked Publics.* University of California, Berkeley.

boyd, d. (2014). *It's Complicated: The Social Lives of Networked Teens.* London: Yale University Press.

boyd, d., & Hargittai, E. (2010). Facebook privacy settings: Who cares? *First Monday, 15*(8), Retrieved from: http://firstmonday.org/htbin/cgiwrap/bin/ojs/index.php/fm/article/viewArticle/3086/2589 (accessed November 2014).

Burkell, J., & Saginur, M. (2015). "She's just a small town girl, living in an online world": Differences and similarities between urban and rural girls' use of and views about online social networking. In J. Bailey & V. Steeves (Eds.), *eGirls, eCitizens* (pp. 129–152). Ottawa: University of Ottawa Press.

Connell, R. (2005). *Masculinities (2nd Ed.).* Berkeley, CA: University of California Press.

Englander, E. (2012). *Low Risk Associated with Most Teenage Sexting: A Study of 617 18-Year-Olds, MARC Research Reports Paper 6.* Retrieved from Bridgewater, MA:

Fisk, N. (2016). *Framing Internet Safety: The Governance of Youth Online.* Cambridge: The MIT Press.

Geertz, C. (1973). *The Interpretation of Cultures.* New York: Basic Books.

Glaser, B. G., & Strauss, A. L. (1964). Awareness contexts and social interaction. *American Sociological Review, 29*(5), 669–679.

Gubrium, J., & Holstein, J. (2011). Don't argue with the members. *The American Sociologist, 43*(1), 85–98.

Hasebrink, U., Livingstone, S., Haddon, L., & Olafsson, K. (2009). *Comparing Children's Online Opportunities and Risks Across Europe: Cross-National Comparisons for EU Kids Online.* Retrieved from

Heary, C., & Hennessy, E. (2002). The use of focus group interviews in pediatric health care research. *Journal of Pediatric Psychology, 27*(1), 47–57.

Hinduja, S., & Patchin, J. (2014). *Bullying Beyond the Schoolyard: Preventing and Responding to Cyberbullying (2nd Ed.)*. Thousand Oaks, CA: Corwin.

Kowalski, R., Giumetti, G., Schroeder, A., & Lattanner, M. (2014). Bullying in the digital age: A critical review and meta-analysis of cyberbullying research among youth. *Psychological Bulletin, 140*(4), 1073–1137.

Kozinets, R. (2010). *Netnography: Doing Ethnographic Research Online*. Los Angeles: Sage.

Lenhart, A. (2009). *Teens and Sexting: How and Why Minor Teens Are Sending Sexually Suggestive Nude or Nearly Nude Images via Text Messaging*. Retrieved from Washington, DC: www.pewinternet.org/Reports/2009/Teens-and-Sexting.aspx.

Li, Q. (2010). Cyberbullying in high schools: A study of students' behaviors and beliefs about this new phenomenon. *Journal of Aggression, Maltreatment & Trauma, 19*(4), 372–392.

Livingstone, S. (2008). Taking risky opportunities in youthful content creation: Teenagers' use of social networking sites for intimacy, privacy and self-expression. *New Media & Society, 10*(3), 393–411.

Livingstone, S. (2009). *Children and the Internet: Great Expectations, Challenging Realities*. Malden, MA: Polity Press.

Livingstone, S., & Sefton-Green, J. (2016). *The Class: Living and Learning in the Digital Age*. New York: New York University Press.

Madriz, E. (1997). *Nothing Bad Happens to Good Girls: Fear of Crime in Women's Lives*. Berkeley: University of California Press.

Madriz, E. (2000). Focus groups in feminist research. In N. Denzin & Y. Lincoln (Eds.), *Handbook of Qualitative Research* (2nd Ed., pp. 835–850). Thousand Oaks: Sage.

Maher, D. (2008). Cyberbullying: An ethnographic case study of one Australian upper primary school class. *Youth Studies Australia, 27*(4), 50–57.

Marker, B. (2011). *Sexting as Moral Panic: An Exploratory Study into the Media's Construction of Sexting*. (Masters of Science), Eastern Kentucky University, Richmond, Kentucky.

Marwick, A., & boyd, d. (2011). I tweet honestly, I tweet passionately: Twitter users, context collapse, and the imagined audience. *New Media & Society, 13*(1), 114–133.

Marwick, A., & boyd, d. (2014). 'It's just drama': Teen perspectives on conflict and aggression in a networked era. *Journal of Youth Studies, 17*(9), 1187–1204.

Mcmillan, S., & Morrison, M. (2006). Coming of age with the internet: A qualitative exploration of how the internet has become an integral part of young people's lives. *New Media & Society, 8*(1), 73–95.

Morgan, D. (1997). *Focus Groups as Qualitative Research* (2nd Ed.). California: Sage.

Paul, S., Smith, P., & Blumberg, H. (2012). Revisiting cyberbullying in schools using the quality circle approach. *School Psychology International, 33*(5), 492–504.

Pelfrey, W., & Weber, N. (2014). Talking smack and the telephone game: Conceptualizing cyberbullying with middle and high school youth. *Journal of Youth Studies, 17*(3), 397–414.

Sparks, R., Girling, E., & Loader, I. (2001). Fear and everyday urban lives. *Urban Studies, 38*(5–6), 885–898.

Spector, M., & Kitsuse, J. I. (1977). *Constructing Social Problems*. Menlo Park: Cummings Publishing Company.

Stewart, D., Shamdasani, P., & Rook, D. (2007). *Focus Groups, Theory and Practice* (2nd Ed.). London: Sage.

Strauss, A. (1987). *Qualitative Analysis for Social Scientists*. New York: Cambridge.

Strauss, A., & Corbin, J. (1990). *Basics of Qualitative Research: Grounded Theory Procedures and Techniques*. Newbury Park: Sage.

Twinn, S. (1998). An analysis of the effectiveness of focus groups as a method of qualitative data collection with Chinese populations in nursing research. *Journal of Advanced Nursing, 28*(3), 654–661.

Vandebosch, H., & Cleemput, K. V. (2008). Defining cyberbullying: A qualitative research into the perceptions of youngsters. *Cyberpsychology and Behavior, 11*(4), 499–503.

Vandebosch, H., & Cleemput, K. V. (2009). Cyberbullying among youngsters: Profiles of bullies and victims. *New Media & Society, 11*(8), 1349–1371.

West, C., & Zimmerman, D. (1987). Doing gender. *Gender & Society, 1*(2), 125–151.

Chapter 3

Teens online: what and why

Introduction

Media reporting sometimes makes it difficult to consider teens being online as a positive experience. In today's technology-saturated climate, the common perceptions of youth as potential prey raise concerns among parents, guardians, educators, and others about youth safety online and, relatedly, their potential exposure to cyber-risk (Vickery, 2017). Media driven moral panics (Cohen, 2002 [1972]; Goode & Ben-Yehuda, 2009) frequently add fuel to accumulating anxieties highlighting the morose, criminal potentiality of youth accessing cyberspace (e.g., Marker, 2011; Murguía, Tackett-Gibson, & Lessem, 2007). The list of "what can happen" to a youth online frequently dominates media stories about, for example, teen suicides motivated by an invasion of privacy or online harassment and stalking (Grenoble, November 10, 2012); assault and even murder videos (sometimes dubbed "performance crimes") broadcast on social network sites (SNS; Mohney, April 18, 2017; CBC News, April 26, 2017); sexual harassment and sexual assault (including experiences of rape and postings of gang rape on SNS; Heath, 2015; Rentschler, 2014; Shariff & DeMartini, 2015); sexting and cases of "revenge porn" targeting female teens (Karaian, 2012; Poltash, 2013; Stroud, 2014) – to name just a select few.

Online threats facing, and coming from, youth should be taken seriously, as the potentiality – however minimal – remains for the more extreme and caustic online risk outcomes. At the same time, sociologists drawing attention to the social construction of social problems stress that such news items, in seizing and aggrandizing emotions such as shock, horror, and disgust, obfuscate and bely assessments of social problems that take a wider sociological perspective (Cohen, 2002 [1972]; Loseke, 2003; Spector & Kitsuse, 1977). Social constructionists, as such, draw attention to the "formula stories" (Loseke, 1999, 2012) at play that congeal with preconceived notions of what teens are doing online, who are the usual victims and victimizers, and act to reinforce stereotypes and deflect counter-evidence. Anxieties related to these intersecting areas of concern refract and amplify each other, especially those centered on technology and youth in general. In Chapter 7, for example, we highlight concerns tied to "sexting" and the sexual practices of young white, heterosexual females in particular (Karaian, 2014; Milford, 2015).

It is necessary to retain a sociological imagination about the social problems related to teens online, especially when the personal troubles of teens are the focus (Mills, 1959). As Livingstone (2009) notes, there are often polarized approaches to children online, represented as both vulnerable potential victims and competent, even creative agents and even, we would add, sometimes as malevolent victimizers taking advantage of the affordances of cyberspace, especially its anonymity. Moral panics are frequently a reaction to perceptions of wider social malaise and disorder evidenced from the particular activities and actions of groups of youth (Cohen, 2002 [1972]). Youth are, in other words, frequent targets of moral panics. However, the particular forms moral panics take regarding youth are often surprising when taking a wider, historical view. Even the waltz, when first introduced, inspired outcry over its potential to incite "lascivious behaviour" in teens (see Livingstone, 2009). Although this seems a humorous atavism of the past from our present-day vantage, it remains that while the content inducing panic may change over time, the formula is predictable: a new phenomenon not yet fully understood draws fevered excitement and addictive attention amongst teens, who we seek to protect against their "base" desires, especially during the hormonal onslaught of puberty – thus there is moral panic. While Mary Shelly's novel *Frankenstein* was one of the first to alert us to the twin fascination and terror new technologies often inspire, the advent of the Internet during the 1990s, and especially its more recent "web 2.0" iteration in the 2000s have ignited, or reignited fears over the various online risks facing teens, especially those exacerbated by the persistence, anonymity and searchability of cyberspace (boyd, 2008, 2014).[1]

Anxiety about the dangers of youth going online often center on particular online behaviors such a cyberbullying, hacking, and sexting, among others. Researchers who have conducted research with youth and online practices, including how youth use technology, for what purposes, and under what circumstances, consistently find that, overall, "the kids are alright." In contrast to the formula stories regarding youth and cyber-risk frequently cited in sensationalistic media, researchers find that the majority of youth have *not* been victimized by cyberbullying or sexting, and many take advantage of the online opportunities for political activism, education, and social connection and awareness (Hinduja & Patchin, 2014; Koskela, 2004; Livingstone, 2008; Marwick & boyd, 2014; Tapscott, 2009).

In this chapter, we set aside, for the time being, many of the central anxieties regarding teens and cyber-risk, focusing instead on the opportunities and enticements they find appealing online. Our ability to address and effectively respond to cyber-risk would be undercut if the wider context of what draws youth online is not considered. The opportunities and risks associated with cyberspace are inseparable, mutually reinforcing aspects of going online

(Livingstone, 2008, 2009). This is not to suggest that concern over issues such as cyberbullying, online stalking and harassment, and so forth are misplaced or not as relevant as the more positive aspects of going online. Rather, like so many of the issues examined in this book, risks and opportunities are intertwined and often, importantly, open to varying subjective experiences and interpretations. Discourses of cyber-risk such as "addiction," "cyberbullying," and "sexting" point to what sociologists describe as sensitizing concepts, which provide the analyst with "a general sense of reference and guidance in approaching empirical instances" (Blumer, 1954: 7). Our approach, in line with Blumer, is to advance knowledge by studying the interpretations youth have regarding these concepts in their lived experiences (which sometimes are made sense of, we may add, in unanticipated ways). This idea is significant for both its methodological and theoretical implications. A word such as "addiction" or "cyberbullying" often carries with it negative association(s), especially when connected to youth and online behavior. However, research with children and youth has the opportunity to reveal how these social constructs are experienced, at times resisted, and attitudes towards them. Indeed, viewing risks and opportunities as flip sides of the same coin – as intertwined realities – is also to level the playing field and take into account not only the coexistence of opportunities and risk, but that both of these need to be examined from the perspective of youth themselves, not just from the point of view of parents, educators, or adult society more generally. Thus, our focus is on understanding why youth go online, their positive associations with being online, and why they find it so engaging.

What draws youth online: social connection and offline peer groups

Youth online engagement has many positive aspects. There is evidence that, despite the risks and negatives associated with the Internet, youth today are more accepting of those different from themselves, are less inclined to alienate their friends, and are more accepting of friends who are not heterosexual. There are also indications of "diminished racial conflict in many contexts" (Gardner & Davis, 2013: 86). Sonia Livingstone's (2009) research on youth online experiences reveal a comprehensive list of online opportunities, which she lists as:

> access to global information, educational resources, social networking among friends, entertainment, games and fun, user-generated content creation, civic or political participation, privacy for identity expression, community involvement/activism, technological expertise and literacy, career advancement/employment, personal/health/sexual advice, specialist groups/fan forums, shared experiences with distant others.
>
> (Livingstone, 2009: 30)

SNS are particularly popular among teens and young adults, used for staying in touch with friends, making plans, becoming familiar with new peers, and presenting the self to particular friends and peer groups (Shapiro & Margolin, 2014). SNS, Facebook in particular, are often used to share problems, social information, and seek affection among teens and young adults, with other platforms such as instant messaging used primarily for maintaining existing relationships (e.g., Quan-Haase & Young, 2010). Our participants – Canadian teens – provided a number of reasons to explain why SNS are so popular, including finding sources of humor and posting humorous content ("I post funny videos, I love sharing funny things," Paige, a 16-year-old female from Cyberville stated during one discussion). Some youth referred to seeking out assistance or resources through social media. For instance, a group of four males from Cyberville, aged 16 and 17, discussed using Snapchat to arrange for a designated driver during a party. Drinking and driving is "very shamed upon around here," Jorge says, "like if we're at a party and we see someone leave, like getting in a video if they're drunk, it's a big deal." Myles adds, "a lot of people even … if they're partying on the go … people will be DD [designated driver], they'll be on Snapchat, like anybody needs a ride, message, cash." SNS, in this context, represents a tool for locating essential information, albeit for safety needs (e.g., a designated driver), but also for school projects and assignments. Fatima, aged 15 from Cyber City, explains:

> if I have like a school project, and I don't have the phone number or something and we need to talk or like arrange something, and most likely then I'll be friends with them on Facebook and then I can contact them that way.

Some participants referred to the ways in which SNS can connect people, thus bringing them together and helping them to stay in touch around the world. For instance, Demetry, a 17-year-old male from Cyber City, discussed the appeal of both Facebook messenger (a messaging service often preferred over use of the full "regular" platform) and Instagram because of their perceived utility in connecting people:

> [Facebook] messenger is very useful for friends that are outside of the country, cuz you can't text them, so it's good, things like Facebook bring people together, if used properly, same with Instagram, you actually get to see what people do. Like my best friend lives in New Zealand, so he Instagrams pictures of the beach and things, and I like them because it looks great right, I'd do the same thing.

Social media is "potentially global," articulates Abigail, 19-years-old, from Cyber City: "so if you're having problems with something specifically in your personal life and go online and can't find that acceptance that you're looking for." She adds, "if there's so many people in the world, there is guaranteed to be something or someone out there who can understand what you're going through."

While Facebook remains popular for the majority of our participants, its use is waning or, more accurately, our participants are accessing it less frequently yet more carefully, with respect to managing impressions of particular audiences (see Chapter 6; see also boyd & Hargittai, 2010). Facebook has long been used by teens to maintain mostly weak, low commitment ties (Ellison, Steinfield, & Lampe, 2007; Lewis & West, 2009). Lewis and West (2009), for example, interviewed United Kingdom-based university students who joined Facebook when it first became available to universities in 2005. For these students, Facebook served as "a supplement to other forms of communication, especially between close friends, and a useful way of touching base occasionally with others" (Lewis & West, 2009: 1223). The most popular platforms actively used by the teens we spoke with are, however, Snapchat and Instagram – not Facebook. A factor influencing this gravitation away from active Facebook use is teen concerns over privacy and privacy management (see also Piwek & Joinson, 2016; Utz, Muscanell, & Khalid, 2015), which we examine in further detail in Chapter 6.

Privacy considerations do help to explain the popularity of new SNS, like Snapchat, yet a full appreciation of their use comes with recognizing their role in facilitating *social connection*, especially among offline peer groups. In fact, *social connection or connecting with others is the most frequently raised motive linked to SNS use among our participants* (17N; 36R). Moreover, participants made such references relatively evenly across ages; said another way, there is a rather equal emphasis placed on social connection among younger or older teens. However, females in all female focus groups made three times as many references to social connection as males in all male focus groups (21 vs. 7). Despite the higher number of all female focus groups, this may suggest social connection can be understood as a vocabulary of motive (Mills, 1940), more salient among female teens than males (as found in face-to-face studies of gender differences and self-presentation (see Haferkamp, Eimler, Papadakis, & Kruck, 2012). That is, while social connection may be equally important to teens, wider norms of traditional interpretations of masculinities (Carrigan, Connell, & Lee, 1985; Connell, 1995; Gill, Henwood, & McLean, 2005; Kimmel, 1990; Ricciardelli, Clow, & White, 2010) may lead some males to self-imposed restrictions on how they use social media, or use it differently than females (Siibak, 2010). Notably, double the references to social connection were made among Cyber City residents than Cyberville residents (24 vs. 12). This is notable since a greater proportion of groups were held in Cyberville (see Chapter 2). Care should be taken in interpreting this finding. We do not argue that social connection online is more relevant for those living in urban location. Rather, this could simply indicate that online access (especially to "web 2.0" communications technologies) is less available in rural areas, so teens are less reliant on these technologies for social connection (see also Burkell & Saginur, 2015).

The offline peer group: "friends"

In a co-ed group of 17- and 18-year-olds from Cyber City, Frederick's response, when asked what is appealing about Snapchat and Instagram, revealed the importance of social connection as shaped by the affordances of the applications: "I think it's more like instead of just texting your friends, you can actually show them what you're doing, or you can put it on your story so you can show all your friends cool stuff that you're doing".[2] It is important to underscore that, despite reflecting upon what they do online, by "friends," as revealed through Frederick's words, teens often are referring to their offline peer networks, e.g., friends they see at school on a daily basis, spend time with during extracurricular activities, and invite over to each other's homes. For instance, some participants referred to gravitating away from platforms such as Twitter based on keeping in contact with close, offline peers. For example, 19-year-old Serena from Cyber City reveals that "part of the reason I'm not on Twitter is because none of my friends are really on Twitter, so that's why I don't really have it." Later in the discussion, asked about whether Facebook was still relevant, Serena disclosed: "I deleted Facebook, at the end of high school just cuz I didn't think I needed it, was like, I didn't post anything, it wasn't, I don't know, none of my friends were really on it." In the same group Carmen, 19, also reveals that her lack of interest in Twitter is also influenced by her offline peer groups:

> I've just seen Twitter usually more like of, more [an] American thing I would say, and likewise as [Serena], none of my friends really use it, and I've kind of just like, use social media to stay connected with my friends who might not be in [Cyber City] and like close to me right, so, I'll use a, we'll use a mutual form of social media to stay connected to one another.

Although noting a different SNS, when asked what forms of social media are preferable, Carmen's answer was consistent with other participants: "usually Facebook, just Skype, stuff like that, just the chat, keep in contact."

The salience of *offline peer groups* in relation to connectivity online is in line with research finding youth usually use online communication to maintain already established local friendships, especially through social media today (Boneva, Quinn, Kraut, Kiesler, & Shklovski, 2006; Ellison et al., 2007; Gross, 2004; Livingstone & Brake, 2010). This finding echoes a 2005 Canadian Media Awareness Network report, which found "young people use their social skills online primarily to participate in and extend their real-world social networks" (Steeves, 2005: 8). In contrast to Carmen, while other participants preferred Twitter over Facebook, they did so in relation to connections to offline peers. For instance, Yasmin, 18, from Cyber City, explains:

> I don't ever really check like my actual like feed on Facebook, because I, there's so much stuff I don't really care about, but so I mostly usually use it as a contact, but since most of my friends … are on Twitter, that's more so what I use it for.

Recent studies have identified the general gravitation away from Facebook among teens (at least in terms of where their *dominant* SNS is concentrated), and their preference for newer platforms such as Twitter, Tumblr, and Instagram (e.g., Bailey, 2015; boyd, 2014; Gardner & Davis, 2013). Facebook is less relevant for Yasmin, not so much due to preference of features or "affordances" of the technology; rather Twitter is where her closer, offline peer networks are found. Again, the saliency of offline peer groups among teens is important to underscore here. As Steeves and Webster (2008) argue:

> when these kids are talking online, they are typically talking with people whom they have met through their real-world social networks. Respondents reported that most of their friendships were made in real-world environments, including school (i.e., 94.3% indicated making or meeting new friends at school), parties (75.4%), and playing sports/clubs (74.9%).
>
> (Steeves & Webster, 2008: 10)

The offline non-peer group: parents

The importance of social connection was also raised in discussions of parenting, especially how some parents rely on the deprivation of technology as a punishment for their children. Although this strategy was criticized by several groups, such as one coed group of three males and two females, aged 14 and 15, from Cyber City, Logan admits "you would witness a lot of tantrums" in his house during such a punishment. Asked if such a punishment is very serious, Aiden agrees: "you lose connection" (Ava, female, concurs with a "yeah"). Aiden elaborates:

> If you're so used to like, I'm 15 now, I've probably had social media since I was 12, since I was in grade six or so, and that's three years of being used to seeing statuses and seeing what's going around; it's kind of like turning on the TV never watching the news for two years, what happens when you don't know that there was a shooting in Paris, you don't know all this stuff, you lose connection to what's actually going on, it's [how] one literally can access information is [sic] through social media.

Isabella, also 15, adds "not having my phone for two days, I don't get to access people, I can't do a lot of things, I can't get homework from someone else, I can't get help." Besides Aiden's prescient remarks about being left uninformed about world news and current events, Isabella's statement also points to how ubiquitous the use of technology is for teens. Connection with friends is certainly one aspect, but using the same devices for school work, frequently disseminated using online course management software, is inextricable from their other leisure and social functions. Overall, while our participants pointed to social connection being the driving force drawing them to using particular online platforms such as SNS, the need for connection led to considerations of the darker edge of this drive: addiction and the fear of missing out.

Addiction, social acceptance, and the fear of missing out

The opportunities, enticements, and risks available through technology and social media do not run alongside each other; rather they are intermeshed. Participants discussed the lure of SNS, often expressing concerns about what is being posted online by close peer groups, especially what is being posted about oneself. This fear of how people may be "talking about oneself" online was juxtaposed with the *fear of missing out*. This latter fear, sometimes abbreviated by teens as FOMO (Przybylski, Murayama, DeHaan, & Gladwell, 2013), is alluded to by a 13-year-old male teen interviewed for a special CNN report *#Being 13: Inside the Secret World of Teens*, who confessed "even though I was at school, I would still check my phone because I mean, people post things at school and stuff, so you always worry."[3] Another female interviewed for the report, asked how often she checks her phone on a daily basis, responded: "The most times I check it (my phone) in a day? I lose track. It's just a need. Like I need to." Similarly, in Cyber City, Lexi, 15, connected her "need" to check based on FOMO principals: "sometimes you really do need it to like, not be out of the loop I guess and then like maintain contact with your friends." Framing it differently, 14-year-old Holly from Cyber City, states,

> if you don't have the social medias [sic], you're really like out of it everything, cuz everybody posts everything and they like text you, so you don't really know what's going on if you don't have social media and stuff.... if I'm not on it for a day, then I don't know like anything.

Ashima replies to Holly, agreeing: "yeah, you miss a lot of information, it just gets passed through, and then everyone, you'll go to school the next day, and they'll be like oh remember that one thing ... and then I'm no [sic]." Ashima, here, also gives insight into the notion of teens being concerned over being "left out" if they are not actively keeping up to date with social media and the related postings of those in their closest peer groups.

Interestingly, the theme of FOMO is also raised during discussions on the various strategies teens use to manage privacy online. Lexi's group, consisting of four females aged 14 and 15, discussed the effectiveness of blocking unwanted users and their messages to manage trusted friendship networks. Also in the group, Nancy observes that blocking, while effective would ironically undercut one's social connectivity:

> like you can block [unwanted messages], ... but a lot of the problem is, nobody really wants to block them because when you block them, then you're outside the circle, with, where everybody else knows all the information, and you just block them so you don't know anything.

Ashima replies to Nancy's comment, clarifying that blocking is an option preferred for those unfamiliar to the person, not close or even more distant friends. She states "you only use that [blocking] if you don't know the person, and they're like trying to get your information, ok you're blocked, I don't want to talk to you." Here too, the relevance of offline friends is highlighted, indicating that FOMO is primarily a concern regarding close peer networks, and may bear upon which strategies teens use − or choose not to use − when managing their privacy and online presence. This emphasis on the saliency of offline friendship groups also offsets the emphasis often found in cyber-safety materials directed at teens that inform about risk of strangers and "predators" online (boyd, 2014; Livingstone, 2008). Although teens may have hundreds if not thousands of "friends" on particular SNS, they are also far more likely to invest their emotional energies towards those who post content linked back to their everyday offline lives or peer groups.

Concerns for being socially cut off are also expressed in a group of three 17-year-old females from Cyberville. Expressing anxiety over not being in control over what gets posted about them online, Ally suggests "if you don't have any accounts, that's the only way you're safe." Zoey agrees but adds the caveat: "yeah, even that, if someone can upload a picture of you, then it's worse than you're not patrolling [your account], if you don't have the account." Concerns over being left out of conversations that impinge upon one's reputation and friendships are thus expressed by both Cyber City and Cyberville residents. This suggests another similarity alongside what SNS both urban and rural teens use most often and the reasons they provide for their popularity (Burkell & Saginur, 2015). Significantly, advice regarding eliminating or limiting online use and employing various strategies for managing privacy may well be ignored by teens who feel persistent pressure to constantly check up on what is being posted about themselves and their inner circle of friends (see also Chapter 8 for further discussion of policy implications).

Factors influencing addiction

Conversations about FOMO often gravitated to the topic of addiction, where some groups raised the topic themselves; others were asked more directly if they considered themselves addicted to SNS and the various applications or "apps" teens are using. Here we highlight the interpretations of addictive behavior among teens, including the factors pushing them to engage with technology in ostensibly addictive ways. Addiction to online environments is often linked as a "major factor" to cyberbullying, sexting, and a lack of attention in the classroom (Fisk, 2016: 141). Addiction, which can be readily linked back to teens' FOMO, may also be associated with depression and anxiety (Oberst, Wegmann, Stodt, Brand, & Chamarro, 2017). Research with teens sometimes appears to corroborate such problems. One 13-year-old female interviewed for CNN's *Being 13* report, for example, bluntly states "I would rather not eat for a week than get my phone taken away. It's really bad," alluding to internet addiction being more caustic than eating disorders such as anorexia and bulimia. A Canadian MediaSmarts national survey of over 5,000 teens found "39 per cent of students said they sleep with their cellphones, just in case they get a text or call during the night," indicating the connection between the FOMO and addiction explicitly. At the same time, however, only a third of the sample worry about how much time they spend online. While half of the participants stated they would be upset if they were to go offline for everything but school work, 46% reported they would not care if they were "unplugged" for a week (Loney, January 22, 2014).

Among our own participants, the frequency of discussions about online addiction reveal some distinct trends. A fairly uniform number of references are made across all ages. The majority of references – both to solicited questions and open discussions where addiction is spontaneously raised – is concentrated among female participants in all female groups (55 references). Although we did expect fewer references among males given the greater number of females in the sample, we anticipated more than the five references to addiction made by males, which include confessions about being addicted to social media. Our findings suggest a gendered patterning of how experiences of addiction are interpreted. More tellingly, 66 references to addiction come from participants living in Cyber City, with only 16 references from those residing in Cyberville, perhaps again a result of access issues in rural areas and thus the less pronounced role of social media in said areas as a result. As elsewhere, this finding is notable considering the relatively greater number of groups held in Cyberville where the theme of addiction would arise rather frequently.

During focus group discussions, social media was colorfully described as a "really big-time sponge" (Carmen, 19, Cyber City), sometimes interpreted as a means to cope with awkward in-person situations. For example, in a coed Cyber City group of 14- and 15-year-olds, Logan argues "it kind of has something to do with your hands, that's the thing, if you're bored, have nothing to do, you have a phone, you can really do anything." Ava agrees, suggesting contexts where this strategy works, such as sitting alone at a bus stop or spending time with someone where the situation becomes awkward, in which case, Isabella adds, "you can pull out your phone." Logan, in agreement, adds:

> If you don't have your phone, that's [*sic*] give you a really uncomfortable feeling, cuz if it's constantly on you and you don't have it, you're probably going to panic, to be honest (Ava: "it's true"), every 30 seconds, you probably have a little bit of a heart attack!

Logan's words here expose the clear anxiety tied to being 'phoneless' in the modern world. For those who agreed, when asked, if they consider themselves to be addicted to the internet, some elaborated on the feelings they associated with their interpretation of being addicted. For instance, Helen, 16-years-old from Cyber City, discloses "it's like, I feel anxious if I don't, like if it's a long period of time goes by and I like, I don't check it, I get anxious, like what's happening, kind of thing." Mya, also 16, "kind of" agrees, stating that she is not "super anxious," but admits

> I've got into the habit of looking at it, so I'm just "oh, I wanna check my phone," "oh this person [is] saying that" and I'm like "ok," but I don't like check it too often, but if it's the weekend or it's a break, then I'll be on my phone like all the time.

As these youth reveal, and is further clarified from the number of youth who admitted to feelings of anxiety over what is being posted about them, their 'addiction' is driven by a need to "check to make sure nothing['s] happening" (Cassidy, 17, Cyber City), again linking back to the FOMO and anxieties that underpin impression management. Such anxieties are centered more on issues of social comparison, the FOMO, and managing one's online identity than on addiction to technology per se. Nevertheless, the need to check content related to oneself and one's peer groups is undeniably driven by the *negative potential driving addictive behaviour*, rather than positive potential.

Not surprisingly then, when asked about frequency of phone use, it was often a qualification rather than a set number of hours provided, sometimes with a trace of humorous exaggeration: "whenever you are bored" (Cecilia, 14, Cyber City); "like all day ... my phone's never not in my hand, I sleep with it in my hand" (Mia, 17, Cyber City); "probably more than I should be" (Cassidy); "I cannot go a day without checking like, or like you know even an hour, I feel like I always have to check, even if it's nothing important, it's just like, it's a bad addiction" (Christine, 19, Cyber-City). Nancy recalls a typical day: "I come home, first thing I do, I pull out my phone and scroll through all social media before I do anything else." Other members of Nancy's group elaborate that the reason they do so is to check "what is happening" (Ashima), and compare it to watching "the news, but for your school or something" (Nancy).

In addition, some participants referred to how various affordances (i.e., the technical features and structure) of technology acts to structure their anxieties and sense of addiction. Critics of early techno-enthusiasm during the initial development of the internet in the 1990s, such as computer scientist–philosopher Jaron Lanier (2010), point to the ways users adjust and in some ways "reduce" themselves to fit the affordances of particular online platforms. This echoes the axiom that "we shape our tools, and thereafter our tools shape us" (Culkin, 1967) and the arguments consistent with Giddens' theory of structuration (Giddens, 1986). For example, some groups referred to using Snapchat's popular "Snapstreak" feature. Snapchat's (a SNS mobile application) core feature is that images and messages sent between users are only available for a short period of time before they are deleted and no longer retrievable. The Snapstreak feature works as an incentive to promote users to keep actively using Snapchat. Snapstreaks are established when two users have "snapped" each other an image or message within 24 hours for more than three consecutive days. Snapstreaks are maintained when users transmit images or messages frequently; if either party fails to respond within 24 hours the "streak" is lost.[4] In this sense, the technology is encouraging the user to reproduce behaviors which are then reproducing the popularity of the technology and vice versa in a dynamic "back and forth" process.

While our participants ostensibly dismissed Snapstreak as a gimmick that they are not lured by, when pressed, many admitted to finding themselves "locked in" to using the feature given the affordances of Snapchat (in this case, the requirements of maintaining a Snapstreak). Emily, 19-years-old from Cyber City, characterizes the anxiety: "it's like 'oh my god, we're about to lose our 500-day streak, do something about it,' it's like 'ok, hold on, hold on,' well yeah, I think it's about maintaining streaks now, and maybe having a decently cool story." Reid, also 19, adds "I think it's about popularity … it seems like a popularity contest on Snapchat, people have to make their stories all the time, you know." Talking about the audiences Snapchat streaks are geared toward, all participants in this focus group agreed that streaks and stories are most often directed to particular friends online. However, was also becomes relevant is the impressions these exchanges make among friends at school. As Emily puts it: "but like people when they go, you know when you're on Snapchat and there's someone beside you and they see them and they're like 'Yo, you're so popular'!" Here again, it becomes apparent how relevant offline audiences are to influencing online activities and, as emphasized here, how they are interpreted. Affordances, such as Snapchat's Snapstreak, therefore amplify teens' felt need to frequently check on social media to see what is being posted about them, or simply what is going on or what they may be missing out on. At its core, this relates to offline peer groups and an ongoing search for acceptance and belonging.

Searching for acceptance

Inevitably the need for social connection translates into a need for social approval and acceptance. Adolescence is well recognized as a period where the judgements of one's peers weighs heavy on one's sense of identity and self-esteem, both of which are in a liminal stage of development (Harter, Stocker, & Robinson, 1996; Lerner & Steinberg, 2009). Aiden, a 15-year-old from Cyber City, directly made this point in relation to contemporary SNS: "I think that social media has come down to the fact that we're looking for acceptance from our peers," of which the others in the coed group of five 14- and 15-year-olds agreed. At heart, the search for acceptance involves a recognition, or confirmation from others regarding one's identity. Our participants referred to the importance of receiving acknowledgement from peers online to figure out, fundamentally, who they are. Madison, 16-years-old from Cyber City, summarizes this view presciently:

> I think it matters how people see you … *I have to know how people see me, but maybe because I don't know how I see myself*, so if I don't know how I see myself then, maybe they could give me the answers to that, but I think in our age group … we have to know how people see us, that we know if it's good or bad. [emphasis added]

Asked if this involves seeking social approval, Madison refers to the "different ranks" of peers that she seeks social approval from, including "popular kids," "the rich and poor … so … we have to know where we stand."

This raises the question of how social approval is recognized when received online. Perhaps the most recognizable indicator of social acceptance on SNS is through receiving a "like" on Facebook, in response to something one has posted. Two 19-year-old males from Cyberville exemplified this when asked if there is "pressure to have a lot of friends on Facebook or no?" Keegan responds

> not really, more like "likes," a lot of people want likes on Facebook…. people just want likes, I know my mom does that, I know a lot of people do that, and … for people on Facebook, how many likes you get I guess is how popular you are, a lot of people I know is like that.

Asked to confirm that it is the "likes" on Facebook that is important, not the number of friends, Keegan confirms "yes"; Fernando, the other group participant, reiterates "number of likes," confirming his agreement with Keegan. It should also be noted that despite discussing Facebook, the site remained associated with older adults, as indicated by Kegan when he explained that "my mom does that."

Despite the suggestion that "likes," not number of friends, is the ultimate judge of popularity on Facebook, not all groups agreed with the emphasis. Instead, points of resistance to the logic of pursuing likes emerged. For instance, Ashima questioned the underlying motivation for "chasing likes":

> When people post a picture, sometimes yeah, they'll want to see how many likes, but then I feel like it should be, it should be used for like, to remember things and like, remember those times and like share with your friends, so they can remember it, rather than "I'm the best and you should like my picture" and they end up deleting it anyway in the end.

It may of course be relatively easy for teens to take a non-conformist attitude towards what they perceive to be the dominant, mainstream use of SNS; here Ashima may still very much care about personally receiving "likes" on Facebook, but expresses resistance and critiques the notion in the context of a focus group discussion. Despite some participants resisting the significance of receiving likes to confirm social approval, it remains obvious how much this still matters to teens, despite the gravitation away from active Facebook use, in preference of Instagram, Snapchat, and other more recent SNS. Here too, the *affordances* of Facebook limit the ways users can interact with each other to express approval and disapproval alike. These affordances, meshed with the FOMO and need for social approval, drive a seemingly perpetual comparison among teens that fuels addictive behaviors to SNS and related technologies.

Gender and social approval

Prior researchers have consistently found female teens to be highly aware of the potential risks they face online and, in response, engage proactively in a variety of risk management strategies (Bailey & Steeves, 2015; Marwick & boyd, 2014). Some studies also reveal females to be concerned about social approval, related to what they post online (e.g., Bailey & Steeves, 2015; boyd, 2008). Similarly, among our participants, several gender differences emerged in discussions around social approval. For example, Fiona, 18 years-old from Cyber City, argues girls are concerned more with "what do I look like, how are they going to look at me, like is my eyebrow nice today, like do my eyelashes look long." In contrast, she argues males are more object-oriented, posting pictures of their car or video game and "it's just like they just want to share it, where girls are like 'what do I look like?,' 'will my followers think that I look bumping in this photo' kind of thing." In the same group, Serena, 19-years-old, agrees:

like girls look more for approval from others that they look good and their form of approval is "likes" the more "likes" you get, the more love you get for your photo, that's giving you approval … but for guys it's like "I did something cool," "here's a photo of it."

She continues to describe how differently Instagram is used between males and females, characterizing the images male's post as "random photos … because they think it's right in the first place," whereas females take time to post elaborate borders with consideration for "aesethically [appealing] so perfect." Unlike males, "for girls, it's more like seeking approval." This gendered self-presentation dynamic on Instagram is elaborated in recent research (see Doherty, 2017).

This view is reiterated in a number of groups, with some elaborating on the pressure experienced by females in particular, as well as the fear of negative judgement. For instance Christine, 19-years-old from Cyber City, discusses at length the pressure on females in particular to present a perfect image on Instagram. She refers to the need for "the caption … to be right, the filter like, does this look ok, does it flow with the rest," adding that she used to post on Instagram for fun, being interested in photography, but it has since:

> become something like I'm overthinking, not posting photos because I'm scared of how you get judged over social [media] you know … it has to get … like you hashtag so people will like it, … like it's become very much a, like a [sic] unwritten competition on social media that girls think specifically, oh she got a 100 "likes" on this, or oh look her profile picture got like 100 "likes" in the first like 2 minutes.

She concludes that she has not used social media "to its full potential" given her fear of "the judgement that comes behind overusing it."

Some groups actively challenged the gendered association of primarily female teens using social media to seek and obtain social approval rather than males. That is, some participants suggested that male teens are just as likely to be concerned about social approval, but either express it differently, or else try to hide their concerns. For instance, in one co-ed group from Cyber City, 14-year-old Julien (male), argues "guys basically it's more pressure" since males will "gang up on" each other if they lack knowledge about certain "rites of passage" such as pornography. Another co-ed group (three males, two females) in Cyber City, aged 14–15, voice concern about what others post about them. The males in the group were asked if they would have anxieties if anyone posted "party pics" of them online. Aiden argued that it does in fact matter for male teens:

> Yeah cuz people can see it, but if it's like two people that I know, if it's the people at [the] party seeing it I don't honestly see that being a big

deal … but I think … there is not control of the audience on social media, just because we think there is, there is none, there is zero. Every person you could possibly think of could look up a photo and can see you half naked, drunk at a party, so it's just, taking steps to prevent it from beginning and don't do it again.

Other groups of all male participants expressed the same attitude: "I'd be concerned about [having drunk party pictures posted about me]" admitted Deshawn, 15, from Cyber City. Female groups also agreed, suggesting that masculine gender norms also shape self-presentation strategies for deflecting concern online. If their reflections are true, it would suggest males still feel the pressures of traditional gender norms that suggest select appearance concerns are still culturally read as feminine rather than masculine (Pope, Phillips, & Olivardia, 2000; Ricciardelli et al., 2010; Wolf, 1991). As such, they practice the idea that males should not reveal the degree of effort they place in their appearance outwardly, yet must still invest in their body and self (Featherstone, 1991; Ricciardelli, 2011; Shilling, 2003). For instance, Carmen, 19, from a group of four female undergraduate students in Cyber City, aged 18 and 19, argued:

> guys … like present off a good image, but they try to make it look unintentional … kind of like "oh, I woke up like this," that's the kind of like, they try to pull it off easy, easy going swagger I guess, just like it looks, but they still like, you can tell they're still trying to look good and stuff.

Yasmin, 18, agrees with Carmen's remarks, arguing "it may not be equal, but it's close." She adds that a lot of her "guy friends … try really hard" to present themselves ideally in posted photos online, taking "half an hour to take the photo so that they can post it." The caveat, however, Yasmin believes is that "there's a *lot more public ridicule for women* and their photos on Instagram, whereas like if there's a photo of like, on a guy's Instagram, I think there's a lot less like hate that's going to towards it" [added emphasis]. Yasmin thinks further on the gender dynamics of online presentation of self, and thoughtfully observes that it may be true to an extent that "guys just don't care" about what they post and how what they post will be received. However, she states,

> I think it's also … expected of women to care, but it's not [expected of] guys and so some of my guy friends won't post photos of themselves or of something that they do want approval of, because they're going to get looked down upon and their other friends will be like "why did you post that?" "That doesn't really, that's not what you're supposed to post."

The concern Yasmin describes among male teens anticipating "they're going to be judged for what they post" suggests that desiring approval yet not seeking it due to wider gender norms shapes gendered perceptions of self – a reality that requires further examination to understand if online spaces are advancing or hindering gender equalities in self-presentations and body positioning particularly as body ideals are ever changing and increasingly unattainable (Connell & Messerschmidt, 2005; McCabe & Ricciardelli, 2004; Ricciardelli & Clow, 2009; Ricciardelli & White, 2011).

The majority of such comments came from participants of Cyber City, but this does not necessarily mean that they do not apply to rural regions. One group of two 14-year-old females from Cyberville was asked whether online "drama" is something affecting more males or females. Christy answers "both"; Raquel agrees. Pressed further whether drama is different between males and females, Christy elaborates: "people think it's more the girls, but I've seen a lot of guys that [are] like depressed and stuff when they're on Instagram ... you don't really know the drama."

Conformity to gender norms online includes the distillation of gender performances that are culturally read as appropriate (Bailey, 2015). Our participants reveal the influence of gender norms in explaining experiences regarding finding social acceptance online. At the same time, they illuminate a process of reflexive cogitation that challenges the assumption that online actions reflect offline motive. Specifically, both female and male teens suggest that males may often be as anxious about what is being posted about them online as females, and may avoid engaging with online exchanges to appear aloof. Yet, our participants also highlight the ongoing reality that the social and psychological stakes are either higher or interpreted as higher for females, who frequently face more negative social repercussions (e.g., ridicule, de-legitimation, "slut shaming," etc.) in comparison to males (Bailey, 2015; Fairbairn, 2015). We explore these double standards with regards to sexting in more detail in Chapter 7.

Discussion: the amplification of anxiety

Despite the ongoing media rhetoric frequently sensationalizing the risks teen face online, we show in this chapter that the search for social connection is the primary driver for teens. This need for social connection is part and parcel of the processes of maturation and self-discovery synonymous with adolescence. The primary medium for friendship and connection has shifted online, where teens connect with their offline peer groups, and this consideration has fueled societal concerns and moral panics due to the notion of online stranger-danger and luring. Sociologists and criminologists remind us that, although these incidents due occur, young people are more likely to be harmed by someone known to them offline than online (Gardner & Davis, 2013). The real risk here is in interpreting such relatively isolated incidents as typical of the everyday realities of teens online (boyd, 2014).

The gravitation of teens away from Facebook towards newer, more popular platforms such as Snapchat and Instagram has been widely observed and applies likewise to Canadian teens (e.g., Bailey, 2015; boyd, 2014; Gardner & Davis, 2013). A major factor explaining this gravitation involves privacy management. However, platform preferences remain strongly linked to which platforms are used by offline peer groups (Valkenburg & Peter, 2007; Valkenburg, Peter, & Schouten, 2006). Mcmillan and Morrison (2006: 79), drawing on autobiographical essays written by teens about their experiences and personal histories going online, found most described "the internet as a place that helped them solidify their offline identities." The fact that female participants made more references to being online for social connection may reflect the saliency and need for social connection among female teens, in comparison to males, though such a conclusion is likely an oversimplification considering the impact of wider gender norms and practices. This becomes particularly evident during our focus group discussions on social acceptance.

Males in our groups expressed concerns for "drunk party pics," and some female participants reflexively considered that males may share such concerns about both being accepted and about what is being posted about them online, yet may feel they cannot express these feelings. Wider culture and gender norms regarding masculinities shape both reactions and perceptions of youth and cyber-risk, where, as one of our participants presciently remarked, females are more frequently (and for longer time periods) ridiculed based on what they post online than males. That a greater number of references to social connection among our participants are made among Cyber City residents than Cyberville residents may also suggest that rural regions offer other offline points of comparison for teens and may de-emphasize, to a degree, the weight given to what is posted online. Relatedly, Burkell and Saginur (2015) found that female teens living in rural areas had "smaller, more interconnected offline networks," facilitating the "primary importance" of "offline relationships" (Burkell & Saginur, 2015: 145). The saliency of offline networks among rural residents should not be underestimated; nevertheless, the desire for social connection and acceptance among teens is ubiquitous across urban and rural regions. Most research on teens and online technologies is conducted in urban centers, despite the exceptions noted above. While our sample included teens from a rural Canadian region, our own findings remain tentative. Further qualitative and quantitative research with rural teens is needed, especially studies which incorporate comparison groups in urban regions.

While there *are* particular substantive risks which are of concern to one extent or another among our participants (e.g., cyberbullying, sexting, online "drama" and hacking, to which we turn to in the following chapters), the opportunities for social connection are strongly linked to social factors which animate a set of latent risks associated with the need for acceptance online and the FOMO. Teens express an ongoing need to keep 'in the loop' regarding events local to them – i.e., at their school, among their peers, and especially to keep apprised of what is being said about them. These elements explain the curious phenomenon sometimes observed where teens, seated together in offline physical space, are still conversing with each other online (usually through smart phones). The extent to which teens worry appears to verge at times on paranoia, for instance, evidenced through the desire to not block other users for fear of social repercussions and being ostracized and, in a literal sense, ex-communicated from salient peer networks. Efforts to subdue the FOMO are often thwarted due to the various affordances of technology, which act to "lock" teens into social patterns online (e.g., the "snapstreak" feature on Snapchat, receiving and seeking "likes" on FB). Exacerbating this process is the assumption – expressed by some of our participants – that peers are living perfect lives exemplified by their online postings (e.g., pictures on Instagram). This alludes to the fundamental looking glass process of self-development that is engendered through SNS and other social platforms online (Cooley, 1902). The long-standing features of adolescence – identity formation based on the assumption of how one is being perceived – underpin such processes. The online medium, however, amplifies these processes and creates in many respects a more complex terrain to navigate. The comparisons made, moreover, are perpetual and frequently negative.

More optimistically, boyd (2014) critiques off handed ascriptions of teens being 'addicted' to online platforms. She argues that concerns for the online addiction of 'screenagers' (Rushkoff, 2006) divert attention from how sensationalistic media coverage engenders moral panics over "zombified social media addicts" who are not in control of their own lives (boyd, 2014: 78). Moreover, as boyd (2014: 78) argues, "the language of addiction sensationalizes teens' engagement with technology and suggests that mere participation leads to pathology. This language also suggests that technologies alone will determine social outcomes." She continues to disambiguate the idea of online addiction from that of 'flow', originally coined by psychologist Mihaly Csikszentmihalyi, referring to "the state of complete and utter absorption" – comparable to "being in the zone" (boyd, 2014: 80). boyd highlights the positive draws of social media and "being in the zone," including social connection and socialization, and buttresses her critique by reminding us that the original term, "internet addiction disorder," was in fact facetiously coined by psychiatrist Ivan Goldberg in a satirical essay written in 1995. As she rightly notes, "most teens aren't addicted to social media; if anything, they're addicted to each other" (2014: 80). While boyd offers a crucial critique of mediated discourses and stereotypes of teens online, we argue that there are important aspects to growing up online today that are amplifying concerns teens have and perhaps have always had to varying degrees, regarding their position relative to their peers. Understanding the context of these concerns next to the opportunities online communities offer is important; diffusing moral panics over the more serious cases of offending and victimization related to online activities is crucial; yet ignoring what appears to be a *deeply rooted and gendered paranoia regarding social status that is amplified by the affordances of SNS today is equally problematic*. Policy responses to these problems (see Chapter 8) must be situated by an appreciation of the balance which needs to be struck.

Notes

1 Web 2.0 refers to high speed bandwidth access enabling an "architecture of parti-cipation," especially regarding its multimedia content (O'Reilly, 2007). It includes video chat platforms such as Skype as well as social media such as YouTube, Twitter, Facebook, Tumblr, and more recently Snapchat and Instagram.
2 Both Snapchat and Instagram feature a "story," which can combine photos and videos into a slideshow or "reel" to create a coherent narrative or story to share with particular audiences.
3 CNN's *Being 13* report can be found at: www.cnn.com/2015/10/05/health/being-13-teens-social-media-study/index.html.
4 For details on Snapchat's "Snapstreak" feature, see: https://support.snapchat.com/en-US/a/Snaps-snapstreak.

References

Bailey, J. (2015). A perfect storm: How the Online environment, social norms, and law shape girls' lives. In J. Bailey & V. Steeves (Eds.), *eGirls, eCitizens* (pp. 22–46). Ottawa: University of Ottawa Press.

Bailey, J., & Steeves, V. (Eds.). (2015). *eGirls, eCitizens*. Ottawa: University of Ottawa Press.

Blumer, H. (1954). What is wrong with social theory? *American Sociological Review*, *19*(1), 3–10.

Boneva, B., Quinn, A., Kraut, R., Kiesler, S., & Shklovski, I. (2006). Teenage com-munication in the instant messaging era. In R. Kraut, M. Brynin, & S. Kiesler (Eds.), *Computers, Phones, and the Internet: Domesticating Information Technology* (pp. 201–218). Oxford: Oxford University Press.

boyd, d. (2008). *Taken Out of Context: American Teen Sociality in Networked Publics*. Berkeley, CA: University of California.

boyd, d. (2014). *It's Complicated: The Social Lives of Networked Teens*. London: Yale University Press.

boyd, d., & Hargittai, E. (2010). Facebook privacy settings: Who cares? *First Monday*, *15*(8), Retrieved from: http://firstmonday.org/htbin/cgiwrap/bin/ojs/index.php/fm/article/viewArticle/3086/2589 (accessed February 2018).

Burkell, J., & Saginur, M. (2015). "She's just a small town girl, living in an online world": Differences and similarities between urban and rural girls' use of and views about online social networking. In J. Bailey & V. Steeves (Eds.), *eGirls, eCitizens* (pp. 129–152). Ottawa: University of Ottawa Press.

Carrigan, T., Connell, R. W., & Lee, J. (1985). Towards a new sociology of mascu-linity. *Theory and Society*, *14*(5), 551–604.

Cohen, S. (2002 [1972]). *Folk Devils and Moral Panics* (3rd Ed.). London: Routledge.

Connell, R. W. (1995). *Masculinities*. Cambridge: Polity Press.

Connell, R. W., & Messerschmidt, J. (2005). Hegemonic masculinity: Rethinking the concept. *Gender & Society, 19*(6), 829–859.

Cooley, C. (1902). *Human Nature and the Social Order*. New York: Scribners.

Culkin, J. M. (1967). A schoolman's guide to Marshall McLuhan. *Saturday Review*, 51–53, 71–72.

Doherty, T. (2017). *The Presentation of Self in 'Online' Life: A Content Analysis of Instagram Profiles*. (Master of Arts Thesis), University of Calgary, Calgary.

Ellison, N., Steinfield, C., & Lampe, C. (2007). The benefits of Facebook "friends": Social capital and college students' use of online social network sites. *Journal of Computer-Mediated Communication, 12*(4), 1143–1168.

Fairbairn, J. (2015). Rape threats and revenge porn: Defining sexual violence in the digital age. In J. Bailey & V. Steeves (Eds.), *eGirls, eCitizens* (pp. 229–280). Ottawa: University of Ottawa Press.

Featherstone, M. (1991). The body in consumer culture. In M. Featherstone, M. Hepworth, & B. Turner (Eds.), *The Body: Social Process and Cultural Theory* (pp. 170–196). London: Sage.

Fisk, N. (2016). *Framing Internet Safety: The Governance of Youth Online*. Cambridge: The MIT Press.

Gardner, H., & Davis, K. (2013). *The App Generation: How Today's Youth Navigate Identity, Intimacy, and Imagination in a Digital World*. New Haven: Yale University Press.

Giddens, A. (1986). *The Constitution of Society: Outline of the Theory of Structuration* (Vol. 349). California: University of California Press.

Gill, R., Henwood, K., & McLean, C. (2005). Body projects and the regulation of normative masculinity. *Body & Society, 11*(1), 37–62.

Goode, E., & Ben-Yehuda, N. (2009). *Moral Panics: The Social Construction of Deviance* (2nd Ed.). Malden: Wiley-Blackwell.

Grenoble, R. (November 10, 2012). Amanda Todd: Bullied canadian teen commits suicide after prolonged battle online and in school. *Huffington Post*. Retrieved from www.huffingtonpost.ca/entry/amanda-todd-suicide-bullying_n_1959909.

Gross, E. (2004). Adolescent internet use: What we expect, what teens report. *Applied Developmental Psychology, 25*(6), 633–649.

Haferkamp, N., Eimler, S., Papadakis, A.-M., & Kruck, J. (2012). Men are from mars, women are from venus? examining gender differences in self-presentation on social networking sites. *CyberPsychology, Behavior & Social Networking, 15*(2), 91–98.

Harter, S., Stocker, C., & Robinson, N. (1996). The perceived directionality of the link between approval and self-worth: The liabilities of a looking gladd self-orientation among young adolescents. *Journal of Research on Adolescence, 6*(3), 285–308.

Heath, S. (2015). Security and insecurity online: Perspectives from girls and young women. In J. Bailey & V. Steeves (Eds.), *eGirls, eCitizens* (pp. 361–383). Ottawa: University of Ottawa Press.

Hinduja, S., & Patchin, J. (2014). *Bullying Beyond the Schoolyard: Preventing and Responding to Cyberbullying* (2nd Ed.). Thousand Oaks, California: Corwin.

Karaian, L. (2012). Lolita speaks: "Sexting," teenage girls and the law. *Crime Media Culture, 8*(1), 57–73.

Karaian, L. (2014). Policing "sexting": Responsibilization, respectability and sexual subjectivity in child protection/crime prevention responses to teenagers' digital sexual expression. *Theoretical Criminology, 18*(3), 282–299.

Kimmel, M. S. (1990). After fifteen years: The impact of the sociology of masculinity on the masculinity of sociology. In J. Hearn & D. Morgan (Eds.), *Men, Mmasculinities, and Social Theory*. London: Unwin Hyman.

Koskela, H. (2004). Webcams, TV shows and mobile phones: Empowering exhibitionism. *Surveillance & Society, 2*(2/3), 199–215.

Lanier, J. (2010). *You Are Not a Gadget: A Manifesto*. New York: Alfred A. Knopf.

Lerner, R., & Steinberg, L. (Eds.). (2009). *Handbook of Adolescent Psychology, Volume 1: Individual Bases of Adolescent Development*. Hoboken, NJ: John Wiley & Sons.

Lewis, J., & West, A. (2009). "Friending": London-based undergraduates' experience of Facebook. *New Media & Society, 11*(7), 1209–1229.

Livingstone, S. (2008). Taking risky opportunities in youthful content creation: Teenagers' use of social networking sites for intimacy, privacy and self-expression. *New Media & Society, 10*(3), 393–411.

Livingstone, S. (2009). *Children and the Internet: Great Expectations, Challenging Realities*. Malden, MA: Polity Press.

Livingstone, S., & Brake, D. (2010). On the rapid rise of social networking sites: New findings and policy implications. *Children & Society, 24*(1), 75–83.

Loney, H. (January 22, 2014). Canada's youth are highly connected, girls face different rules online: study. *Global News*. Retrieved from http://globalnews.ca/news/1098160/canadas-youth-are-highly-connected-girls-face-different-rules-online-study/.

Loseke, D. (1999). *Thinking about Social Problems*. New York: Aldine de Gruyter.

Loseke, D. (2003). Constructing conditions, people, morality, and emotion: Expanding the agenda of constructionism. In J. A. Holstein & G. Miller (Eds.), *Challenges and Choices: Constructionist Perspectives on Social Problems* (pp. 120–129). New York: Aldine De Gruyter.

Loseke, D. (2012). The empirical analysis of formula stories. In J. Holstein & J. Gubrium (Eds.), *Varieties of Narrative Analysis* (pp. 251–271). Los Angeles: Sage.

Marker, B. (2011). *Sexting as Moral Panic: An Exploratory Study into the Media's Construction of Sexting*. (Masters of Science), Eastern Kentucky University, Richmond, Kentucky.

Marwick, A., & boyd, d. (2014). "It's just drama": Teen perspectives on conflict and aggression in a networked era. *Journal of Youth Studies, 17*(9), 1187–1204.

McCabe, M. P., & Ricciardelli, L. A. (2004). Body image dissatisfaction among males across the lifespan: A review of past literature. *Journal of Psychosomatic Research, 56*, 675–685.

Mcmillan, S., & Morrison, M. (2006). Coming of age with the internet: A qualitative exploration of how the internet has become an integral part of young people's lives. *New Media & Society, 8*(1), 73–95.

Milford, T. (2015). Revisiting cyberfeminism: Theory as a tool for understanding young women's experiences. In J. Bailey & V. Steeves (Eds.), *eGirls, eCitizens* (pp. 55–81). Ottawa: University of Ottawa Press.

Mills, C. W. (1940). Situated actions and vocabularies of motive. *American Sociological Review, 5*(6), 904–913.

Mills, C. W. (1959). *The Sociological Imagination*. Harmondsworth: Penguin.

Mohney, G. (April 18, 2017). Murder on Facebook spotlights rise of "performance crime" phenomenon on social media. *ABC News*. Retrieved from http://abcnews.go.com/US/murder-facebook-spotlights-rise-performance-crime-phenomenon-social/story?id=46862306.

Murguía, E., Tackett-Gibson, M., & Lessem, A. (2007). *Real Drugs in a Virtual World: Drug Discourse and Community Online.* Lanham: Lexington Books.

News, C. (April 26, 2017). Attackers threaten to kill victim in video linked to Serena McKay homicide. *CBC News.* Retrieved from www.cbc.ca/news/canada/manitoba/sagkeeng-first-nations-facebook-video-attack-1.4086169.

Oberst, U., Wegmann, E., Stodt, B., Brand, M., & Chamarro, A. (2017). Negative consequences from heavy social networking in adolescents: The mediating role of fear of missing out. *Journal of Adolescence, 55,* 51–60.

O'Reilly, T. (2007). What is web 2.0: Design patterns and business models for the next generation of software. *Communications & Strategies, 65*(1), 17–37.

Piwek, L., & Joinson, A. (2016). "What do they snapchat about?" Patterns of use in time-limited instant messaging service. *Computers in Human Behavior, 54,* 358–367.

Poltash, N. (2013). Snapchat and sexting: A snapshot of baring your bare essentials. *Richmond Journal of Law & Technology, XIX*(4), 1–24.

Pope, H., Phillips, K., & Olivardia, R. (2000). *The Adonis Complex: How to Identify, Treat and Prevent Body Obsession in Men and Boys.* New York: Simon and Schuster.

Przybylski, A., Murayama, K., DeHaan, C. R., & Gladwell, V. (2013). Motivational, emotional, and behavioral correlates offear ofmissing out. *Computers in Human Behavior, 29*(4), 1841–1848.

Quan-Haase, A., & Young, A. L. (2010). Uses and gratifications of social media: A comparison of Facebook and instant messaging. *Bulletin of Science, Technology & Society, 30*(5), 350–361.

Rentschler, C. (2014). Rape culture and the feminist politics of social media. *Girlhood Studies, 7*(1), 65–82.

Ricciardelli, R. (2011). Masculinity, appearance and consumerism: A look at men's hair. *Canadian Review of Sociology, 48*(2), 181–201. doi:10.1111/j.1755-618X.2011.01261.x

Ricciardelli, R., & Clow, K. A. (2009). Men, appearance, and cosmetic surgery: The role of confidence, self-esteem and comfort with the body. *Canadian Journal of Sociology, 34*(1), 101–131.

Ricciardelli, R., Clow, K. A., & White, P. (2010). Masculinity portrayals in men's lifestyle magazines. *Sex Roles: A Journal of Research, 63*(1), 64–78. doi:10.1007/s11199-010-9764-8

Ricciardelli, R., & White, P. (2011). Modifying the body: Canadian men's perspectives on appearance and cosmetic surgery. *The Qualitative Report, 16*(4), 949–970.

Rushkoff, D. (2006). *Screenagers: Lessons In Chaos From Digital Kids.* Cresskill, NJ: Hampton Press.

Shapiro, L. A. S., & Margolin, G. (2014). Growing up wired: Social networking sites and adolescent psychosocial development. *Clinical Child and Family Psychology Review, 17*(1), 1–18.

Shariff, S., & DeMartini, A. (2015). Defining the legal lines: eGirls and intimate images. In J. Bailey & V. Steeves (Eds.), *eGirls, eCitizens* (pp. 281–305). Ottawa: University of Ottawa Press.

Shilling, C. (2003). *The Body and Social Theory* (2nd Ed.). London: Sage Publications.

Siibak, A. (2010). Constructing masculinity on a social networking site: The case-study of visual self-presentations of young men on the profile images of SNS Rate. *Young, 18*(4), 403–425.

Spector, M., & Kitsuse, J. I. (1977). *Constructing Social Problems*. Menlo Park: Cummings Publishing Company.

Steeves, V. (2005). *Young Canadians in a Wired World, Phase II: Trends and Recommendations*. Ottawa: Media Awareness Network.

Steeves, V., & Webster, C. (2008). Closing the barn door: The effect of parental supervision on Canadian children's online privacy. *Bulletin of Science, Technology & Society, 28*(1), 4–19.

Stroud, S. (2014). The dark side of the online self: A pragmatist critique of the growing plague of revenge porn. *Journal of Mass Media Ethics, 29*(3), 168–183.

Tapscott, D. (2009). *Grown Up Digital: How the Net Generation is Changing Your World*. New York: Mcgraw-Hill.

Utz, S., Muscanell, N., & Khalid, C. (2015). Snapchat elicits more jealousy than Facebook: A comparison of Snapchat and Facebook use. *Cyberpsychology, Behavior, and Social Networking, 18*(3), 141–146.

Valkenburg, P., & Peter, J. (2007). Preadolescents' and adolescents' online communication and their closeness to friends. *Developmental Psychology, 43*(2), 267–277.

Valkenburg, P., Peter, J., & Schouten, A. (2006). Friend networking sites and their relationship to adolescents' well-being and social self-esteem. *CyberPsychology & Behavior, 9*(5), 584–590.

Vickery, J. (2017). *Worried About the Wrong Things: Youth, Risk, and Opportunity in the Digital World*. Cambridge, MA: The MIT Press.

Wolf, N. (1991). *The Beauty Myth*. London: Chatto and Windus.

Chapter 4

Youth attitudes and experiences towards parental and school surveillance

Introduction

Technological advancements have engendered the world with ubiquitous surveillance devices, within which new generations of citizens are embedded. Indeed, as early as infancy smart phones are used to control monitoring devices that "keep an eye" on sleeping newborns. Youth comfort with and dependence on technology is increasingly evinced among youth who grow up in a virtual world, connected to peers and fixated on happenings within their inner social circles and the greater netizen landscapes – in essence their world both shrinks and grows (Livingstone, 2009; Tapscott, 2009). Issues of who to trust and how to be safe online, however, are common concerns and topics of interest among law enforcement, justice circles, educators, parents and those focused on youth welfare (Fisk, 2016; Hinduja & Patchin, 2014; Livingstone & Sefton-Green, 2016). "Cyberspace" may be presented as "the new frontline" yet it is shaped by a virtually "limitless victimization risk" (Blakemore, 2012: 16; Hinduja & Patchin, 2009: 24).

Sociological researchers, however, suggest that despite evidence of real risks, public concerns (e.g., among parents and educators) are often based on perceptions of risk that are disproportionate to the realities facing children and teens (boyd, 2014; Vickery, 2017), especially female teens (Bailey & Steeves, 2015; Cassell & Cramer, 2008). These perceptions are compounded by media driven moral panics (boyd, 2014; Cohen, 2002 [1972]; Vickery, 2017) that only fuel accumulating anxieties and highlight the potentiality for youth in the online world to become criminalized or victimized; the prey or the predator (e.g., Marker, 2011; Murguía, Tackett-Gibson, & Lessem, 2007).

In today's technology-saturated climate, the common perceptions of youth as potential prey raise concerns among parents and educators (e.g., teachers, counselors) about youth online safety or exposure to cyber-risk (Vickery, 2017). Specifically, in response to open-ended survey items asking parents to share their biggest concern with their children's online activities, they consistently list "sexual predators," "child molesters," "pedophiles," and "sex offenders" as primary concerns (boyd, 2014: 109) – a list seemingly influenced by media headlines and the societal infused hate directed toward those who sexually prey on youth (see Ricciardelli & Spencer, 2017). Arguably, such perceptions appear driven by emotional assessments of risk, rather than statistical data that instead shows relatively low risk levels tied to cyberbullying and strangers online (Bailey & Steeves, 2015; boyd, 2014; Vickery, 2017). Researchers investigating parental challenges faced when raising children today suggest that, motivated in part by fear of cyber-risks or the pending detriment of teens being left with "idle hands" online, many teens' activities are regulated through various school, volunteer, sports, and other recreational activities, leaving little downtime (boyd, 2014). Parental concern over, and monitoring of, their children's online activities both at home and in school is well documented (Bailey & Steeves, 2015; boyd, 2014; Livingstone, Haddon, Görzig, & Ólafsson, 2010). In response, surveillance by parents and educators has become a routinized aspect of childhood and youth (Steeves, 2010, 2012), with parents rationalizing monitoring out of "tough love" (boyd, 2014) while educators monitor based on a fusion of pedagogical and security motives (Fisk, 2016).

Surveillance is defined as "any collection and processing of personal data, whether identifiable or not, for the purposes of influencing or managing those whose data have been garnered" (Bruno, 2012: 344). Said another way, it is the collection and analysis of data with the intention to maintain awareness over those individuals. In the United States, for instance, researchers report both a heightened concern on the part of parents and willingness to use surveillance to address their concern. For example, authors of a PEW Research Institute report on parents and social media found "33% of parents have had concerns or questions about their child's technology use in the past 12 months," with "mothers and fathers … equally likely to have had concerns and questions" (Duggan, Lenhart, Lampe, & Ellison, July 2015: 23). Moreover, concerns are more likely for parents who have children under five years of age. Another PEW report found that "most parents check what their teen does online and on social media," and that parental concerns about potential harm online inform a "hands-on approach" to the monitoring of their children (Anderson, January 2016: 2). Anderson here reported that 61% of surveyed parents indicated they have checked the websites their child or children visit; 60% ever checked their social media profiles; 56% ever "friended" or followed them on a SNS such as Facebook or Twitter; 48% looked through their phone or text message records.

With fear as a driving commercialized force, some parents supplement their efforts at mediation by using "spyware" software to trace their children's online activities (Anderson, January 2016; Fisk, 2016; Marx & Steeves, 2010). Use of spyware and other technologically geared surveillance tools, accessible from parents' cellular phones and computers, arguably provides parents with a sense of control that minimizes their perception of risk (Fotel & Thomsen,

2002). Resources, such as booklets and pamphlets, websites for various surveillance applications, and videos on YouTube, with testimonials from parents – usually mothers – purport the efficacy of such technologies (e.g., NetNanny and PC Tattletale, among others; see Williams, 2013). Parents are introduced to spyware and the justification for its use in schools, for example during parent–teacher meetings involving presentations from police officers, school teachers, and counselors. In his U.S.-based research with students in grades 6 to 12, as well as parents and school administrators, Nathan Fisk (2016) attended such presentations, which ended with information about online monitoring strategies and the promotion of software such as Net-Smartz. He noted that through such presentations, "all teens seeking privacy or otherwise enjoying themselves on the computer are made to appear as risky or suspicious" (Fisk, 2016: 74). Tellingly, in conducting focus groups with parents, Fisk (2016) found a self-imposed moral policing of 'good parenting' whereby parents who did not adhere to the putative norm of online surveillance were "positioned as bad, disinterested parents" (126). Similar research in Canada is rare, though Johnson's (2015) Canadian focus groups with parents similarly revealed that parents often feel "pressured to take any steps they could to keep their children safe, including subjecting them to constant monitoring" (Johnson, 2015: 339; see also Steeves, 2013).

In addition to parental monitoring, so-called "surveillance schools" – schools "characterised by an array of routine practices … [that] identify, verify, categorize and track pupils" – are becoming established around the world (Taylor, 2012: 2). Their common features include Closed Circuit Television (CCTV), fingerprinting, iris scanning, school ID cards with Radio Frequency Identification (RFID), and even "smart uniforms" which monitor student whereabouts both on and off school property (Taylor, 2013). While it remains too early to empirically state the implications of such a degree of surveillance on youth and learning environments, we feel the increased degree of surveillance in the name of "safety" may have unintended yet rash consequences on student well-being and development. Nonetheless, through research with students, parents and school administrators in the United States, Fisk (2016) found some schools possessed "an extensive surveillance system to monitor and restrict the activities of students throughout the school day," including CCTV and audio monitors in bathrooms and locker rooms (Fisk, 2016: 159). Similarly, through research with 13- and 14-year-old students in an urban secondary school in London, Livingstone and Sefton-Green (2016) found it "striking … how the class was almost constantly under surveillance, recorded, and evaluated – both interpersonally and digitally" (140).

Canadian schools today are benefitting from the federal government's commitment, made in the 1990s, to ensure Canada stays internationally competitive in their networked communications. This commitment was actualized through, for example, the "wiring" for the internet in all public schools by the end of the 20th century (Steeves, 2006). However, these advancements in the 1990s came alongside moral panics over school shootings such as Columbia, Colorado, and Taber, Alberta (Steeves, 2010). CCTV cameras, argued to be "at the forefront of embedding communications technologies into everyday teaching and learning," soon became "common" across Canadian schools too (Steeves, 2006: 183; see also Steeves, 2010). School administrators draw from a variety of surveillance technologies, including "draconian use policies, filtering software, and monitoring," that make surveillance the "default response" to any harm potentiality (Steeves, 2010). In the early 2000s, "dystopian accounts" of technologies impact on youth, especially female teens, helped justify "expanded state and law enforcement powers, especially powers of surveillance" (Bailey & Steeves, 2015: 3). Indeed, the comfort apparently thought garnered through surveillance may have continued to fuel its increasing implementation.

But, how, then, are teens responding to an arguably draconian climate of omnipresent surveillance? There is no overarching answer, though many researchers point to overt antagonism coupled with creative strategies to help mitigate and circumvent surveillance by parents and educators (e.g., Fisk, 2016; Taylor, 2013). In 2006, Taylor (2013) found the students she interviewed in British schools to be "incensed about the lack of privacy they were afforded, not just in the school but more broadly a result of surveillance technologies" (64). Likewise, Giroux (2003: xvii) highlighted the "deep distrust" apparent across U.S. schools' employees in their interactions with students, whom he argued have become a "generation of suspects". Most recently, Fisk (2016) found some students in the United States complaining about content their schools block, citing increased difficulties in completing class projects as a consequence. The Canadian female teens interviewed by Bailey and Steeves (2015) felt surveillance by particular groups to be more of a problem than solution. They write, "many of our participants expressed as much or more concern about online surveillance by family members, employers, and peers as about surveillance by unknown adults" (39). According to multiple researchers, young "digital natives" often demonstrate creative strategies to resist governance, thwart attempts at control, and circumvent restricted access (Barron, 2014; boyd, 2014; Livingstone, 2008). For instance, Fisk (2016) found students told not to text in class simply did so in washrooms and locker rooms (perhaps explaining school-deployed audio monitoring of these spaces), while Steeves (2010) addressed the Canadian context, arguing:

> although the surveillance capacities of networked computing have been used to deepen the neoliberal tendency to treat students as suspects, the effect of this on the social relationships in the classroom has been ambiguous, and the wired classroom remains a contested site in which students can resist the teacher's authority.

Teens, in short, "wish to avoid paternalistic adults who use safety and protection as an excuse to monitor their everyday sociality" (boyd, 2014: 56). Thus, the suggestion here is that teens disambiguate the notion of safety and protection as disjointed from that of control and scrutiny.

A teenaged panoptic wasteland

Theoretically, scholarship on surveillance often incorporates (to one extent or another) Foucault's model of governmentality, i.e., the "conduct of conduct" enacted through "the particularities of governmental projects" (Haggerty, 2006: 40). The broad goal of such scholarship is population management in order to ensure their well-being (Li, 2007); here too, for our study, the focus is on the well-being of youth as impacted by surveillance practices. Foucault's panopticon "conjures a 'docile' subject, rendered disciplined through being aware of the potential of surveillance at all times" (Kanai, 2015: 88). Such positioning aligns well with the ideal neoliberal citizen; a prudential person considered to be calculative of dangers and avertable of risks (Rose, 1996a, 1996b). Yet neither Foucault nor Rose seem to place any emphasis on how youth are socialized into the role of the ideal prudential person. We may expect this process to be highly fragmented, discontinuous, and not at all isomorphic, yet such expectations are only notional.

We thus echo Haggerty's (2006) observation that models of contemporary surveillance, often presuming top-down forms of governance, exclude the "actual experiences of people being subjected to different governmental regimes," and that "modestly realist projects" are required "that analyze the politics of surveillance on the experiences of the subjects of surveillance" (42). We extend this idea in our examination of Canadian youth perceptions and responses to attempts to govern their online conduct by parents and educators. Indeed, our study responds to those who suggest scholarship on governance and "governmentality" – the examination of the efforts by various sectors of society to govern conduct – would greatly benefit from grounded empirical research (Haggerty, 2006; Li, 2007; Nadesan, 2008).

Surveillance itself may be considered a contested concept among teens. Scholars examining parental mediation of children' activities have challenged the often-conflated notions of surveillance and monitoring practices. For instance, in Stattin and Kerr's (2000) seminal critique of the parental monitoring literature, they argue that teens' trust in their parents has received insufficient attention in the literature on parental monitoring: "whether they feel that their parents are willing to listen to them, are responsive, and would not ridicule or punish if they confided in them" (1083–1084). They also argue parental monitoring is conceptually distinct from more overt and abjured (from the perspective of children) surveillance practices; the former, which includes "parent-child communication is more beneficial than surveillance and control" (2000: 173). In the context of digital surveillance, the latter involves more covert efforts to track the activities of children with or without their consent, for instance using particular tracking software packages. In sum, active (i.e., regular and effective) communication is linked to children's good performance, while surveillance is linked to bad performance (Kerr & Stattin, 2000; Stattin & Kerr, 2000). Comparably, Steeves and Webster's (2008) large survey of Canadian teens between the ages of 13 to 17 sought to examine the relationship between parental "supervision" and children's privacy-risky behaviors online. They operationalized supervision through a 3-point scale measuring children's frequency of internet use at home with a parent or other adult, and the presence of house rules against interacting with strangers online and divulging personal information. While they found that high levels of parental supervision did reduce privacy-risky behaviour, they also reported that:

> even among those respondents experiencing the highest level of parental supervision, those young people with the greatest social interaction … continued to be more likely than those with the least social interaction … to be most willing to disclose personal information [and] … continued to be more likely to display the least privacy-protective behavior than those with low levels of social interaction.
>
> (Steeves & Webster, 2008: 13)

From these findings, it is clear that we need more insight into youth perspectives if we are to create and implement effective policies related to parenting and school practices. Said another way, how do youth interpret supervision?

Media headlines decrying youths' lack of concern for privacy have been long debunked by scholarship on the creative strategies taken to guard against personal disclosure online (boyd & Hargittai, 2010). However, a handful of scholars highlight an emerging trend of teen dismissal of privacy as a concern. In our own sample of teens, we found that as Canadian teens age, they come to internalize an ethos of self-responsibilization, evidenced through their claim, when asked about issues related to privacy and surveillance, to not "doing anything wrong" and therefore having "nothing to hide" (see Chapter 6; see also Murumaa-Mengel, Laas-Mikko, & Pruulmann-Vengerfeldt, 2015; Nau, 2014; Solove, 2011). This seems to be directly related to an acquiescence to panoptic surveillance. By 2013, Taylor also noticed a shift in attitude amongst Australian university students, who expressed a "so what?" attitude towards the intensification of surveillance in schools (see Taylor, 2013). Does this trend indicate teens are increasingly unconcerned for privacy and surveillance given their view that they are not "doing anything wrong?" To what degree is the trend of panoptic hegemony – the reality of omnipresent and effective surveillance being taken as common sense and "just the way things are" – evident in the attitudes of teens today?

Parental monitoring: best intentions, coercive surveillance, and having nothing to hide

It quickly became evident in our focus group discussions that teens actively delineated between monitoring and surveillance. Since the level of acceptance or antagonism regarding parental mediation is contingent on the gradations of its various types, several group discussions centered on what qualifies as "monitoring," specifically, what is being monitored, under what conditions and with what intentions?

With some reservations, youth expressed more tolerance toward parental monitoring that they deemed relatively non-invasive, was engaged in with their tacit consent, and motivated by their parents' need to protect them from harm. When compared with the number of youth who made reference to having parents who scrutinize their social media, a sizable percentage sympathized with their parents, at least to a degree. Expressions of sympathy for parental monitoring are concentrated amongst Cyber City residents (23 references versus seven from Cyberville residents). Female groups made far more references (24) than male groups (4). Despite the greater proportion of females in the study, this skew, alongside the concentration of sympathetic references in urban areas, points to the significance of gender in shaping experiences of parental monitoring.

Reservations regarding parental monitoring are tempered through a discourse of having 'nothing to hide' among our participants (for elaboration on this privacy mindset, see Chapter 6). For instance, despite being sympathetic toward parental monitoring, 15-year-old Chantelle from Cyberville mentioned during a discussion of parental monitoring that her mother checks her Instagram and Snapchat activity weekly. Chantelle says she does not mind her mother's frequent monitoring "because I don't really do anything bad," – a discursive position found more prominently among our older participants (see Chapter 6). From one of our younger groups, Valerie, age 13 from Cyberville, discloses she would "feel so uncomfortable" if her parents "went through all [her] pictures on [her] phone," especially if it involves pictures with her friends "doing something." She adds "not that I have anything to hide, but if they had to go through it I wouldn't mind, it's just I feel so uncomfortable, like I take, *that's practically my life*, just looking through it" (added emphasis). The emotional and personal emphasis Valerie places on the pictures on her phone suggests an acute need to guard privacy, and exposes a subtle vulnerability tied to how her photographs may be interpreted by her parent(s), with the begrudging rationalization that parental monitoring, while not welcome (and perhaps not always comforting), is nevertheless 'understood'. It is notable that parental monitoring, although designed for safety, is not necessarily comforting to youth, in that safety and 'comfort' are not synonymous – monitoring may help assure physical safety but impinge on personal comfort.

Perhaps such vulnerabilities underlie why some teens in our discussions expressed considerable exasperation at their own attempts to develop trusting relationships with their parents, despite parental debasement of trust – albeit unintentional. For instance, Yasmin, 18-years-old from Cyber City, speaks of her "kind of open" relationship with her mother, while with her father,

> every time I get a text message he'll like lean over and read it, and like that kind of thing … it might just be my friend being … and I'm like "what do you want to know? Just ask me and I'll tell you."

A social sense of privacy (James, 2014; see also Chapter 6) is evidently important to both Yasmin and Fatima: that anyone, whether family or otherwise, can peer over to see what a child is doing online does not absolve them of the responsibility of asking permission to do so. Our participants often declared, again with a note of exasperation: "trust me, please, just ask and I'll tell you" to parents and educators alike. Empathy for parental monitoring, then, depends on the extent of open communication, respect and trust. "If parents monitor their kids, it should be in a way that's respectful you know, not just like getting info," argues Fiona, age 18 from Cyber City. Clearly, the message she advises to parents is to overcome the urge to infiltrate their communications – particularly by exerting their authority and thus ability to simply "take" what would be personal information. Asked what such a respectful relationship would look like, she elaborates:

> I feel like you should always like sit down and talk to your child and say like, I want your password for this because of this reason and only use it for that reason that you specified, not any other reason … just for safety reasons to have their passwords and stuff.

The frustration that some of our participants expressed towards parents reveals not only their desire for open communication but also their distaste for more overt but "underhanded" or deceptive attempts to peer into their online lives, despite acknowledging parents' best intentions.

As alluded by our participants' statements above, some teens are concerned that even when they feel parental monitoring is well intentioned, parents will not understand the context of what is being posted online (boyd, 2008). Serena, a 19-year-old university undergraduate student from Cyber City put it this way:

> Not that there [is] anything bad [about parental monitoring], but it's just, you know you talk about so many things with your friends that your parents just wouldn't understand, or would ask for an explanation and you would have no idea how to explain it or whatever.

As Serena's words reveal, for many youths it is the mundane, everyday exchanges becoming misinterpreted by parents that concerns them far more often than their parents finding them engaging in illicit activities. In response to other participants in her focus group, Serena adds that she is "not that tight" with her parents, and does not "open up to my parents as much as some people do, which I wish I could but I can't because my parents won't understand half the things I do." Her remarks suggest that factors, including level of communication, trust, and attitudes of parents towards technology in general and online monitoring in particular, help shape teens' views of parental mediation (i.e., whether viewed as monitoring or surveillance). The dialogue in our group discussions show that teens who have higher degrees of trust with their parents are quicker to justify parental monitoring, though notably these youth also express reservations about intrusiveness. For example, 14-year-old Nancy from Cyber City revealed that when her parents "ask me what's going on" and since "they kind of trust me," she will "show them my phone, and they'll, they'll be fine with it. Like there's sometimes that still even if it's nothing bad … I still don't like showing my phone to everybody, but uhm … wouldn't do any harm either." Nancy, who trusts her parents and justifies parental monitoring, still reveals a personal vulnerability tied to "showing" her phone.

In contrast to monitoring, which is at least tolerated given a respectful disclosure of the rationale parents have to monitor their children's online activities, surveillance practices were described as more coercive than monitoring – such as use of spyware – and a breach of privacy and trust (Racz & McMahon, 2011; Stattin, 2001; Stattin & Kerr, 2000). Participants recalled being "creeped out" by nosey parents using social media to track their location and "stalk" them, as expressed by Cecilia, age 14 from Cyber City. Explicit antagonism towards parental surveillance (with reference to invasions of privacy) is concentrated among female groups (11 references, versus only one reference from a male group) and, overall, references are concentrated in Cyber City (15), versus Cyberville (2). This concentration may suggest more informal and close-knit connections in rural areas that foster greater amounts of communication and trust with parents, though at the same time a fair number of urban youth also made reference to parental trust. Nonetheless, many teens argue that surveillance violates their privacy. Significantly, Anna, a 19-year-old undergraduate student, provides a representative statement of finding the balance between what could be described as parental "intrusion" into privacy and their efforts to provide a safety net:

> I don't necessarily feel like parents should be logging in all the time. I feel like there needs to be a level of trust, but I also do feel like having the option to check in should something be wrong, is also helpful.

It is more likely that many teens are not knowledgeable about the exact surveillance practices their parents engage in, including the associated technologies. Many of our participants appeared to believe that both parents and teachers could surveille them through Wi-Fi servers. Cecilia, for example, responding to a question about how exactly her parents surveille her online activities, admits "I don't know how do they do it. They check through the Wi-Fi server … they can read my texts without having my phone, it's wild." Her friend Vivian, 15, is surprised by this: "That's terrible, tell me not to swear when I text you!" A typical response to parental use of spyware comes from Amber, age 15 from Cyber City. She has general sympathy for parents' concern for their children's online activities, arguing that the frequency and intensity matter:

> I think it's good that like parents occasionally check up on what their kids are doing on social media but *I think constantly doing it and spying on them I feel like it would be an invasion of privacy.* I wouldn't like it, personally I wouldn't like it … but at the same time I'd let them look through my stuff if they need to, or if they wanted to cuz *there's nothing to hide* but, like at the same it's just I don't know, I don't really like it, it's not just my parents, I wouldn't let anyone go on my phone and like spy on me any hour of the day. [added emphases]

Amber is typical of many of our participants in acquiescing to a certain amount of monitoring if only to appease intrusive parents (and, as we discuss below, educators), though more overt spying is not acceptable. Her attitude is emboldened by her argument for having "nothing to hide," which may be considered a vocabulary of motive that appears to be more readily internalized as teens mature (see Chapter 6; see also Cannataci, 2015; Keeler, 2006; Mills, 1940).

Ironically, some participants critiqued parental surveillance practices for the vulnerabilities its use exposes parents themselves to. One co-ed group of four, aged 17 and 18, were asked if they knew of any parents using software to surveille their children. Evidencing a strong IT background during his focus group Seth, a 17-year-old from Cyber City, opted to warn parents about such software technologies. He responded:

> I know of some parents who've done that, but the issue that I have with that is it's a double-edged sword, and it may be true you're keeping watch of your kids, but the fact of the matter is that it's one of the most dangerous things you could do in terms of privacy for that kid and for yourself in fact as well.

He elaborates that spyware "has to go through a secondary service" to collect information on a child and make "copies of all the information that your kid has on their phone." However, he adds, "anything that you access from there, they can have reverse access to whatever you have [as parents] as well." The consequences, Seth argues, involve not only "annoyed" children who are "probably not ever going to let you back in further on down the road at least in terms of, if you ask them about online safety later on," but also parents who inadvertently open themselves up for revealing their own data using the same software. "It's much more dangerous of a thing than people realize," Seth concludes. Seth provides much insight on how "disguised" control and information seeking can have long term negative impacts on trust and other aspects of child–parent relationships, despite best intentions. Second, he reveals how ubiquitous surveillance tools can, ironically, surveille those who seek to surveille others (Andrejevic, 2005; Regan & Steeves, 2010), suggesting the polymorphous nature of power and process in relation to surveillance under contexts of panoptic hegemony. The consequences for both youth and parents, as put forth by Seth, appear more damaging than the possible benefits in terms of control, safety, and relationships.

School-based mediation: obedience, resistance, and belief in surveillance efficacy

Across focus groups, discussions centered on experiences with parents and technology naturally gravitated to experiences in school. During these discussions, some participants revealed that some of their teachers restricted access to their cell phones in class. In the United States most teachers informally permit students to possess cell phones for safety reasons (i.e., in response to the Littleton high school shooting in 1999), with official policies varying by school district; some schools have cell phone bans to curb cyberbullying, others embrace technologies for the educational opportunities it affords students (Earl, May 18, 2012; Fisk, 2016; Higgins, August 7, 2013). Similarly in Canada, partly in response to the school shooting in Taber, Alberta, in 1999, school boards often have policies in place declaring their "right to monitor all electronic communications" of students, who are often told they have their online activities recorded (Steeves, 2010). Some scholars have argued the majority of school boards in Canada treat cell phones "as a scourge," though more recently the Toronto District School Board (the largest in Canada), among others, have reversed restrictive policies in favor of "permissive smartphone" usage, in line with views of students' use of cell phone for connectivity and learning (Mcquigge, February 26, 2017). Suggestive of these trends, our participants revealed no overarching trend regarding policies on technology in the classroom; instead, policies seem to be more a product of individual teacher decisions than school or school board policy (or, where such policies exist, students reveal variation by teacher regardless). Some teachers attempt to strike a balance, as recalled by 18-year-old Fiona, from Cyber City:

> Some teachers had a 5-minute technology break in the middle of class so that you could just [go] on your phone and answer whatever you needed and do whatever you needed to do, and then they went back to where your phones had to go away.

While some participants felt that restrictions placed on technology are effective, references are minimal compared with those who felt such restrictions are not effective. Understandably, the majority of references regarding having a class with restrictions on technology are concentrated among 13- to 14-year-old participants, given the assumption that teachers may have more restrictive policies for younger students. Overall 21 references are antagonistic to technological restrictions (usually cell phones are discussed), with only two supportive. Moreover, the majority of antagonistic references (16) come from female groups. There are no significant differences in the concentration of references between Cyber City and Cyberville (i.e., antagonism was expressed relatively equally in both regions).

Kevin from Cyberville, aged 13, offered a practical view about teachers collecting phones during class: "Well yeah I guess [it works], cuz if your phone's not with you, you can't exactly go on it." Though he admits students are able to relatively easily circumvent this policy: "There's some people, yeah, who go to the bathroom like every five minutes, they go on their phone." Teachers who aim to restrict access to cell phones then face challenges to student ingenuity. Participants antagonistic towards cell phone restrictions in the classroom often made reference to strategies such as keeping their phones on them with the ringer turned off, or having a friend keep their phone for a while, while others suggested that teachers do not follow through with their directives, as they are able to keep their phones openly on their desk to charge. Lexi, 15-years-old from Cyber City, offers a representative view pointing to the lack of deterrent effect of restrictive policies:

> I think there's rules implemented, but very few students listen to them, so then in one year, I would have say four teachers, one teacher would be so strict, would follow the rules and would actually collect the cell phones and another teacher would just not care if you're even using them, so generally the rules are told to us, but when we don't follow them there's not necessarily any punishment for it.

Thus, not only did phone-related policy appear inconsistent across classes, teachers, and school, but phone policies that did exist did not appear to be consistently enforced.

Many participants also expressed strong antagonism in response to school-based internet restriction policies, specifically blocking Wi-Fi access to students. No patterns by age or gender emerged here, though interestingly the majority of references to schools having a Wi-Fi restriction policy come from rural Cyberville participants (17 versus only four from Cyber City), with Cyberville youth presenting as slightly more antagonistic towards such policies. These discussions reveal how significant access to technology is for many teens. Some students from Cyberville, during wider discussions of technology in the classroom, revealed that their school principal had placed restrictions on cell phone and Wi-Fi access in response to transgressive student incidents such as the non-consensual distribution of nudes (i.e., "sexting"; see Chapter 7). One student, 13-year-old Valerie, critiqued the school's response as overbearing: "so now we have no internet in the school, so I think that really ticked everyone off, because now we have to use our 3G and stuff. ... I hate not having my phone on me." Valerie refers to being restricted from school Wi-Fi and thus using cell phone data, which many participants felt placed significant restrictions on their online access. Like Valerie, Ally, a 17-year-old from Cyberville, also discloses that she "went over 50 bucks on my data like yesterday, because I don't have Wi-Fi, it sucks." Others – from both Cyberville and Cyber City – argued that access to their phones is essential to completing school assignments, especially as many are assigned and managed using online course management databases. Here too Ally offers a representative statement: "usually people do research projects on their phone and they get them done like that, because everyone wants to be on their phone, but the Wi-Fi's gone now, and a lot of people can't do it." The lack of free Wi-Fi was an identified challenge for many students, especially in Cyberville, who often have cell phone plans with limited or restricted data. Data plans were identified as very expensive (versus free Wi-Fi access), and often there is no cell signal or very poor-quality signal strength in said areas.

Wi-Fi restrictions in schools, then, may have more of an impact on rural teens than those living in urban centers. Raquel and Christy, both 14 and living in Cyberville, express great reservation towards schools restricting Wi-Fi access. Raquel reveals that she does not bring her phone to school and "a lot of my friends don't have functioning cellphones." Christy agrees, adding "where my friends are they don't have cell service." 3G, 4G, and LTE bandwidth data access are understandably taken-for-granted by teens living in urban regions. However, for those without such access in rural areas, Wi-Fi access takes on greater importance.

Perhaps ironically, students who are "forced" to use data instead of Wi-Fi may well have their illicit activities displaced rather than eliminated, given the sense they are not being observed. William, aged 17 from Cyber City, argues that even if directly aware of being surveilled by their schools, some students will simply search for illicit content on their data plans. "Even if people are even conscious about the fact [that they are being surveilled], they'll just do it on the data on their cell phones." Teens "will to misbehave" usurps any efforts by schools, he argues: "If people are going to do it, then they're going to do it always." Another group of two 13-year-old boys from Cyberville complained about their school's restricting Wi-Fi access, remarking (apparently sincerely) "so now we have to send nudes over 3G." Such remarks clearly evidence that school-based Wi-Fi access restrictions fail to provide any genuine deterrent, at least in the context of sending nude images. The only real and likely unintentional consequence of such restrictions is to perpetuate differentiation between students based on socio–economic status (i.e., students who can afford data will be able to use online resources to assist with school work, and will not be socially hampered by being unable to access social media).

Of note, during focus group discussions, it became evident how strongly some participants felt the schools are able to surveille their activities online. One group of females from Cyber City, ages 14 and 15, raised the issue of the "panoptic" powers of school-based surveillance. Holly says "yeah during school hours … once you're logged in the [school] network, they can look at everything." Nancy adds "they can go [on your phone] and look at anything with an app." Ashima suggests that the monitoring is due to bullying, "because they want to know who's bullying who and why, and when." As a result, "now they're like if I see your phone, like it's gone." Participants in some groups recalled vivid memories of the moment that they realized they were being surveilled. Serena recalled using a computer lab in junior high school, where "there is one computer that is only for the teacher which could see what every computer was doing." She recalls doing school work one day in the lab, though having

> an extra internet tab open on some weird website … and then my teacher started typing on my Word document, I could see it on my screen, and it was [Serena] please start typing your work and do your work and I was like whoa, that was scary, she was typing [from] her computer and it was showing up on my Word document, so that's how intense that was monitored!

In addition to being startled, this sudden realization of being watched caused Serena to re-focus on her school work: "I started working after that because I realized someone was watching me." Notably, the surveillant means towards this end (i.e., good student behavior) is not an easy compromise for Serena: "I think it's smart but it was very creepy, and very scary."

We argue that it is reasonable to consider student anticipation over the overarching panoptic surveillance powers of schools is highly exaggerated. Nevertheless, from an educator's standpoint, licit behavior is instilled through an *expectation* of being surveilled. Moreover, this recognition of how easily one can be surveilled by someone that is completely undetected can further extend the expectation of being surveilled and the associated resulting sense of vulnerability, even violation, due to the privacy breach. Despite the discomfort, surveillance is justified based on its potential to instill a safe and secure environment. Some of our participants, then, tended to censor their online behaviors based on the over-arching possibility that that they were surveilled at school, which falls directly in line with Foucault's argument of surveillance efficacy (Foucault, 1977; Garland, 1997).

Discussion

At the beginning of his influential book *The Culture of Control*, David Garland presciently writes "we quickly grow used to the way things are" (Garland, 2001: 1). He refers to the broad ways that, over time, a penal climate can sediment itself such that the array of penal technologies, including punitive and rehabilitative responses, seems atemporal and transcultural – just "the way things are." The same historical progression can be claimed for the ubiquitous presence of surveillance technologies, especially those used by parents and educators (i.e., teachers and counselors) to track the activities of children and students, respectively. Panoptic hegemony refers not only to the omnipresence of surveillance technologies, but the wider expectation of their deterrent efficacy and embedding within society as "the way things are," so as to stymie critical responses of the current system (Gramsci, 1971). Yet despite what we know about how teens often actively resist efforts of social control within the online spaces they inhabit (Barron, 2014; boyd, 2008; Livingstone, 2008), here we highlight the range of teen responses that together reveal a spectrum of orientations toward the 'governable subject' (Rose, 1996a, 1996b) – the ideally socialized, compliant and therefore "safe" child/student.

In line with prior research on parental monitoring (e.g., Stattin & Kerr, 2000), our focus group discussions reveal more sympathy – sometimes laced with reservation – for parental monitoring that is fully disclosed and "understood" to occur given parental concern for child safety and security. Research on parental monitoring is unequivocal: high parental knowledge of children's activities is consistently linked to measures of good adjustment. The question becomes how such knowledge is acquired. Trust is maintained through ongoing communication and children's spontaneous disclosures of information rather than parental tracking and surveillance (Kerr & Stattin, 2000; Racz & McMahon, 2011; Stattin, 2001). Our participants conveyed that their concerns for parental monitoring are centered on potential misunderstandings of the content they are posting online, rather than concern over parents discovering illicit activities. While media continues to highlight the latter, it is mundane communications with (usually offline) peer networks, where teens manage context and meaning, where their privacy matters most (boyd, 2008; Davis, 2014).

In contrast, our participants expressed strong antagonism towards parental surveillance – conceived as less consensual, often undisclosed and a more explicit intrusion into privacy. The fact that the majority of those reporting as antagonistic towards parental surveillance in our sample are females living in Cyber City offers an interesting line of inquiry for further comparative research between urban and rural regions. This finding may indicate resistance from female teens towards messages of cyber-safety and associated "technologies," from parents but also schools and governments, often targeted to females more than males (Bailey & Steeves, 2013; Hasinoff, 2012; Karaian,

2014). It is also possible that rural environments offer more opportunities for parental communication alongside connections with the wider community in ways that instill social capital which are undercut in urban, hyper-atomistic and "not in my backyard" communities (cf. Burkell & Saginur, 2015; Christie, 2004; Putnam, 2000); or, that male children may be less overtly surveilled than females (see Steeves, 2005). Based on our participants' responses, overall, we advocate for parents fostering greater ongoing and empathetic communication with their children, rather than risk breaching trust by adopting surveillance tools that not only are likely to be detected at some point but are also likely to be viewed as violating. Further, as one participant remarked, using such technologies places parents themselves at risk for breaches of their own privacy as well as their children.

Among our participants, stronger reservations are expressed for parental surveillance than for school surveillance. A significant proportion of participants believed in schools' ability to surveille everything they do online, especially through the use of Wi-Fi "perimeters" – despite the likely feasibility of such practices. Tellingly, many thought school surveillance helps instill good behavior, even combatting issues such as cyberbullying. However, others felt that good behavior would only be instilled during the spatio-temporal boundaries of school during school hours, when such surveillance could be applied. Greater antagonism was expressed towards schools restricting Wi-Fi access, especially among rural residents who rely upon Wi-Fi (over data plans), moreso than their urban counterparts.

There is also the overall sense that school-based efforts to restrict technology are ineffective for meeting their ultimate objective of preventing harm, because either teachers are not following through on their policies in the classroom (or are barred from doing so), or due to student ingenuity in circumventing restrictions or hiding their use of technology (e.g., cell phones). In the former, it must be noted that teachers may have the best intentions in terms of their classroom technology policies, however, there remains the potentiality that exceptions requested for or by individual students may make such policy impossible to enact in a way that seems fair and just. Students with special circumstances, for instance those who require access to their phones for health monitoring purposes (e.g., diabetes), or those with custodial issues that have their guardian requesting he/she have a mobile device, make it difficult to enforce a class policy without breaching the confidentiality of the students with such "exceptions."

Significantly, however, some teens take a different approach to those highlighted above – neither rejecting nor approving monitoring and surveillance but arguing that it is not relevant to them as they have "nothing to hide." Some of our participants, then, appear to demonstrate a pattern of anticipatory socialization towards panoptic hegemony, adjusting their attitude from arguing they have high concern for privacy to one that acquiesces to debased privacy and omnipresent surveillance given the attitude that they are not doing anything wrong. Of course, there is a likely disjuncture between what is said and what is done, and further qualitative, ethnographically geared research with youth as well as educators and parents to help shed light on these nuances would provide crucial observational data in Canada that some researchers have been successfully drawing from in the United Kingdom (e.g., Livingstone & Sefton-Green, 2016).

Overall, active resistance to surveillance exists, especially in relation to parental surveillance. Yet, it is often tempered by the internalization of the ideology accompanying panoptic hegemony, most directly in relation to school surveillance. While it is too early to anticipate the long-term impact surveillance or monitoring by parents and educators will have on today's "net generation," the result of panoptic hegemony is likely an erosion of "belief in democratic systems [which] teaches young people that the only means of trust is through technological means, and takes away privacy" (Taylor, 2013: 74). Students may gain a sense of safety and security based on school surveillance practices, though reliance on surveillance as the "default response" may lead to schools losing "the opportunity to help students develop the skills of citizenship and reinforce the neoliberal view of student as suspect" (Steeves, 2010). Steeves (2010) shows that implications need to be carefully considered by parents and educators alike. Cyber-risks involving youth, often conjuring images of cyberbullying and sexting, also involves – perhaps moreso – the debasement of privacy and wider toolkits for active citizenship which, if neglected, may lead to more serious and longer-term psychological and sociological impacts.

References

Anderson, M. (January 2016). *Parents, Teens and Digital Monitoring*. Retrieved from www.pewinternet.org/2016/01/07/parents-teens-and-digital-monitoring/.

Andrejevic, M. (2005). The work of watching one another: Lateral surveillance, risk, and governance. *Surveillance & Society, 2*(4), 479–497.

Bailey, J., & Steeves, V. (2013). Will the real digital girl please stand up?: Examining the gap between policy dialogue and girls' accounts of their digital existence. In J. M. Wise & H. Koskela (Eds.), *New Visualities, New Technologies: The New Ecstasy of Communication* (pp. 41–66). Farnham, Surrey: Ashgate.

Bailey, J., & Steeves, V. (Eds.). (2015). *eGirls, eCitizens*. Ottawa: University of Ottawa Press.

Barron, C. (2014). "I had no credit to ring you back": Children's strategies of negotiation and resistance to parental surveillance via mobile phones. *Surveillance & Society, 12*(3), 401–413.

Blakemore, B. (2012). Cyberspace, cyber crime and cyber terrorism. In I. Awan & B. Blakemore (Eds.), *Policing Cyber Hate, Cyber Threats and Cyber Terrorism* (pp. 5–20). Farnham, Surrey: Ashgate.

boyd, d. (2008). *Taken Out of Context: American Teen Sociality in Networked Publics*. Berkeley: University of California.

boyd, d. (2014). *It's Complicated: The Social Lives of Networked Teens*. London: Yale University Press.

boyd, d., & Hargittai, E. (2010). Facebook privacy settings: Who cares? *First Monday*, 15(8), Retrieved from: http://firstmonday.org/htbin/cgiwrap/bin/ojs/index.php/fm/article/viewArticle/3086/2589 CAccessed February 2018).

Bruno, F. (2012). Surveillance and participation on web 2.0. In K. Ball, K. Haggerty, & D. Lyon (Eds.), *Routledge Handbook of Surveillance Studies* (pp. 343–351). New York: Routledge.

Burkell, J., & Saginur, M. (2015). "She's just a small town girl, living in an online world": Differences and similarities between urban and rural girls' use of and views about online social networking. In J. Bailey & V. Steeves (Eds.), *eGirls, eCitizens* (pp. 129–152). Ottawa: University of Ottawa Press.

Cannataci, J. A. (2015). *The Individual and Privacy*. Farnham, Surrey: Ashgate Publishing Limited.

Cassell, J., & Cramer, M. (2008). High tech or high risk: Moral panics about girls online. In T. McPherson (Ed.), *Digital Youth, Innovation, and the Unexpected* (pp. 53–76). Cambridge, MA: The MIT Press.

Christie, N. (2004). *A Suitable Amount of Crime*. London: Routledge.

Cohen, S. (2002 [1972]). *Folk Devils and Moral Panics* (3rd Ed.). London: Routledge.

Davis, K. (2014). Youth identities in the digital age: The anchoring role of friends in young people's approaches to online identity expression. In A. Bennett & B. Robards (Eds.), *Mediated Youth Cultures: The Internet, Belonging and New Cultural Configurations* (pp. 11–25). New York: Palgrave Macmillan.

Duggan, M., Lenhart, A., Lampe, C., & Ellison, N. (July 2015). *Parents and Social Media*. Pew Research Center. Retrieved from www.pewinternet.org/2015/07/16/parents-and-social-media/.

Earl, R. (May 18, 2012). Do cell phones belong in the classroom? *The Atlantic*. Retrieved from www.theatlantic.com/national/archive/2012/05/do-cell-phones-belong-in-the-classroom/257325/.

Fisk, N. (2016). *Framing Internet Safety: The Governance of Youth Online*. Cambridge: The MIT Press.

Fotel, T., & Thomsen, T. (2002). The surveillance of children's mobility. *Surveillance & Society*, 1(4), 535–554.

Foucault, M. (1977). *Discipline & Punish: The Birth of the Prison* (A. Sheridan, Trans.). New York: Pantheon.

Garland, D. (1997). "Governmentality" and the problem of crime: Foucault, criminology, sociology. *Theoretical Criminology*, 1(2), 173–214.

Garland, D. (2001). *The Culture of Control: Crime and Social Order in Contemporary Society*. Chicago: The University of Chicago Press.

Gramsci, A. (1971). *Selections from the Prison Notebooks*. New York: International Publishers.

Giroux, H. (2003). *The Abandoned Generation: Democracy Beyond the Culture of Fear*. New York: Palgrave Macmilllian.

Haggerty, K. (2006). Tear down the walls: On demolishing the panopticon. In D. Lyon (Ed.), *Theorizing Surveillance: The panopticon and beyond* (pp. 23–45). Mill Street, Uffculme: Willan Publishing.

Hasinoff, A. (2012). Sexting as media production: Rethinking social media and sexuality. *New Media & Society, 15*(4), 449–465.

Higgins, J. (August 7, 2013). More schools use cellphones as learning tools. *USA Today.* Retrieved from www.usatoday.com/story/tech/personal/2013/08/07/views-shift-on-cell-phones-in-schools/2607381/.

Hinduja, S., & Patchin, J. (2009). *Bullying Beyond the Schoolyard: Preventing and Responding to Cyberbullying.* Thousand Oaks, CA: Corwin Press (Sage).

Hinduja, S., & Patchin, J. (2014). *Bullying Beyond the Schoolyard: Preventing and Responding to Cyberbullying (2nd Ed.).* Thousand Oaks, CA: Corwin.

James, C. (2014). *Disconnected: Youth, New Media, and the Ethics Gap.* Cambridge: The MIT Press.

Kanai, A. (2015). Thinking beyond the internet as a tool: Girls' online spaces as post-feminist structures of surveillance. In J. Bailey & V. Steeves (Eds.), *eGirls, eCitizens* (pp. 83–106). Ottawa: University of Ottawa Press.

Karaian, L. (2014). Policing "sexting": Responsibilization, respectability and sexual subjectivity in child protection/crime prevention responses to teenagers' digital sexual expression. *Theoretical Criminology, 18*(3), 282–299.

Keeler, M. (2006). *Nothing to Hide: Privacy in the 21st Century.* Lincoln, NE: iUniverse.

Kerr, M., & Stattin, H. (2000). What parents know, how they know it, and several forms of adolescent adjustment: Further support for a reinterpretation of monitoring. *Developmental Psychology, 36*(3), 366–380.

Li, T. (2007). Governmentality. *Anthropologica, 49*(2), 275–281.

Livingstone, S. (2008). Taking risky opportunities in youthful content creation: Teenagers' use of social networking sites for intimacy, privacy and self-expression. *New Media & Society, 10*(3), 393–411.

Livingstone, S. (2009). *Children and the Internet: Great expectations, Challenging Realities.* Malden, MA: Polity Press.

Livingstone, S., Haddon, L., Görzig, A., & Ólafsson, K. (2010). *Risks and Safety for Children on the Internet: The UK report.* Retrieved from London: www.eukidsonline.net.

Livingstone, S., & Sefton-Green, J. (2016). *The Class: Living and Learning in the Digital Age.* New York: New York University Press.

Marker, B. (2011). *Sexting as Moral Panic: An Exploratory Study into the Media's Construction of Sexting.* (Masters of Science), Eastern Kentucky University, Richmond, Kentucky.

Marx, G., & Steeves, V. (2010). From the beginning: Children as subjects and agents of surveillance. *Surveillance & Society, 7*(3/4), 192–230.

Mcquigge, M. (February 26, 2017). After years of trying to ban cellphones, many schools are now trying to make them work in the classroom. *The Toronto Star.* Retrieved from www.thestar.com/news/canada/2017/02/26/after-years-of-trying-to-ban-cellphones-many-schools-are-now-trying-to-make-them-work-in-the-classroom.html.

Mills, C. W. (1940). Situated actions and vocabularies of motive. *American Sociological Review, 5*(6), 904–913.

Murguía, E., Tackett-Gibson, M., & Lessem, A. (2007). *Real Drugs in a Virtual World: Drug Discourse and Community Online.* Lanham: Lexington Books.

Murumaa-Mengel, M., Laas-Mikko, K., & Pruulmann-Vengerfeldt, P. (2015). "I have nothing to hide." A coping strategy in a risk society. In L. Kramp, N. Carpentier, A. Hepp, I. T. Trivundža, H. Nieminen, R. Kunelius, T. Olsson, E. Sundin, &

R. Kilborn (Eds.), *Journalism, Representation and the Public Sphere* (pp. 195–207). Bremen: edition lumière.

Nadesan, M. (2008). *Governmentality, Biopower, and Everyday Life.* New York: Routledge.

Nau, J. (2014). *"Why protest? I've got nothing to hide." Collective Action Against and Chilling Effects of Internet Mass Surveillance.* (Master of Arts in Peace and Conflict Studies), University of Kent, Marburg.

Putnam, R. (2000). *Bowling Alone: The Collapse and Revival of American Community.* New York: Simon and Schuster.

Racz, S., & McMahon, R. (2011). The relationship between parental knowledge and monitoring and child and adolescent conduct problems: A 10-year update. *Clinical Child and Family Psychology Review, 14*(4), 377–398.

Regan, P., & Steeves, V. (2010). Kids R Us: Online social networking and the potential for empowerment. *Surveillance & Society, 8*(2), 151–165.

Ricciardelli, R., & Spencer, D. (2017). *Violence, Sex Offenders, and Corrections.* New York: Routledge.

Rose, N. (1996a). The death of the social? Re-figuring the territory of government. *Economy and Society, 25*(3), 327–356.

Rose, N. (1996b). Governing "advanced" liberal democracies. In A. Barry, T. Osborne, & N. Rose (Eds.), *Foucault and Political Reason: Liberalism, Neo-Liberalism and Rationalities of Government* (pp. 37–64). London: UCL Press.

Solove, D. (2011). *Nothing to Hide: The False Tradeoff Between Privacy and Security.* New Haven: Yale University Press.

Stattin, H. (2001). Candid, not monitored, children run less risk of becoming delinquent. *Lakartidningen, 98*(25), 3009–3013.

Stattin, H., & Kerr, M. (2000). Parental monitoring: A reinterpretation. *Child Development, 71*(4), 1072–1085.

Steeves, V. (2005). *Young Canadians in a Wired World, Phase II: Trends and Recommendations.* Ottawa: Media Awareness Network.

Steeves, V. (2006). It's not child's play: The online invasion of children's privacy. *University of Ottawa Law and Technology Journal, 3*(1), 169–188.

Steeves, V. (2010). Online surveillance in Canadian schools. In T. Monahan & R. Torres (Eds.), *Schools Under Surveillance: Cultures of Control in Public Education* (pp. NA; Kindle Ed.). New Brunswick: Rutgers University Press.

Steeves, V. (2012). Hide and seek: Surveillance of young people on the internet. In D. Lyon, K. Haggerty, & K. Ball (Eds.), *The Routledge Handbook of Surveillance Studies* (pp. 352–359). New York: Routledge.

Steeves, V. (2013). *Young Canadians in a Wired World, Phase III: Talking to Parents and Youth About Life Online.* Ottawa: MediaSmarts. http://mediasmarts.ca/sites/media smarts/files/publication-report/full/ycwwiii-youth-parents.pdf (accessed February 2018).

Steeves, V., & Webster, C. (2008). Closing the barn door: The effect of parental supervision on Canadian children's online privacy. *Bulletin of Science, Technology & Society, 28*(1), 4–19.

Tapscott, D. (2009). *Grown Up Digital: How the Net Generation Is Changing Your World.* New York: Mcgraw-Hill.

Taylor, E. (2012). The rise of the surveillance school. In K. Ball, K. Haggerty, & D. Lyon (Eds.), *Routledge Handbook of Surveillance Studies* (pp. 225–231). New York: Routledge.

Taylor, E. (2013). *Surveillance Schools: Security, Discipline and Control in Contemporary Education*. New York: Palgrave Macmillan.

Vickery, J. (2017). *Worried About the Wrong Things: Youth, Risk, and Opportunity in the Digital World*. Cambridge, MA: The MIT Press.

Williams, M. (2013). *Is My Face in Cyberspace? Keeping Your Child Safe Online*. Kollege and Kareer 4 Youth (www.12kaky.com). Retrieved from www.amazon.ca/My-Face-Cyberspace-Keeping-Online-ebook/dp/B00JVANF20/ref=sr_1_1?ie=UTF8 &qid=1530546781&sr=8-1&keywords=is+my+face+in+cyberspace.

Chapter 5

Relational aggression

Introduction

In this chapter, we turn our attention to concerns explicitly raised by teens in response to questions about what is concerning to them online, and if they have any concerns related to social network sites (SNS) and applications. Participants identified three major areas of primary concern (and anxiety) online: cyberbullying and drama, "sexting," and hacking. The concern raised most frequently during focus group discussions is related to digital sexual expression (i.e., sexting), either during open-ended questions about what most concerns participants or independently by participants in the course of conversation. Every group raised the issue of sexting at some point (all 35 focus groups), making 193 references (see Chapter 7 where we detail this salient theme). Cyberbullying is the second most frequently referenced theme, with 26 groups making 110 references, followed by addiction (22N; 82R) and anonymity (28N; 77R). Drama, however, is also frequently raised as a salient theme *apart from* cyberbullying, often directly linked to relational aggression (29N; 75R), which we define and discuss below, as well as hackers (20N; 36R) and privacy concerns.

Overwhelmingly, we show that youth central concerns online rest on relational aggression, most often found among offline school peer networks. Online concerns, in other words, are most frequently connected to offline social contexts and problems. Relational aggression, unfortunately too often associated with girls and women, is defined as the manipulation of relationships with the explicit intention to hurt others (Coyne, Linder, Nelson, & Gentile, 2012). It applies to "inadvertent" actions, "with the goal being not to hurt others but to draw attention to oneself" (Regan & Sweet, 2015: 175). To this end, we show that concerns over seemingly disparate social problems such as cyberbullying and hacking are better appreciated as forms of relational aggression connected to immediate peer groups in offline contexts. We also unpack another reason relational aggression is a useful way to capture these concerns, that teens may not identify their personal experiences with larger institutionalized discourses such as cyberbullying. In other words, while journalists, politicians, and various other experts may draw from recognizable and arguably catchy concepts such as "cyberbullying," teens often reject such descriptors, preferring more idiosyncratic (and gendered) terms, such as "*drama.*"

Cyberbullying and drama: frequency and saliency

In our sample, the issue of cyberbullying (often discussed as a potential risk) is raised most by teens aged 15 to 17 (52 references), trailed by older teens aged 18–19 (27 references). The majority of references are made in all female groups (83 references) vs. all male groups (only 11 references). While there are a greater proportion of females than males in our sample, this particular skew suggests the risk of cyberbullying resonates more with female participants. Some Canadian researchers indicate that female teens are more likely targets of cyberbullying in comparison to males, with, for example, male teens pressuring female peers into taking and sending nude photos (Bailey & Steeves, 2015a; Li, 2007). However, some researchers' findings remain inconclusive regarding the role of gender and cyberbullying (see Brown, Demaray, & Secord, 2014). Even more striking than gender, despite the greater proportion of groups held in Cyberville (rural Atlantic Canada), significantly more references to cyberbullying are made from participants residing in Cyber City (urban Western Canada): 16 vs. 94 references respectively. Before we discuss why this may be the case, we stress that while some of our participants recalled incidents of bullying and cyberbullying in their past, most of our participants did not identify as cyberbullying victims or perpetrators.

Internationally, researchers have found variation in the prevalence and frequency of cyberbullying (see Hinduja & Patchin, 2014 for a detailed review of existing research). Some U.S.-based research involving statistically significant samples finds up to one-third of students have become victimized at some point from cyberbullying (e.g., Cassidy, Brown, & Jackson, 2012; Cassidy, Faucher, & Jackson, 2013), and roughly 11% to 17% have engaged in cyberbullying someone else (Wade & Beran, 2011). Similar figures are found in research from the United Kingdom and Canada (see Li, 2007). That said, the question of phenomenological experience turns more to issues of discourse and definition.

Cyberbullying is an elusive concept that, at first glance (especially as it is often presented in media), appears amenable to common sense understandings. A commonly employed definition was first proposed by Swedish psychologist Dan Olweus in the 1970s, who emphasized the imbalance in power between the victimizer and victim when delineating general youth aggression and bullying, arguing the latter involves a deliberate and repeated aggression among peers (Olweus, 1978, 1993). While adults may invoke the term cyberbullying in reference to general meanness and cruel behaviors among youth, teens often are reticent to refer to the term, distancing their own experiences from the concept as it is used in society more broadly (Pelfrey & Weber, 2014). Teens, especially those in high school, often claim bullying is not a serious issue among their own peer group (boyd, 2014). Indeed, the "lack of salience that internet safety concepts holds" (Fisk, 2016: 149) for teens suggests why some are so resistant to anti-cyberbullying messages in school (see Chapter 8 for more extensive discussion on policy and online safety).

In one U.S.-based study spanning six school districts, to exemplify, students in grades 6–12 responded to open-ended survey questions about their concerns over the course of a school year (Fisk, 2016). Their responses included reference to issues with homework and grades, social status and extracurricular activities, with some not mentioning any concerns, and with rare mentions of technology or the internet (Fisk, 2016). Only two students directly referenced cyberbullying, specifically anxieties over things posted online being taken out of context and producing "drama" (Fisk, 2016; see also boyd, 2008; Marwick & boyd, 2014). Indeed, Fisk (2016) found "active resistance among students to the term bullying, calling it 'annoying' and arguing that it is not often intentional and knowing, but begins with a comment or offhand snide remark that gets out of control" (177).

One interpretation of such findings is that teens are in fact experiencing relational aggression, but are simply not defining it through the lens of institutionalized discourses such as cyberbullying. Drama, for instance, is a term teens often use to describe their experiences with relational aggression, especially among females.

Cyberbullying and drama: offline saliency

Among our participants, when asked if they had personal experiences or general thoughts about cyberbullying, many quickly veered to the interpersonal dynamics of drama. Teens are much more likely to use the term 'drama', reflecting relational aggression online, when discussing experiences that range from "insignificant joking around to serious jealousy-driven relational aggression" (boyd, 2014: 137). With Marwick, boyd expanded her definition of drama to include "performative, interpersonal conflict that takes place in front of an active, engaged audience, often on social media" (Marwick & boyd, 2014: 5). Such understandings of drama are evident among our participants, like 16-year-old Saylee from Cyber City, who expressed being anxious when "people decide to … post things about me, and think that I don't find out, and then confronting the person just makes it worse." She adds "and yeah I get messages like, name calling, people telling me something that somebody said or … just a bunch of drama for nothing." For Saylee, offline friendship networks retain psycho-emotional saliency, but "drama" has a higher emotional valence than the more abstracted and formal notion of "cyberbullying."

The amorphous nature of the concept of cyberbullying for teens is evident from some of our participants' discussions. Asked if cyberbullying is a problem at her school, Kiana, a 16-year-old female from Cyber City, states "yeah, recently yeah, people will be on Snapchat or whatever, and zooming in on people's faces when they make funny faces or something, I think that's the biggest issue here." The behavior Kiana describes bears little resemblance to the formal definition of cyberbullying, instead it suggests the relatively loose ways the concept is applied to experiences of online risk. Moreover, why zooming in on a face can be viewed as 'bullying' further suggests that what is considered or experienced as hurtful among teens online today may require a revisiting by future researchers to unpack why such an act, which may at first glance appear rather benign, is hurtful.

Some participants referred to differences between "traditional" bullying in the 1980s and cyberbullying in the present, suggesting how the affordances of information communications technologies today augment and amplify bullying behavior. For instance, Ashley, 13-years-old from Cyber City, argued cyberbullying today is different compared to the offline and thus localized bullying of the 1980s and 1990s:

> It's like, there's more, there's still bullying like, in the 80s but it's just more [today] cuz it's online and they think that they can hide themselves and they don't know who it is, so it's anonymous and that's like the problem, and I think that's why there's a lot of bullying and I think that's why a lot of people are trying to stop it and stuff because there's quite a lot more, (Emma in the group agrees: "yeah") cuz I know I was talking to my mom, mom listen, was there any bullying? [She told me] of course there was bullying, but it just, you recognize it more back then because it's people doing it to each other and you know who it is, instead of [how people can be] doing it now, so when you get bullied on social media now, you never really know who it is (Emma agreed again, saying: "yeah").

Ashley's concerns are underscored by the affordances of social media, specifically those of anonymity, persistence, searchability and replicability (boyd, 2008), that encourage novel permutations of bullying online (for further debates over whether cyberbullying is "old wine in new bottles," see Hinduja & Patchin, 2014; Li, 2007). Concerns for anonymous comments may seem to weaken the association of online relational aggression from traditional definitions of bullying (i.e., where offline bullying involves repeated aggression from a known person or persons); explained by participants' references to the link between anonymous cyberbullying and drama. However, researchers consistently find that the cyberbullying encounters youth face most frequently involve someone they know personally, rather than a stranger (Kowalski, Limber, Limber, & Agatston, 2012). Despite indications suggesting cyberbullying offers novel permutations when compared with 'traditional', offline bullying, that the roots of cyberbullying are found predominately in offline social networks suggests that wholly technologically-focused solutions miss the mark. Anonymity, for instance, may be a unique aspect germane to cyberbullying. However, "while anonymity may be a distinguishing factor in some instances of cyberbullying, we should not ignore the fact that the majority of victims do know the person who is cyberbullying them" (Cassidy et al., 2013: 579). Ironically, despite the vast concerns over 'stranger-danger', it remains people who know each other who are able to cause each other the most pain and hurt.

Our participants' often linked cyberbullying to concerns over judgement from closer, offline peer groups. A group of four 13-year-old males from Cyberville, were asked "for the bullying stuff, does anything come of it? Like people say stuff online, does it translate back at school?" Cole confirms, "yeah, they're all in my class." Craig adds: "it's usually these three and another person that usually get bullied." The group continues to discuss their experiences dealing with bullying, which relate to one participant being teased for his father's death, and another being called "gay" for not having a girlfriend. Homophobic-infused bullying appears to be common for male teens, as heteronormative gender and sexual roles and norms are reproduced online (Bailey, 2015; Fairbairn, 2015; Katz, 2012).

Some of our female participants expressed concern over judgement related to being cyberbullied. For example Judy, a 15-year-old female from Cyber City, disclosed: "doing something that people judge you for, like bullying and then like yeah, that's like a concern every time." Judy is then asked why what anonymous commenters online say matters. She replies, "I guess they could go off and tell like one of your friends that you said something about them." Interviewer: "Right, and come back to the friends who you do hang out with?" Judy: "Yeah." It is clear from such discussion that it is not useful to think of negative judgement emanating from anonymous cyberbullying or offline, "traditional" peers as mutually exclusive. The concern here is that what may start as anonymous taunts online is transmitted and responded to by personal peer networks, including school classmates.

Cyberbullying and drama: gender norms

Beyond the link between offline peers and drama suggest by our participants, focus group discussions also revealed that the experience of drama varied between male and female peer groups. Said another way, drama online is undeniably gendered. Although not a surprising finding, given drama is consistently found to be an, arguably, female practice (boyd, 2014; Marwick & boyd, 2014; Regan & Sweet, 2015), what is very pronounced among our participants is that progress made in mainstream society regarding gender understandings, equalities, and practices appear slackened in the online world.

Even the idea that females engage in "drama" and males, in contrast, frequently refer to similar behaviors online as "pranking" or "punking" (body, 2014: 139) suggests that interpretations of actions and practices online are heavily gendered – a reality we return to in the subsequent pages.

Although our participants did not refer specifically to "pranking" or "punking," indicative of just how quickly discursive fashions change among teens, they did refer to gender differences in relational aggression. For instance, participants suggested that relational aggression often manifested among females online, yet when offline the females involved in a conflict held up "poker faces" – they did not reveal the conflict. Thus, the relational aggression is both discrete in that it is hidden in offline interactions yet also hurtful and seemingly underhanded in online spaces (e.g., engaged in by females with the power and protection of cyberspace). In contrast, males often "resolved" rather than hid their problems offline, for example by calling for a physical fight after school (see also Regan & Sweet, 2015). Eleanor, age 19 from Cyber City, explained males and females have "different concerns" regarding cyberbullying:

> I feel like guys don't fight on social media, but girls definitely do (Emily, also 19, agrees with an "oh yeah"). A lot of like cyberbullying is girl-based. Guys will just fight in person, girls will just be really mean to each other.

It may also be that the constellation of behaviors describing relational aggression online is described more often as 'drama' by female teens, though such experiences do resonate for males as well. While the *frequency* of references to cyberbullying is higher among our female participants, we cannot dismiss the effects of relational aggression on males. It is entirely possible that the processes of male socialization make it unlikely for males to either recognize or talk about cyberbullying, particularly using descriptors that are culturally read as tied to feminine behaviors (e.g., drama). As such, although relatively rare in our discussions, the fact that some males did reveal being deeply affected, both cognitively and emotionally, by relational aggression is telling.

True to form, males in our sample tended to have a discursive preference for using more precise terms like "rumors", as Amir did in a group of three 14-year-old males from Cyberville. Amir admits "it still hurts like the first time you hear about it [online rumors]." Travis offers advice to Amir: "well you gotta just feel like 'why would people do this to me?' And then I get over it." Amir responds positively to Travis' support: "I did nothing wrong." Travis reciprocates: "and I'm like oh wait its people … people do this, I'm not the only one." When groups of female teens were asked whether they thought males were also being victimized by cyberbullying but perhaps not coming forward, responses, such as those by Helen, Mya and Lucy, ages 16 and 17, from Cyber City, affirmed this possibility. Helen responds: "Yeah, cuz they don't want to be seen [as] less manly in a way"; while Lucy concedes that

> cuz if they're being bullied and that's really bugging them, for a girl a lot of time girls are seen in society as weaker, so if a girl's like "'I'm being bullied," it's like oh "ok," console them right, but if a guy's being bullied, another guy will be like "oh you're being a baby, man up."

Also in agreement, Mya elaborates, making explicit reference to the wider societal norms of masculinity:

> That's the whole thing "you're a guy, you have to be strong, you can't cry." You're the one that's supposed to be protecting the lady or the damsel in the distress; you're supposed to save her. They're kind of shown when they're younger to like, they're not allowed to be feminine, they're not allowed to be emotional, and I think that can go for both ways, because usually you get judged for your emotions…. But for girls, they're kind of more open about it I'd say, cuz it's not, cuz they're like "oh you have to be more feminine."

Abigail, a 19-year-old university undergraduate student, expressed similar sentiments, also pointing to the broader societal influence on gender differences in reporting cyberbullying:

> particularly I think girls are more likely to come forward [to report being victimized online] because it's socially acceptable to share your feelings, and society kind of puts women in a place where it's, it's ok to show your emotion; you're a girl, don't punch girls … they're weaker. I don't know, but I think it's like where men are socially reinforced every day from childhood that they're supposed to be macho. They're not supposed to show emotion so, so I think women are more likely to come forward.

Similar to discussions related to the drive for social acceptance and the fear of missing out (see Chapter 3), both phenomenological experiences and reactions to relational aggression are fundamentally augmented by gender norms, especially the heteronormative norms governing the performance of masculinity (Connell, 2005; West & Zimmerman, 1987). This is presciently captured by the discussions highlighted above, referring to the ways in which wider societal norms regarding gender are frequently reproduced – if not more deeply entrenched – online (Bailey & Steeves, 2015b).

Moreover, some social media platforms are argued to be particularly insidious for female youth. One such platform is Ask.fm, a SNS and "honesty app" where users create profiles to ask each other questions anonymously and pseudo-anonymously and receive responses from others, also ostensibly anonymously, online (Hinduja & Patchin, 2014; Woo, October 5, 2017). While Ask.fm has recently been "rebranded," with efforts to promote safety and positive interactions among users (including initiatives to allow users to report cyberbullying), Ask.fm has been associated with anonymous "trolling" and bullying, once dubbed "the most controversial social media platform used by teens" that some argue is tied to some incidents of death by suicide among teens (Hinduja & Patchin, 2014: 30; see also Hern, 19 August 2014; McGinn, January 21, 2016). The popularity of sites like Ask.fm can be attributed, at least in part, to the need teens (and people more generally) may have to know how others perceive them (see Cooley's (1902) classic work on the "looking glass self"). Ask.fm users often pose questions about their personal circumstances, seeking advice or an opinion about one's appearance or personal experiences. Anonymous questions, moreover, are assumed to promote honest responses and feedback. The view that Ask.fm is particularly caustic was shared by both male and female participants during our discussions. For instance, 18-year-old Edward from Cyberville recalls that "with Ask[.fm] for sure there was lots of, you know, drama between young girls and stuff." Asked what kind of drama, he elaborates:

> sometimes we'll get like, ... I read about on CBC [Canadian Broadcast Corporation], about someone made a poll for the ugliest girls in a certain grade and posted it on Ask anonymously, yeah.... just mean stuff really, really petty stuff happens on there.

In another group, Lucy, age 17 from Cyber City, reflects on Ask.fm:

> I thought the whole concept of it was stupid from the start, like a site where you go on and people can anonymously comment on anything. I thought it was so stupid, cuz of course you're going to get people who are just like "oh I'm going to go call this person fat and like make their life miserable," and ... there was no point to that, so I didn't go on it from the start, but I know some of my friends have done that. But the whole point of Ask.fm I find it so stupid, because, especially for girls, a lot of girls are pretty sensitive and they go on there thinking oh, who knows, and then when they get that kind of hate from other people and the mean stuff, they take it to heart, which is like, *it kind of sucks because they put themselves in that situation*, but they don't know [how] to just get rid of it and then the hate will go away, but most people just kind of take it and then it slowly really gets to them.
>
> (Added emphasis)

Lucy reveals a neoliberal logic of self-preservation here, explicitly that teens, especially young females, should "know better" than to place themselves in a circumstance where they "invite" anonymously posted trolling and harassment. Yet, her words also show this underlying 'addiction' and need many youths have to know what is going on among their peer group (or perhaps even fear that if they remove themselves from a social media site they may lose control over the gossip spread about them). Some participants who disclosed accounts of being harassed on sites such as Ask.fm, usually as a younger teen, argued that they were eventually able to distance themselves from this particular site because of its anonymous nature. Drama, then, appears to be a more salient concern among younger teens and 'tweens' in comparison to older (Burkell & Saginur, 2015). Janiya, 18 years-old from Cyber City, thus argued that the ability to ignore a hateful message depends on the context and source: "if I'm getting hate on Ask.fm it's probably not from someone I know, so it doesn't matter." Here too, risk perception is influenced by whether or not offline peers are using particular social media platforms. As we show elsewhere, anxieties about what is being posted online, and staying "in the loop" through a fear of missing out is often related to the impact among offline peers (see Chapter 3).

Digital self-harm: a side note

In the early phase of our research, after a participant introduced the phenomenon of "cyberbullying oneself," we became interested in asking teens whether they had heard of this form of digital self-harm. Cyberbullying oneself is a less publicized variant on cyberbullying that involves directing negative attention towards oneself, anonymously, online. Elizabeth Englander, who has researched the phenomenon, dubs it "Digital Munchausen" based on its resemblance to the psychiatric disorder Munchausen's Syndrome (Englander, June 2012). She writes "the Syndrome's central identifying symptom is the patient's infliction of self-harm in a quest for sympathy, attention, and admiration for their ability to cope with their (so-called) 'victimization'" (Englander, June 2012: 2). The anonymous affordances of contemporary SNS thus beget a version attuned to teens' current practices online. dana boyd (2014) discussed this phenomenon in the context of the SNS Formspring, the anonymous question and answer "truth" SNS which was the predecessor of Ask.fm. boyd began investigating Formspring after media reports drew attention to incidents of cruelty. With the cooperation of Formspring representatives, boyd found in the more severe cases of 'bullying' that both anonymous questions and the responding answers were linked to the same IP address (i.e., using the same account). Those engaging in digital self-harm are not engaging in self-sabotage; instead, they do so to elicit *positive* feedback from others (often strangers) online – they want someone to come to their defense and be there for them. To explain, initial negative 'roasts' or 'trolling' replies may be initiated by the same user who posted the question, but often what is sought is validation from others; people who disagree with the negative comments. Englander's (June 2012) study found 9% of the 617 U.S. youth surveyed reported "self cyber-bullying" with about a third feeling they felt better as a result. boyd (2014) argues that the practice of digital self-harm seems to be evident only among a relatively small minority of teens, yet it does blur the boundaries between attention-seeking behavior and bullying.

Given the emphasis on the rarity of digital self-harm, we were surprised to find the concept did not come as a surprise to most of our participants. While none reported any personal experiences with digital self-harm, participants quickly pointed to particular SNS platforms which they identified as more frequently associated with the behavior, and offered explanations and motivating factors to explain why some people engaged in such actions. They often argued that digital self-harm revolves around attention seeking objectives. For instance, Helen argues "human nature is to be sympathetic to most people," and, following this logic, if someone is experiencing harassment online, posting anonymized attacks directed at oneself should elicit sympathy from others:

> you get the attention and sympathy that you want and a lot of people, a lot of times will bully themselves in order to try to get attention from others so that they seem they're more the spotlight of the show, instead of just a background singer.

In another group, similarly asked what motivates people to commit self-harm online, Eleanor replies "I think they want attention, which isn't bad, like if you need attention, you need attention that's just not the way to go about it, and to get sympathy and stuff like that." Here digital self-harm is related to visibility and agency online for those who may feel otherwise powerless to respond to cyberbullying and other forms of relational aggression. Eleanor also recalls seeing "people sending themselves hate, like you see it on Tumblr sometimes, they'll forget to hit anon, and you can see that it was like themselves, so you get pity and stuff." She adds that those engaged in digital self-harm do so to search for sympathy and pity, in order to create an imagined audience that paves the way for the "victim" to cope with and, arguably, heal from their painful experiences. Of note, discussion about digital self-harm centered on personal attention seeking behavior and not about the possible unintended consequences of such acts for others who may become suspicious of someone posting questions on SNS. Indeed, such acts were presented as entirely individualistic and discussion failed to move beyond the individual to the greater harm such actions could impose upon family, close friends, offline peers and particularly known persons of conflict (e.g., a former romantic partner or a friend with whom a falling out has occurred).

Beyond Ask.fm, other groups made reference to additional SNS that seem to invite online self-harm, such as the Reddit (a news-content and discussion website) forum "roastme." Eleanor recalls very few cases of "self-trolling" or self-hate recently on Ask.fm. Her recollection suggests that the frequency of self-harm online may be dependent on the popularity of particular SNS. Group members here all agreed that it is now less of an issue than in the past, though Eleanor adds that it still remains salient "with people who are trying to build social media profiles for themselves as a career." She uses the example of those aiming to establish an online media presence on YouTube who simultaneously post self-directed hate on sites such as Guru Gossip: "People will post hate about themselves, on the other website [Guru Gossip], and then they talk about it in their YouTube videos, and people will feel sympathy for them and watch their other videos." In consequence, the lines between victim and victimizer are increasingly blurred given such social dynamics. On a spectrum, serious incidents of relational aggression and "trolling" oneself to gain online followers could not be more disparate; yet the form connecting both phenomena is the seeking of connection, popularity, and perhaps most of all, visibility and recognition. Moreover, the rarity of digital self-harm is likely related to the greater emotional weight usually given to valuations by immediate and close friends, rather than anonymous strangers online.

Hackers and privacy breaches

On the surface, the issue of hacking may not seem directly connected to relational aggression. Media reports, for example, most frequently follow criminal incidents of hacking with an increasingly large societal impact, sometimes involving global geopolitical dynamics (e.g., Gertz & Beacon, August 30, 2017; Newman, October 21, 2016). To complicate matters, the discourse of hacking no longer carries with it a solely negative, even criminal, connotation. Among some youth, "hacktivist" efforts to promote and instigate social change offer positive opportunities for political activism and expression of dissent, easily facilitated through various online platforms and that can take on a range of forms (Jordan, 2002; Kleinknecht, 2003; Taylor, 2005; Yar, 2013). Consistent with the contemporary emphasis on neoliberalist promotion of individualization and self-responsibilization (Brenner, Peck, & Theodore, 2010; Kelly & Caputo, 2011; Rose, 1996), youth express a preference for more individualized forms of activism, including computer hacking, culture jamming, and brand boycotts over the more traditional collectivist social movements of the past (Harris, Wyn, & Younes, 2010). Livingstone and Bober (2003) found that UK teens referred to downloading content, such as movies and music, as well as hacking, among their lexicon of "alternative skills" – a part of their "peer culture" and valued above traditional educational skills (2).

It is noteworthy, then, that among our 35 focus groups, 20 groups expressed concerns over hacking, making 36 references, often in response to general questions about what is most concerning to them about going online.

The references are concentrated among female participants: only eight male groups expressed concerns over hacking, versus 23 references in female groups (the remainder of references are found in a small number of co-ed groups). In addition, the majority of references are made by those living in Cyber City (25, vs. 11 from Cyberville). To make sense of these findings, we distinguish between two variants of hacking, which elicited different responses among our participants. On the one hand, participants report being relatively unconcerned about hackers in general. When pressed to explain why, participants often refer to hackers targeting big name multinational corporations and organizations, seeing themselves as 'little fish' that are not on the radar of such groups or individuals.

On the other hand, forms of hacking that *do* generate concern are those most closely linked to relational aggression among offline peer groups, specifically hacking linked to interpersonal drama and aggression. Eleanor's co-ed group of three 19-year-old undergraduate students in Cyber City exemplified this attitude. Eleanor argues:

> I feel with hacking it typically ends up happening more so to bigger channels or people. I see them more with people who I found on Instagram, they happen to have more than a [*sic*] 100,000 followers or something like that and then they get hacked and then the people deletes everything and they unfollow everyone, and then they lose their entire following, and then they have to remake the page again.

Emily agrees with Eleanor's remarks: "cuz I don't usually find that with people like us, we're just normal people." Reid elaborates in agreement: "yeah I think it's mostly higher up people cuz people want to like slander you and make you look bad, but for the rest of us, we're just regular people." Eleanor follows through: "so there's nothing to accomplish by hacking the three of us!" Her remark causes all three members to laugh. Eleanor and Reid go on to specify that they are "worried" more about viruses and privacy in relation to commercial transactions (i.e., using credit cards for online shopping).

Their reports about privacy concerns echo findings from research with users of the online chat client ICQ who were asked questions about privacy concerns (Paine, Reips, Stieger, Joinson, & Buchanan, 2007). The researchers found that users top four concerns were viruses, spam, spyware and hackers (about three quarters of those sampled were under 30). Indeed, research more explicitly geared to explore teen perceptions and attitudes often reveal teens' concern about viruses, "worms," and malware; all of which are concerns that at root are tied to the invasion of their privacy (e.g., Fisk, 2016; for details regarding computer viruses see Yar, 2013) or the harming of their technology (e.g., making their phone or computer unusable).

Our participants mirrored these concerns and expressed further annoyance at targeted advertising and "pop up" ads on SNS. Some admitted that their concerns were related to the "risky" websites they visit to access movies and music that are believed to leave them more susceptible to hackers. "Viruses [are] a big thing," said Edward, admitting "I download all kinds of like music and stuff off these shady websites, so my laptop got a pretty bad virus there now." Others pointed to untrustworthy websites that will "hack you through ads and stuff" (Angie, 18, Cyberville), and encourage users to "click" in places they may not desire: "then you go hit the x button but you missed the x button, cuz it's like two." Here Angie refers to certain affordances of technology that make it difficult to avoid targeted advertisements, or identify where the "close window" button is located on pop-up advertisement that may lead to yet more pop-up advertisements or being redirected to risky or unwanted websites.

Teens' concerns over hackers are enmeshed in wider anxieties over privacy (e.g., who can access their information online) and privacy management – and of course the uninterrupted functionality of their devices (e.g., smart phone, iPad, tablet, and computer). Krasnova, Günther, Spiekermann, and Koroleva (2009), who surveyed university students' concerns over privacy and identity online, argue that "the accessibility of the information is the necessary precondition for all other threats" (50). Researchers in Canada indicate that these threats include the interrelated issues of hacking and identity theft. In one study, for instance, the authors found undergraduate students were slightly more at risk for identity theft, but better informed than non-students of comparable (young adult) age (Winterdyk & Thompson, 2008). However, knowledge regarding Canadian teens' attitudes towards hackers in the context of cyber-risk, privacy, and security remains negligible. In one extensive project on Canadian female teens' experiences with cyber-risk, only one 15-year-old participant mentioned the need for greater security measures to prevent hacking in response to questions about how online platform providers can help improve privacy (Bailey, 2015; Bailey & Steeves, 2015b).

For our participants, the form of hacking that provoked the most concern was any variant of identity theft, including someone creating a fake account by hacking into SNS and smartphones. Christine, a 19-year-old undergraduate student from Cyber City, revealed she is "terrified" of people who "will steal your photos off of your thing, and then create a fake social media [account] and like catfish someone" (i.e., pose as someone they are not on social media). Christine elaborates:

> you see also on like social media, like stories of girls who their photos get stolen off … any sort of social media and then people have a collection of that and then they create like a fake profile, with your name, or with a different name, but with your photos and I think that's my biggest fear.

One potential consequence of this, Christine argues, is to have friends develop a "negative connotation" of her based on the hacker using a fake account. Again, the concern youth have about how others perceive them reappears when discussing "hackers." For example, Christine continued to explain that any time she posts a photo to social media, she reminds herself "there's a risk that anyone … could end up using it for bad things, so it's kind of like nerve wracking in that sense of that, *you're your own person, but someone could be taking that away from you*" (emphasis added). While Christine's concerns are centered on potential strangers hacking into her social media accounts, the potential negative impact extends directly to peers who may not be aware she has lost control of her online identity.

Another variant of this concern centered on friends, rather than strangers, hacking one's online accounts. Brian, age 17 from Cyberville, expressed this succinctly: "I just don't want [my friends] logging on my Facebook and posting all kinds of shit." A more elaborate statement comes from 16-year-old Janelle from Cyber City, who recalls having former friends create a fake account posing as herself:

> Two friends of mine that are not really friends of mine anymore, they made a fake account on my thing, they spelt my name wrong and everything, and they're just messaging, adding random people I didn't know, and like starting all this stuff and pretty soon I got messages on my other Facebook account saying like oh, "we're going to come get you."

Janelle's case suggests how identity theft can occur and be related to relational aggression amongst offline peers. The idea that Janelle's former friends were open to violating her online self-presentation and cause her undue hardship exposes the degree of relational aggression that can unpin online interactions, particularly negative interactions. Janelle is being exploited, her privacy invaded, her reputation challenged, and her online image manipulated by persons whose intentions are negative. Those observing the imposter Janelle's actions may not recognize the difference between the authentic Janelle and the imposter, thus further harming Janelle both on and offline. This harm is exacerbated by the permanence and searchability of what is posted online (boyd, 2014). The saliency of offline peer groups in this situation became obvious when Janelle was asked how she resolved the situation. She shared how she told her other friends "nobody add this person, nobody talk to this person, it's not me, and everyone was like ok … and eventually it got knocked down." Ironically, Janelle relied upon the help of a friend with some expertise in hacking:

> my one friend hacked [the fake account] and deleted it all. … Eventually I found out the two girls that did it … it was like, two girls that I really hate and they just wanted to get people after me.

Dealing with drama with personal peer groups involved Janelle becoming the victim of a form of hacking (identity theft and creating a fake account), and it is telling that her resolution was not direct (i.e., offline) confrontation but to hire another hacker to hack the doppelganger account and delete it. Also, interesting from Janelle's experience is her reliance upon a number of close friends to distinguish between her real and fake accounts. Offline peer networks may help promulgate drama, but they are also sources of social support and contextualized understanding. Janelle's former friends tried to publicly shame Janelle – the very experience many teens arguably fear most online. However, Janelle's offline friends helped her cope with the fact that her two former friends treated her so poorly and in such a public manner; a fact that cannot be lost in discussions of hacking and relational aggression.

Participants in several groups, responded "getting hacked" to questions about their "biggest online safety concern," and in these cases other group members tended to agree. Helen explained that, on a regular basis, "I might make sure all of my accounts are really secure, or like [try to control when to allow access] because … technology has really grown, and people can hack you whenever and get all your information." Others agreed. When asked if a particular SNS is more susceptible to hacking, Helen identified Facebook over other platforms such as Instagram and Snapchat that she considers more secure, "cuz there's more information that you give" on Facebook relative to the others. Later in the discussion she reveals that she "always see[s] [hacking] happen" at her school: "sometimes it's just like you know … friends, 'oh you're hacked,' well like I've seen a few, I've seen like one really nasty one" involving a hacker posing as a friend and posting "really horrible things … but it wasn't really them." Here identity theft among offline peers is again a prominent theme.

For our participants, concerns over cyberbullying were sometimes fused with negative experiences of, or general anxieties towards hackers – specifically regarding breaches of privacy engendered by the anonymity of cyberspace. Christine is one of the few participants who voiced serious experiences of victimization from cyberbullying. After being aggressively and continuously harassed by peers at one public school, she transferred to a private school where the cyberbullying ceased until she began to be accused of certain illicit activities from an anonymous source online. In her recollection of this incident she states that the victimizer was a new female friend who became jealous of an older, longer-term friendship established by Christine – thus suggesting the cyberbullying stemmed from a situation of relational aggression. Through an investigation, which necessitated the school accessing Christine's private social media accounts and email, the school eventually recognized her innocence and exonerated her of any culpability. Summarizing the emotional toll resulting from her experience, Christine highlights the ability of aggressors to take advantage of the affordances of SNS when engaging in cyberbullying including aggressive or even criminal harassment:

It's kind of concerning if someone, *if someone has it out for you, they can very much destroy your life* with either sending a private message, or putting you as the attacker. There's hackers who can like send the IP address to your computer, regardless if you did anything. That's concerning.

(Emphasis added)

Here Christine refers to a hacker sending out malicious attacks and content posing as Christine, and doing so by making it appear as if the messages are coming from Christine's computer (traceable to her IP address). She adds that unlike in the past were animosity between friends may have resulted in some "traditional" gossiping ("face-to-face"), "now it's all hidden behind screens, it kind of leaves this grey area, like who is the real person hiding behind the screen, and so that's the really dangerous part." She concludes decisively: "social media can ruin your life. It can be great, but it can ruin your life in seconds, because of what it does, the power it has to ruin your name, ruin anything … cuz nothing gets deleted." As Christine's words express, the impact of online slandering and cyberbullying on social media can be inescapable; it can penetrate across offline and online peer groups, include strangers, and can follow a person for the rest of their life – viewable by future 'friends and colleagues' and wider social networks. This apparent inescapability also suggests that unlike the experiences of youth in prior generations, many may never have an opportunity for a genuinely fresh start."

Discussion

Given a small minority of our participants self-identified as victims of online aggression, our sample of Canadian youth falls in line with most studies of cyberbullying and relational aggression (e.g., Bailey & Steeves, 2015b; Hinduja & Patchin, 2014). What our focus group discussions reveal are significant insights into (1) the salience of relational aggression online in a broader sense, including "drama" but also hacking among offline peers; (2) the gendered nature of relational aggression (i.e., the relevance of drama among female teens but also the likelihood that males may sometimes share these experiences but hold a reticence in expressing them); and (3) the significance of offline peers in situating anxieties that appear at first to represent disparate forms of relational aggression online.

We highlight the fact that most often participants from Cyber City, not Cyberville, reference cyberbullying. References to drama, on the other hand, are found in fairly equal proportion among both Cyber City and Cyberville residents (31 vs. 44 references respectively). Other Canadian research has found few differences in terms of youth experiences with drama between urban and rural residents. Burkell and Saginur (2015), for example, found that both urban and rural teens indicated that drama is often triggered by photographs and played out in terms of traded comments visible to the entire social network ... [and] that people not involved follow the online drama just to see what is happening (a form of entertainment).

(142)[1]

Some researchers have indicated that females are more frequently victims of cyberbullying than males (e.g., Li, 2007). Nonetheless, care must be practiced before drawing conclusions from such findings, not only since gendered patterns of victimization are not found consistently in research (see Brown, Demaray, & Secord, 2014), but also the assumption may mask relational aggression and victimization experienced by male, non-cisgender and gender-neutral youth. In our sample of self-reported male and female youth, our participants' statements revealed the likelihood that males, drawing on normative practices of masculinities, do not disclose harm when they experience hurt online because, perhaps, such harm fails to align conceptually with definitions of cyberbullying or gendered interpretations of what should be harmful for males (Connell & Messerschmidt, 2005). boyd (2014: 140) observes:

> Teens may not accept the mantle of bullying because they don't want to position themselves as victims, but that does not mean that they don't feel attacked. They smile and laugh off the pain in public because they feel this is what their community expects. They try to ignore any negative emotional response to drama because they don't want their peers to see them as weak.

Heeding the influence of gender on teen responses to online drama, boyd's remark applies just as much, perhaps even moreso, for male than female youth. As noted by Brown et al. (2014: 20) and her colleagues, "males and females may interpret and respond to online behaviors differently." Ybarra's (2004) U.S.-based study found male students to be more than eight times as likely to be victims of cyberbullying, especially those who reported symptoms of a mental disorder, such as those indicative of depression (see also Pedersen, 2013). Cappadocia, Craig, and Peplar (2013) also found no gender differences in terms of experiencing cyberbullying, though females were more likely to *report* being a victim of cyberbullying than males. The bulk of attention which centers on female victims of online relational aggression should therefore expand its consideration to how males may also be negatively affected and victimized but either shrug off such experiences under, for example, a façade of male bravado or fail to even recognize the negative effects given the norms of masculinities directing their perceptions and behaviors. Johnson's (2015) focus groups with Canadian teens reveal significantly more girls than boys (49 percent compared to 39 percent) felt that the internet was an unsafe space for them, and 82 percent of girls – compared to just 63 percent of boys – feared they could be hurt if they talked to someone they didn't know online.

(340)

At the same time, societal conceptions of drama often adhere to a "mean girl" discourse, which acts to "pathologize feminine social aggression and implicitly treat male aggression as neutral" (Bailey & Steeves, 2015a: 10). Our female participants also suggested that such practices apply during online communication, especially regarding "sexting" (see Chapter 7). The fact that interpretations of female and male online behaviors are rooted and shaped by processes of socialization, patriarchal teachings, and related dominant discourses is undeniable. However, it is not as simple as changing interpretations of youth actions; instead it must also be recognized that said realities underpin relational aggression and the ways in which youth communicate. Indeed, in our sample, some females appeared most invested in staying out of online "drama," while others did engage or at minimum "follow" online happenings within their peer groups.

Apart from findings related to gender, what also appears clear from our focus groups discussions is that regardless of the specific form of relational aggression, be it cyberbullying, drama, or hacking, concerns center on how close youth peer groups receive and response to individuals online. While hacking, for example, may not first appear as relevant to interpersonal conflict, it is the forms of hacking involving offline peers that matters the most to teens. The "big game" hackers who target large organizations and governments are not so much on the radar. Neither are the many concerns over so-called "digital self-harm," which seem more pertinent to those seeking to solicit feedback from anonymous strangers online. Our participants' concerns regarding hacking, instead, are embroiled alongside experiences of interpersonal drama and conflict. Wider societal "formula stories" (Loseke, 2012) regarding the criminal actions of hackers targeting large organizations, corporations and infrastructural targets are simply not as relevant. Moreover, hackers among offline peers are not always construed as bad – sometimes teens may call upon supportive peers with hacking skills to help them preserve their identity online, most importantly, their reputation and dignity among close friends. Overall, the salient risks highlighted here underscore further the ongoing negative comparison and need to assay how one is being judged online.

Note

1 This statement is telling also given our own participants' responses indicated a fear of missing out – an interest in keeping tabs on what is being said about them online; see Chapter 3.

References

Bailey, J. (2015). A perfect storm: How the online environment, social norms, and law shape girls' lives. In J. Bailey & V. Steeves (Eds.), *eGirls, eCitizens* (pp. 22–46). Ottawa: University of Ottawa Press.

Bailey, J., & Steeves, V. (2015a). Introduction: Cyber-Utopia? Getting beyond the binary notion of technology as good or bad for girls. In J. Bailey & V. Steeves (Eds.), *eGirls, eCitizens* (pp. 1–17). Ottawa: University of Ottawa Press.

Bailey, J., & Steeves, V. (Eds.). (2015b). *eGirls, eCitizens*. Ottawa: University of Ottawa Press.

boyd, d. (2008). *Taken Out of Context: American Teen Sociality in Networked Publics.* Berkeley, CA: University of California.

boyd, d. (2014). *It's Complicated: The Social Lives of Networked Teens.* London: Yale University Press.

Brenner, N., Peck, J., & Theodore, N. (2010). Variegated neoliberalization: Geographies, modalities, pathways. *Global Networks, 10*(2), 182–222.

Brown, C., Demaray, M., & Secord, S. (2014). Cyber victimization in middle school and relations to social emotional outcomes. *Computers in Human Behavior, 35,* 12–21.

Burkell, J., & Saginur, M. (2015). "She's Just a Small Town Girl, Living in an Online world": Differences and similarities between urban and rural girls' use of and views about online social networking. In J. Bailey & V. Steeves (Eds.), *eGirls, eCitizens* (pp. 129–152). Ottawa: University of Ottawa Press.

Cappadocia, M. C., Craig, W., & Pepler, D. (2013). Cyberbullying: Prevalence, stability, and risk factors during adolescence. *Canadian Journal of School Psychology, 28*(2), 171–192.

Cassidy, W., Brown, K., & Jackson, M. (2012). "Under the radar": Educators and cyberbullying in schools. *School Psychology International, 33*(5), 520–532.

Cassidy, W., Faucher, C., & Jackson, M. (2013). Cyberbullying among youth: A comprehensive review of current international research and its implications and application to policy and practice. *School Psychology International, 34*(6), 575–612.

Connell, R. (2005). *Masculinities (2nd Ed.).* Berkeley, CA: University of California Press.

Connell, R., & Messerschmidt, J. (2005). Hegemonic masculinity: Rethinking the concept. *Gender & Society, 19*(6), 829–859.

Cooley, C. (1902). *Human Nature and the Social Order.* New York: Scribners.

Coyne, S., Linder, J., Nelson, D., & Gentile, D. (2012). "Frenemies, fraitors, and mean-em-aitors": Priming effects of viewing physical and relational aggression in the media on women. *Aggressive Behavior, 38*(2), 141–149.

Englander, E. (June 2012). *Digital Self-Harm: Frequency, Type, Motivations, And Outcomes.* Bridgewater, MA: Massachusetts Agression Reduction Center.

Fairbairn, J. (2015). Rape threats and revenge porn: Defining sexual violence in the digital age. In J. Bailey & V. Steeves (Eds.), *eGirls, eCitizens* (pp. 229–280). Ottawa: University of Ottawa Press.

Fisk, N. (2016). *Framing Internet Safety: The Governance of Youth Online.* Cambridge: The MIT Press.

Gertz, B., & Beacon, W. F. (August 30, 2017). Government warns North Korean cyber attacks continue. Retrieved from www.washingtontimes.com/news/2017/aug/30/government-warns-north-korean-cyber-attacks-contin/.

Harris, A., Wyn, J., & Younes, S. (2010). Beyond apathetic or activist youth: "Ordinary" young people and contemporary forms of participation. *Young, 18*(1), 9–32.

Hern, A. (19 August, 2014). Ask.fm's new owners vow to crack down on bullying or shut the site. *Guardian.* Retrieved from www.theguardian.com/technology/2014/aug/19/askfm-askcom-bullying.

Hinduja, S., & Patchin, J. (2014). *Bullying Beyond the Schoolyard: Preventing and Responding to Cyberbullying (2nd Ed.).* Thousand Oaks, CA: Corwin.

Johnson, M. (2015). Digital literacy and digital citizenship: Approaches to girls' online experiences. In J. Bailey & V. Steeves (Eds.), *eGirls, eCitizens* (pp. 339–360). Ottawa: University of Ottawa Press.

Jordan, T. (2002). *Activism!: Direct Action, Hacktivism and the Future of Society.* London: Reaktion books.

Katz, A. (2012). *Cyberbullying and e-Safety: What Educators and Other Professionals Need to Know.* London: Jessica Kingsley Publishers.

Kelly, K., & Caputo, T. (2011). *Community: A Contemporary Analysis of Policies, Programs, and Practices.* Toronto: University of Toronto Press.

Kleinknecht, S. (2003). *Hacking Hackers: Ethnographic Insights into the Hacker Subculture-Definition, Ideology and Argot.* (Master of Arts), McMaster University, Hamilton.

Kowalski, R., Limber, S., Limber, S., & Agatston, P. (2012). *Cyberbullying: Bullying in the Digital Age (2nd Ed.).* Oxford: John Wiley & Sons.

Krasnova, H., Günther, O., Spiekermann, S., & Koroleva, K. (2009). Privacy concerns and identity in online social networks. *Identity in the Information Society, 2*(1), 39–63.

Li, Q. (2007). New bottle but old wine: A research of cyberbullying in schools. *Computers in Human Behavior, 23,* 1777–1791.

Livingstone, S., & Bober, M. (2003). *UK Children Go Online: Listening to young People's Experiences.* London: LSE Research Online.

Loseke, D. (2012). The empirical analysis of formula stories. In J. Holstein & J. Gubrium (Eds.), *Varieties of Narrative Analysis* (pp. 251–271). Los Angeles: Sage.

Marwick, A., & boyd, d. (2014). "It's just drama": Teen perspectives on conflict and aggression in a networked era. *Journal of Youth Studies, 17*(9), 1187–1204.

McGinn, D. (January 21, 2016). Your kid is on ask.fm? Be afraid, very afraid. *The Globe and Mail.* Retrieved from https://beta.theglobeandmail.com/life/parenting/your-kid-is-on-askfm-be-afraid-very-afraid/article28308222/?ref=www.theglobeandmail.com&.

Newman, L. (October 21, 2016). What we know about Friday's massive east coast internet outage. *Wired.com.* Retrieved from www.wired.com/2016/10/internet-outage-ddos-dns-dyn/

Olweus, D. (1978). *Aggression in the Schools: Bullies and Whipping Boys*. Oxford, UK: Hemisphere.Olweus, D. (1993). Victimization by peers: Antecedents and long-term outcomes. In K. Rubin & J. Asendorpf (Eds.), *Social Withdrawal, Inhibition, and Shyness in Childhood* (pp. 315–341). New York: Psychology Press.

Paine, C., Reips, U.-D., Stieger, S., Joinson, A., & Buchanan, T. (2007). Internet users' perceptions of "privacy concerns" and "privacy actions." *International Journal of Human-Computer Studies, 65*(6), 526–536.

Pedersen, S. (2013). UK young adults' safety awareness online – is it a "girl thing"? *Journal of Youth Studies, 16*(3), 404–419.

Pelfrey, W., & Weber, N. (2014). Talking smack and the telephone game: Conceptualizing cyberbullying with middle and high school youth. *Journal of Youth Studies, 17*(3), 397–414.

Regan, P., & Sweet, D. (2015). Girls and online drama: Aggression, surveillance, or entertainment? In J. Bailey & V. Steeves (Eds.), *eGirls, eCitizens* (pp. 175–197). Ottawa: University of Ottawa Press.

Rose, N. (1996). The death of the social? Re-figuring the territory of government. *Economy and Society, 25*(3), 327–356.

Taylor, P. (2005). From hackers to hacktivists: speed bumps on the global superhighway? *New Media & Society, 7*(5), 625–646.

Wade, A., & Beran, T. (2011). Cyberbullying: The new era of bullying. *Canadian Journal of School Psychology, 26*(1), 44–61.

West, C., & Zimmerman, D. (1987). Doing gender. *Gender & Society, 1*(2), 125–151.

Winterdyk, J., & Thompson, N. (2008). Student and non-student perceptions and awareness of identity theft. *Canadian Journal of Criminology and Criminal Justice, 50*(2), 153–186.

Woo, M. (October 5, 2017). What Parents need to know about new "honesty" apps sarahah and TBH. *Lifehacker.com*. Retrieved from https://offspring.lifehacker.com/what-parents-need-to-know-about-new-honesty-apps-sara-1819122015

Yar, M. (2013). *Cybercrime and Society (2nd Ed.)*. Los Angeles,CA: Sage.

Ybarra, M. (2004). Linkages between depressive symptomatology and Internet harassment among young regular Internet users. *CyberPsychology & Behavior, 7*, 247–257.

Chapter 6

Privacy mindsets

Introduction

Despite concerns about teen safety online and their use of online social networks technologies (boyd, 2014; Karaian, 2012; Marker, 2011; Tynes, 2007), the belief among some citizens that "youth today" are not at all interested in or neglect considerations of their privacy online seems to retain purchase. The media have underscored this stereotype with headlines and editorializing that suggest youth are shameless and have no sense of privacy (boyd, 2014; Livingstone, 2008; Nussbaum, February 12, 2007). Researchers who conducted studies on Facebook soon after the site became available to the general public also empirically support that youth are not concerned about online privacy (e.g., Barnes, 2006). In the United States, Tufekci (2008) found that although undergraduate college students are interested in being publicly visible they balance this interest with selective disclosures designed to balance publicity with privacy. More recently, researchers have also critiqued stereotypes of teen apathy towards online privacy, finding that adolescents and young adults are, in fact, concerned about privacy and take active and creative measures to manage privacy while online (Bailey & Steeves, 2015; boyd & Hargittai, 2010; James, 2014; Livingstone, 2008).

Some have argued teens are facing a "privacy paradox," where statements declaring privacy to be a paramount concern seem to be countermanded by open sharing of personal information through various online platforms (Barnes, 2006; Hargittai & Marwick, 2016). Yet, emerging evidence reveals that some youth, while aware of privacy risks related to their online activities, see the compromise of their privacy as unavoidable, even imperative, in order to connect with peers online and acquire social and personal benefits through accessing social network sites (SNS; Regan & Steeves, 2010). Simply put, "cyber abstinence" is not a viable option for the majority of teens (especially considering the drive for social connection online; see Chapter 3). In response, teens are frequently active in managing their privacy online, often using a number of well documented strategies. These include the creation of multiple or fake accounts, "wall" cleaning on Facebook (referring to reviewing past posts and untagged and/or deleting undesired content), using pseudonyms, and lying about age and location (Bailey & Steeves, 2015; boyd, 2014; James, 2014: 36; Raynes-Goldie, 2010).

Some researchers have explored the relationship between privacy and age. For example, surveying the existing literature, Youn (2005) points to "inconsistent findings" (94), with some scholars finding no relation between age and privacy concerns (e.g., Phelps, Nowak, & Ferrell, 2000) and others, largely focused on consumption practices, showing younger consumers as "more likely to know and use privacy protection strategies than older consumers" (Dommeyer & Gross, 2003; Youn, 2005: 94). Some scholars report a statistically significant relationship between age and privacy concerns, for example that those under 20 years of age were less likely to express concerns over privacy online than those over 20 (Paine, Reips, Stieger, Joinson, & Buchanan, 2007). While, most recently, James (2014: 36) found that younger "tweens" were "naive to the effectiveness of [privacy management] strategies." Collectively, these findings reveal a need for further qualitative exploration that unpack the meanings issues, like privacy and online risk management, have for youth, especially given the rapidly changing social media landscape over the last decade. Consistent with findings in the United States and United Kingdom (boyd & Hargittai, 2010; Livingstone, 2008), we too show that as Canadian youth reach their late adolescent years they become more acutely conscious of privacy issues and the need to maintain a pruned digital identity amenable to future employment (Bailey, Steeves, Burkell, & Regan, 2013; Steeves, Milford, & Butts, March 2010).

In this chapter, we explore three interrelated themes. First, we center on concerns over a lack of agency or control over activities on SNS, especially Facebook. We then delve into the reasons why teens are gravitating away from Facebook (once and in some ways still the dominant SNS used by teens), towards more streamlined alternatives such as Instagram and Snapchat. Finally, we explore how, as teens mature, rather than fine tuning the strategies they deploy, some youth are adopting a mindset of having 'nothing to hide' in relation to online privacy. This seems to be an acquiescence to the perception that privacy is ephemeral online, perhaps influenced by present-day news regarding mass governmental and corporate surveillance programs. We show that both the exodus from Facebook and the "nothing to hide" mindset are connected to what our data reveals to be the primary areas of concern over cyber-risk to our adolescent participants: not having control online and privacy.

Privacy: theoretical approaches and relevance online

Placed in contrast to the collective, conceptualizations of privacy are often linked to individualism in modern liberal democracies (Emerson, 1970). Early formulations stressed control over personal information, placing responsibility on the individual for managing her or his privacy (Westin, 1968). This atomistic conception was subsequently challenged by communitarian scholars who conceived of privacy as quintessentially social – geared towards the 'common good' (Etzioni, 1999; see also Solove, 2011). Here, notions of privacy as a social value or human right are preferred over ones centered on the individual – the latter related to the privacy paradox and the 'trade off' between convenience, access, and safeguarding personal information (Cohen, 2012; Roessler & Mokrosinska, 2015). A third alternative, emerging from the writings of John Dewey, challenges any treatment of privacy that dichotomizes individual and society. Individual rights, here, are valuable insofar as they contribute to collective welfare (see Solove, 2007).

Scholars examining privacy in relation to online practices draw from these broader debates. James (2014: 27), for instance, identifies three broad orientations or mindsets towards privacy management online: "privacy as social, privacy as 'in your hands' and privacy as forsaken online." Privacy as social refers to the expectation that others uphold informally agreed upon precepts regarding appropriate actions; these are not formally enforced nor enforceable, but instead maintained through tacit understanding and mutual respect (see James, 2014). Social privacy, often central to teen concerns online, is in contrast to institutional privacy. Said another way, youth concerns here center more on control over personal information, than on how a company like Facebook and its corporate partners may deploy that information (Raynes-Goldie, 2010).

The mindset that privacy is "in your own hands," James (2014) found, often overshadows the social. This mindset is influenced by internet safety discourses conveyed to youth by parents and educators (see James, 2014). Those who take up the mindset may blame the "victim" for breaches of online privacy, arguing that it is up to the individual to safeguard their privacy online, and if they fail to do so it is their fault. A third and final mindset identified by James (2014), "privacy as forsaken," acquiesces to the idea that privacy is attainable online; that once content is posted, the user no longer has any control over how it is appropriated. James (2014) found that about half of the teen participants in his research, regardless of age, held this mindset. As we will show, there actually emerges a fourth mindset as adolescents mature which is distinct from the typology identified by James (2014).

Feeling out of control online: privacy breaches and strategies

Across all 35 focus groups (30N, 131R), our participants described a lack of control online as one of their most pressing concerns. Relatedly, other pressing concerns centered on the risks associated with the permanence of what is posted online (11N, 28R) and risks underscored by online anonymity (28N, 77R) (see also Chapter 5). Significantly more references to lacking control were made by females than males (87 vs. 17 references), and a greater number of references were made in Cyber City than in Cyberville (95 vs. 36). Again, recalling that there were more female participants in our sample, this may explain at least some of the frequency of statements by gender, but it should still be noted that relatively fewer groups were held in Cyber City than Cyberville, which suggests features of urban contexts may play into amplifying feelings of insecurity online. Here we unpack these concerns as they intersect with the nuances of privacy management.

dana boyd's (2008) influential model of the four affordances of SNS is, as previously explicated in this book, highly relevant. SNS feature persistence or permanency of the data posted to them: content is searchable (e.g., "Googling" information); content can be replicated outside of its' original authentic context; and, finally, users must contend with invisible audiences whereby it is impossible to anticipate those who receive the content posted in networked publics (boyd, 2008). Kathy, age 13 from Cyber City, succinctly summed up concerns over permanency echoed by other groups: "Everything on the internet is always going to be there … it's just you can't control it." She adds that even with attempts to remove content, such as unwanted photos, when you "think it's like 'oh it's off Google,'" then "people screenshot it, they save the photo and it's never ever gone, so something that you don't want on social media, you do not post, it's just that simple." Kathy's strategy for dealing with permanency evokes the privacy as "in your hands" mindset – an individualized response very common among all our groups.

Facebook was often singled out in such discussions. Participants expressed frustration over strangers virtually accosting them on Facebook. During a discussion of general concerns over going online, Kimberly, age 13 from Cyberville, referred to "the whole like stalking … that happens a lot on Facebook." She elaborates: "so you'd be just talking to one of your friends or something and then next thing you know you get this weird message from this person you don't even know. I feel like that's a big problem with Facebook." Some of the groups also expressed anxiety over Facebook's use of location services (i.e., geotagging), especially when accessed through smartphones. Anna, a 19-year-old undergraduate student from Cyber City, admitted to being shocked while messaging her friend on Facebook and finding her precise location by clicking her name on her phone: "so if you just search a name on Facebook, you can find where they are at that exact moment." She elaborates, expressing anxiety over not only her own privacy being potentially breached but those of her friends:

> It's this nearby friends thing, where you can literally see how far away they are, and if I press the button, it will show me where they're walking, where they're going, and with the latest Facebook update, it's just turned

on automatically. I'm pretty sure none of these friends know, yet these are my friends that go to [university name], and they're all one kilometer away. It's creepy.[1]

Anna's message suggests a 'privacy as social' mindset, which, similar to other studies (James, 2014), were rarely made in our discussions.[2] As evident in other studies (e.g., boyd, 2014; Raynes-Goldie, 2010), our discussions involved detailed explications of the various strategies used to manage privacy on Facebook. When asked what strategies are preferred in that regard, the most frequently identified were blocking users, deleting negative comments, and setting profiles to private. These strategies were most often discussed with reference to Facebook. However, another more relevant strategy dominated our discussions: the careful management of one's digital self *across* the more popular SNS today.

Moving beyond Facebook: it's about privacy management

Facebook remains central in adolescents' online lives (Lenhart, April 2015), including among our rural and urban participants. However, as noted, both academic and popular sources have observed Facebook's decline of popularity amongst youth (Lang, February 21, 2015; Marwick & boyd, 2014). A central explanation is that as wider adult sectors of the population – especially parents and relatives – join Facebook, they encroach on what was perhaps once a uniquely adolescent-dominated space. Focus group discussions revealed how much of this transition – the move away from Facebook as the most prominently used SNS – involves concerns over privacy and online impression management (Livingstone, 2008; Marwick & boyd, 2011). This is presciently recognized by Vickery (2015: 289), who argues "the use of different platforms is a deliberate privacy strategy intended to resist the ways social media industries attempt to converge identities, practices, and audiences." Our participants pinpoint who makes up these audiences. A representative summary comes from Christine, a 19-year-old undergraduate student from Cyber City:

> my Facebook is for family and how I want to present myself professionally, and then my Instagram is, I guess how I want to present myself to friends and then, but my Snapchat is where I present myself, my real self I guess, is where they see me doing stupid things.

As expressed by Christine, youth use social media to transition between presentations of their 'front stage' self, referring to the part of the performance of self that is intended for the consumption of particular audiences, which varies with its audience (see Goffman, 1959). Participants felt most able to manage and maintain a sense of authenticity regarding their online self-presentations on applications like Snapchat and Instagram. Here teens may feel more comfortable in presenting a "pseudo back stage" self – referring to a space in which a person is free to express their genuine feelings and actions.[3] Importantly, our discussions reveal that privacy management is less about managing multiple accounts on one platform (Raynes-Goldie, 2010), but instead involves managing a sense of self and authenticity across several SNS to variegated audiences. Chantelle, age 15 from Cyberville, reflects that Facebook is "not really popular, a lot of people don't go on it anymore, they mostly go on Snapchat; but a lot of people like the older people ... they still use Facebook." Thirteen-year-old Cynthia adds succinctly: Facebook is "mostly for older people."

While relatives were expected to be primarily using Facebook, peers who remained exclusively on Facebook were perceived as 'odd'. Judy, age 15 from Cyber City, states "Facebook is more like, yeah relatives, and like we have friends on there too, but you don't really talk to them on Facebook, so"; Janelle, age 16, interjects: "and I think the only time I talk to friends on Facebook, is the only ones that only have Facebook. Like 'I have nothing else, I just have Facebook'; you're like 'oh, ok,' damn!"

Our participants often pointed to breaches of privacy as reasons for avoiding Facebook, or using it in a 'lite' way. For example, to better manage their impressions for various audiences, such as their parents. Largely youth tended to minimize their social networking activities on Facebook. In a group of four 13-year-old males from Cyberville, Craig reveals nervousness about using Facebook, particularly with the challenge of his mother reviewing his posts: "and then now whenever I send something ... to my friends or anything, my mom's able to see it through the messages, so I don't even use Facebook anymore." Cameron adds "I use messenger, my mom can't get on that." Older participants were also attuned to the need to present an idealized profile on Facebook, largely for their parents' viewing needs.[4] David, a 19-year-old male from Cyberville, expressed anxiety over having

> my mom on Facebook ... and my grandmother, and my dad and my aunts, and my uncles, so whatever I puts on there, they're going to see it, so whatever I does, I got to make sure it's the proper thing to do.

Donald, also 19, agrees: "definitely thinking over what you're saying." This more sparing and crafting use of Facebook is geared to project to parents and other relatives an idealized "front stage" self (Goffman, 1959). Evidencing their focus on audience management, participants who use Facebook were acutely aware of the need to continually check their privacy settings. Fiona, 18, from Cyber City, whose mother and aunts are on Facebook, admits to her mom "shar[ing] a lot of things, and I don't think she shares a lot with me, but when she does my settings are also private, so only I'll see it, nobody else will see it." While a few of our participants stated that they no longer (or never did) use Facebook in preference for newer and more popular SNS, the two strategies highlighted above were most salient: more careful and "lite" use, and managing privacy settings to control what can be seen by different audiences.

Such strategies were complemented by the strategic use of other SNS, usually Twitter, Instagram, and Snapchat, which were identified alternatives to Facebook. Participants preferred these sites due to their more focused features and perceived simplicity of use (e.g., sharing pictures and videos). However, our discussions revealed an important underlying draw: the newer SNS enable a stronger sense of agency among participants in terms of their ability to manage privacy and their audiences. For instance, 17-year-old Zoey from Cyberville stated "Twitter you can block people easily, you just hit it, hit your settings, block, then they're gone, but Facebook and stuff it's harder." Christine recollects that initially her Facebook included only "very intimate friends" but has now grown to about 800 people, to which she admittedly does not frequently interact. She compares this with Snapchat, which "is usually connected to your contacts on your phone," enabling her to

> pick who I don't want to see my stories so it's very like, these are the people who I'm like, I trust the most and that's why the privacy settings ... [if] I don't want them to see my story, I can block them from my story or I can ... delete them.

Yet, the practice of "deleting" or "blocking" someone or, more notably, being "deleted" also generated concern. Some participants, for example, worried that blocking others or not using certain SNS would lead to their social exclusion and losing control of their "definition of the situation" online. If central to the social process of going online is "writing oneself into being" (Sundén, 2003), then teens lose the ability to control how others write about their identities if they are not also carefully monitoring what is being posted – a time consuming and worry inducing activity (we highlight examples of this in Chapter 3, regarding the need for social connection). As Raynes-Goldie (2010) illuminates, there is "significant social costs involved in not having an account."

When discussing newer alternatives such as Instagram and, especially, Snapchat – the most popular actively used SNS amongst our participants – strategies, such as blocking, were less salient, perhaps a result of teens having a sense of better security on said sites. This is primarily due to the much smaller and intimate audiences teens communicate with on these platforms. Lucy, age 17 from Cyber City, stated that Snapchat is "more direct" to communicate with well-known persons. Other groups, when asked if Snapchat is more private than Facebook, often strongly agreed, arguing that Snapchat is geared for "personal pictures" (David), where the user feels they have control over who has access to them. From Cyber City, 19-year-old Eleanor provided a representative view: "I post more personal stuff on Snapchat, and nothing personal on Tumblr because I have strangers following me and stuff, so I gotta keep it private" (for a different view on Tumblr see Bailey, 2015). In a different group Bethany, age 19 from Cyber City, said "I use [Snapchat] for my closest friends and then I can choose who it goes to and who sees it."

Some participants pointed to the ephemeral nature of Snapchat as buttress-ing privacy, i.e., that pictures taken last for only a few seconds before auto-matically deleting themselves. An interesting dynamic emerged, however, during focus group discussions centered on Snapchat. Some participants referred to Snapchat's ostensible security, but this was quickly challenged by others. For instance, a group of three 13-year-old females from Cyberville were asked whether they were aware of any "sexting" on Snapchat. Valerie quickly responds "oh my god yeah! ... Snapchat's definitely the worst for that!" Others agree. Valerie elaborates:

> because it's like, you only see the pictures for 10 seconds or you can set them for 1, up to 10 seconds, so I guess if someone asks, you can easily just send it, and it'll be on for 1 second and I guess they don't really have time to screenshot, cuz you can screenshot the picture.

Kimberly then responds: "but then ... say I sent a picture to Valerie and then she screenshots it, I would get the notification that she screen-shotted it." But Valerie retorts:

> Yeah, but there's also an app you can get called Snapsave, and whatever snapchats you get, it saves onto that, so I've heard of boys who have those apps and they get pictures from girls and she'll be like, "I'm sending you so don't screenshot it," and they'll have the app and they're like "no, of course I won't screenshot it, you can trust me and stuff."

Other groups also made reference to Snapsave, describing it as an app that can be used to compromise privacy, especially related to female users engaging in digital sexual expression (see our wider discussion of "sexting" in Chapter 7). In one such group Emily, a 19-year-old undergraduate student from Cyber City, was surprised after hearing about Snapsave: "that's sneaky, I never knew about that, cuz I have nothing to hide, if I screenshot it and they know, like why did you screenshot that." Emily was not alone in suggesting that privacy concerns are less relevant if one has "nothing to hide." In a discussion of Snapsave, this argument was blended with a social privacy mindset. When asked whether the presence of Snapsave is a concern, some participants reinforced the point that they do not post anything of concern, but they also expressed trusting others to not save any images sent that were intended to be temporary. This social trust is then informally policed. For instance, this issue was raised in a humor-tinged exchange amongst females, ages 14 and 15, from Cyber City:

PENNY: Well, it's pretty much just, I don't really send anything bad [in response to the threat of Snapsave].

ORILLIA: It's like [Penny], [Jody], I trust you not to publicly expose my double chins.

PENNY: It's all double chins.

JODY: That's all I send.

While these remarks suggest a continued salience to social privacy mindsets in relation to newer SNS, overall the emphasis placed during our discussions on personal privacy management, especially among older teens, suggested an onus on privacy as "in your own hands" (James, 2014), which we discuss below in relation to patterns related to age and maturation.

Breach of employment and educational prospects

A common theme in discussions about privacy among older teens is anxiety over how future employers may screen their social media profiles during recruitment processes. Concerns about future employment were raised by 11 groups (making 19 references). Perhaps not surprisingly, age presented the clearest trend in relation to concerns over future employment. References (15) are concentrated among participants aged 15–17, no doubt due to their anticipation of graduation from high school and labor force entry. Youth living in Cyber City made three times the number of references than those residing in Cyberville (14 vs. 5); despite the expectation for a natural inflation of references for the latter group, given the slightly higher number of groups conducted with youth in Cyberville. While cyber-risk research comparing urban and rural youth is still rare, Burkell and Saginur (2015) found many similarities between these two groups related to the size and nature of their social network use. The higher number of references to future employment among our Cyber City (i.e., urban) participants may be related to the greater pressures on youth to enter an urbanized economy, though further research is required to explore this theme and geographical trend.

Donald, age 19 from Cyberville, repeated a general sentiment we heard across our focus groups. Asked about general concerns online, the group (of two males) discussed managing privacy by controlling who has access to view certain posts. Donald then added:

Another thing you probably worry about on social media too is employment … say you had a bunch of pictures on there and you were a party animal, right and they go, and they're like [Donald] has a resume entry here, let's check him out and whatever; they goes on my profile and they sees me drinking all the time, and stuff like that, they'll probably be opinionated.

These remarks gel with extant Canadian research revealing that teens are hyper-sensitive to the risks involved to their employability if they present in untoward ways online, for example as having a "party" lifestyle (Bailey et al., 2013; Burkell & Saginur, 2015).

Participants at the cusp of graduating from high school expressed anxiety over how employers may perceive them through their social media profiles and postings. In one group, three 17-year-old females from Cyberville discussed concerns over future employment as well as Canadian college applications during a wider discussion of the permanence of what is posted on social network sites. Rebecca says:

People really take stuff to heart, like back in the day, people would say something and you'd be like "oh that's not true, that's just a rumor," but now it's out there. If someone says something about me I'm obviously going to be offended because it's out there forever ... 20 years from now somebody could look back and be like oh, this is on Facebook about her ... I feel like people are more sensitive but I feel there's a certain rightness to it.

Carolyn agrees, "yeah, if you're applying for a job or something, they're going to look on your Facebook, see what's going on there." Tamara adds, "oh yeah I applied to college and they called and said that they looked on my Facebook and seen all my pictures on Facebook and all that stuff, and they liked it and so I was like ok good." Carolyn: "Like a job, not a job requirement, but like, people hiring you will go on your Facebook, 'who is she's friends with, what is she posting.'" The words of these older teens reveal the pressure they experience to produce a "perfect" online presence. Madison, age 16 from Cyber City, asked if future employment is a concern, replied "that is a concern, because it kind of gets to a stage where you have to think about your future, because next year we are graduating, so we have to be mindful about what we do." She adds that the process of posting content on social media involves "discovering yourself as you go on" but that "how you find yourself" and being online during this process will lead to employers "find[ing] you," which "could be a way of messing up everything, that's a big concern." Particularly revealing in her comment is that concern for managing privacy and one's digital footprint is negotiated alongside "discovering" oneself; each part and parcel of adolescent identity formation and maturation (Livingstone, 2008).

Younger teens may not raise such concerns as frequently because of their life stage; the impact on future employment is still far off from their perspective. Yet, some groups of younger teens did reveal concerns about corporate surveillance of their digital footprint. In a group of four females, ages 13 and 14 from Cyber City, Ashley reflects on losing control of what her peers post online, specifically those who do not consider the consequences of posting pictures of "doing weed" [marijuana]:

> the problem with that, is that you think, "oh I'll just delete [such posts] and it'll be gone forever," but when it's out there, anyone can screenshot it, when companies look for you, they can actually look through that, I know because my mom has taught me this. Because she had a friend who did weed, smoked whatever and then they actually looked through what he posted when he was younger and now he can't get any good jobs, so now he's working at McDonald's or something that. So it's just people don't notice that, and they're like: "oh no, if I delete it's gone forever" and they do tend to get quite cocky about it and they're like "no it's fine," it's like fine, no ruin your life, I don't care.

Ashley also reveals that she has a close relationship with her mother, and values her mother's views regarding safety online and behaviors. Moreover, fewer references to concerns about future employment were made by male participants. This may be due to males not considering future employment as actively as females or that online presentations about safeguarding privacy are less impactful long term for males in comparison to females. The latter, perhaps a consequence of gender norms and socialization processes, suggest part of "growing up" for males may first involve participating in "risky" behaviors and later maturing out of such practices (Berger, Wallis, & Watson, 1995; Lyng & Matthews, 2007; Monaghan, 2001), which would also suggest one's online history is expected to be colorful. It is also possible that male participants may not have felt comfortable revealing any such employment concerns in front of others during focus group discussions (see also Chapter 5 on relational aggression and the influence of gender norms). Nevertheless, several groups of males did reveal how impression management applies across SNS (see above), relegating a professional image for Facebook, where it is perceived that most employers look first and foremost. Referring to impression management on Facebook and Instagram, Demetry, in discussion with his group of 15- and 17-year-old Cyber City males, offered:

> Facebook it's, Facebook and Instagram, usually when you start getting older and you have to get, be more professional, ... I wanna clean mine up a lot, ... just keep it appropriate overall right, and you want to make sure that it doesn't come back to bite you.

Facebook, participants explain, is used more carefully and selectively by older youth. "Wall cleaning" has been staple strategy of adolescents for privacy management on Facebook for a number of years now (Raynes-Goldie, 2010). Here we demonstrate that this strategy, among older adolescents, relates to presenting a more professional image for potential employers, whereas other social network sites offer venues for different facets of ones' personality (see also Bailey & Steeves, 2015; boyd, 2014; Doherty, 2017; Utz, Muscanell, & Khalid, 2015). Our participants still associate potential employer screenings of their internet activity solely with Facebook; no references are made to Snapchat and Instagram in this context. Whether or not employers will begin to gravitate to newer, more popular SNS is an important potential development and will have implications for teens, especially those nearing graduation and those new to the work force.

Overall, these discussions suggest how the life transition tied to entering professional careers and pursuing post-secondary education is associated with becoming more mature and correspondingly presenting in ways deemed compatible with longer term objectives (see also Milford, 2015; Pedersen, 2013). We emphasize here that the pressure to present a professional image on SNS such as Facebook does not necessarily mean that teens' digital footprints, as they mature, are devoid of more casual, silly, strange, and even illicit content. Indeed, that Instagram and Snapchat are seen as platforms for one's "true self," away from the panoptic gaze of adults demonstrates the significance of the privacy paradox, mediated across SNS.

Age and the "nothing to hide" mindset

Perhaps in an effort to adapt to the demands of proper neoliberal citizenship, older teens emphasized an acquiescence to debased privacy that bypasses strategies of privacy management by declaring one has "nothing to hide." References by youth to "having nothing to hide" were concentrated among those aged 15 and older (31 references), with only three references made by youth aged 13 and 14. The majority of references came from females (20) rather than males (3). Overall, 26 references were made by youth in Cyber City, and eight in Cyberville. The contrasts here are more striking – with a concentration of such references among older, urban-based female teens.

The privacy mindset of having nothing to hide online relates directly the neoliberal directive of personal responsibility for one's actions.[5] For instance, participants emphasized their own responsibility to address online risks as they grew older, as opposed to parents and educators. Leah, age 16 from Cyberville, reflecting on the presentations she has attended in schools since the seventh grade, felt that she and her peers are now:

> old enough, we are, we do know this is bad, we know, doing drugs is bad, we know drinking and driving … we know it's bad … I tell my parents all the time, like sure, I understand that you're telling me from

your past experiences that I shouldn't do this, but I also have to learn for myself, like I'm not actually going to know the full effect until I learn for myself.

Leah shows in her words that only so much can be gained from "listening," and instead she is prepared to have her own experiences and, thus, lessons. It is also clear from participant experiences that parenting styles are relevant for helping instill this neoliberal stance; specifically, parents must adjust their behaviors accordingly as their children mature. For instance, three females, age 17 from Cyberville, engaged in a discussion of parental monitoring, raised this issue:

CAROLYN: When I was younger, my mom would like ...
TAMARA: Yeah when we [were] younger it was, ...
CAROLYN: Go through the Facebook friends, and be like "how do you know this person?" ... but like now we're older, I think she thinks you're responsible enough now to know.
REBECCA: My parents don't have any set rules on me *because I don't do anything anyway* [added emphasis].

The notion of "not doing anything anyway," expressed here, buttresses a sedimented notion of personal responsibility for managing risk online and the notion that parents' role in this neoliberal self-management becomes increasingly reduced as children mature. As one participant, rather strikingly, suggests, "I feel it's probably like a 90 individual, 10% parents should also be involved in it" (Helen, 16, Cyber City). Similar remarks were made across our focus group discussions, such as this exchange between two 19-year-old male students from Cyberville:

RESEARCHER: When you think of online messages and safety and all that kind of stuff, do you think it's up to you guys to monitor it?
DAVID: Yes, it is.
DONALD: Yeah.
DAVID: It's our choice to do what we gotta do, to make our news and our things that we put on social media.

Their exchange alludes to the general emphasis on personal responsibility that appears ingrained in individuals by the time they reach their 20s. Said another way, there appears to be a clear individualization and internalization of responsibility for one's online profile. These findings are consistent with those of Youn (2005), whose statistically significant findings revealed that younger teens are more likely to seek help from others regarding how to manage cyber-risk.

More strikingly, while some youth alluded to an expectation of debased privacy, Victoria, age 17 from Cyber City, expressed a "privacy as forsaken" mentality most explicitly:

RESEARCHER: What do you think about these [risks], are you constantly checking old posts, managing your online [presentation]?

VICTORIA: I mean I used to, I used to go back and be like "I need to delete this," but I think I've cleaned it up enough that I don't have to worry about it, but also as I [have] gotten older and more experienced with the internet I guess, I kind of realized, *I don't have any expectation of privacy when I'm posting things*, and I find myself kind of using it less and less, and I kind of stick to more personal social media like Snapchat, and just individually texting people, I don't really post anything on Facebook or Instagram ... *you shouldn't really expect to have privacy in general ... generally if you play it safe it's not a big deal.* [added emphases]

In sum, as evidenced by Victoria and echoed by others, participants generally felt that by high school, "it was just assumed you knew" how to manage oneself regarding youth engagement online (Yasmin, 18, Cyber City).

Despite the fewer number of references among male youth living in Cyberville, some did make remarks that suggest the neoliberal ethos of self responsibilization is also in formation at an early age. For instance, three 13-year-old males from Cyberville were asked if they expected to face different problems as they grew up. Victor replied "probably yeah, we'll probably get into mistakes and that, but we'll just have to deal with it." Already evident here, from Victor's words, is the expectation that "you are on your own" when it comes to being careful online; an attitude that notably preempts the possibility of seeking help from other peers, parents, educators, or other groups.

Discussion

In Canada, Raynes-Goldie (2010) found the position of "privacy pragmatism" was most salient among Canadian teens – mirroring other findings in the United States at the time. This mindset refers to "people who are concerned about their privacy but are willing to trade some of it for something beneficial" (Raynes-Goldie, 2010, n.p.). Researchers, through surveys in the early 2000s, revealed a shift towards privacy pragmatism as opposed to being unconcerned about privacy (see Raynes-Goldie, 2010). While privacy pragmatism remained salient for our participants, it was among older teens that the expressions of unconcern became more pronounced. The "nothing to hide" mindset suggests a fourth typology complementing those identified by James (2014); one that builds on the "privacy as forsaken" mindset but differs since it shuns the notion that privacy is only relevant if one is not "doing anything wrong." Academic focus on the theme of having nothing to hide in relation to privacy management has only recently emerged (see Murumaa-Mengel, Laas-Mikko, & Pruulmann-Vengerfeldt, 2015; Nau, 2014; Solove, 2007, 2011), arguably due to the saliency of this mindset in relation to online sociality. Our findings suggest that this mindset may sediment as youth reach late adolescence.

Our discussions revealed patterns according to age, gender and location (i.e., urban Western vs. rural Atlantic Canada). That significantly more references to feeling a lack of control online and having nothing to hide were made among female participants in Cyber City suggests that societal messages regarding cyber-risk management (primarily from parents and educators) seem to be concentrated on females more than males – which is not novel (see Bailey & Steeves, 2015; Karaian, 2014) – but also to those in urban environments moreso than rural ones. Perhaps teens in rural areas have more close-knit connections that undercut the emphasis on the individual to rely on him or herself; a Durkheimean collective solidarity that has shaped understandings of smaller communities for over a century. Indeed, 13 groups, many from rural Cyberville, made references to having close community ties and familiarity in rural regions, including a few participants who had moved from smaller rural areas to larger urban ones. Future researchers should explore this contrast, mining experiences more specifically related to urban and rural social dynamics (see Burkell & Saginur, 2015).

Youth today are growing up immersed in the expectation of the ephemerality of privacy online, and often express that effectively managing it is impossible. Opting out of social networks may secure privacy, but this is an untenable option for youth for whom electing what information to share through such networks is in itself a form of control over privacy (Bailey & Steeves, 2015; Livingstone, 2008; Marwick & boyd, 2011). Declaring that one has nothing to hide and is therefore indifferent to monitoring, of course, sidelines consideration of situations where one's digital profile can be usurped and privacy breached (e.g., being hacked, "doxxing," "revenge porn" (Stroud, 2014) and so forth). Such a declaration also sidelines the significance of privacy in any number of scenarios youth may wish to engage in, such as digital activism (Wilson & Hayhurst, 2009), consenting digital sexual expression (Koskela, 2006) and managing discreditable stigma (Goffman, 1963). Moreover, atomistic conceptions of risk and privacy obfuscate critical attention to the corporate collection of data and the alignment of social media platforms and "big data" with corporate surveillance and targeted advertising (Marx & Steeves, 2010; Steeves, 2012). Indeed, our participants demonstrated concerns for what can be considered horizontal privacy (i.e., privacy from offline peer groups), and not so much vertical privacy (i.e., privacy from authorities and institutions). In sum, the problem with the question "if you've got nothing to hide, what do you have to fear?" lies in the question itself (Solove, 2007).

The mindset of having nothing to hide links to an atomistic conception of privacy that debases a "pluralistic understanding of privacy" (Solove, 2007: 756) undergirded by more social conceptions geared to collective interests. It is an atomistic notion insofar as it justifies the position that one does not care what happens to others so long as it does not happen to oneself. It is useful to think of the nothing to hide mindset as drawing from a wider "cultural shift in society that does not place an adequate value on privacy and related liberties"; one which acts as a "form of social intimidation to expose those that do not conform" (Keeler, 2006: 25). Moreover, acquiescing to a mindset of having nothing to hide engenders a "pressure towards normalization" and "creates a kind of cultural inertia" that undermines the impetus to and momentum for challenging surveillance practices (Conrad, 2009: 322).

Marx (2003) observed that a person's ability to refuse and ignore surveillance was not a very common response among research participants. This trend may well be reversing for teens growing up with today's SNS. Curiously, however, some of our younger participants (i.e., 13 years of age) seem to have at their disposal the same social vocabulary of motive regarding personal responsibility as older teens. This too behooves further research to clarify the question of whether children and "tweens" entering adolescence are qualitatively different than the "digital natives" (Prensky, 2001) who grew up immersed in technology before them. In this context, we also had a few older participants refer to their younger siblings in contrasting ways: either as more irresponsible online or as more mature. What are the factors that shape these differences, and is more than just age at play? What is certain, however, is that in the rapidly changing technological landscape, it is not clear whether youth are growing up more critically engaged with issues of privacy and cyber-risk. Thus, developing teens' skills is crucial, not only related to privacy management, but a broader sociological imagination regarding their self in relation to society and citizenship.

Notes

1 Participants expressed less concern for their personal safety from location tracking apps and SNS than for the over-abundance of information that could be gleaned about them from friends, emphasizing social privacy considerations. This again suggests less concern over "vertical" breaches of privacy (e.g., from corporations) and more with "horizontal" breaches from often offline peer groups.
2 Unlike our study, where social privacy was not a prominent theme, Johnson (2015) found Canadian teens often rely on these informal social norms around online privacy. More attention to the influence of demographic factors such as age and gender, as well as urban versus rural residence, perhaps even immigration status, etc., would help identify reasons for these differences.
3 Goffman's (1959) "back stage" refers to the part of a performance under preparation and hidden from front stage visibility. It is dialectically related to the front stage in relation to the context of social interaction. Here we refer to online performances involving a "pseudo back stage," signaling that Goffman's (1959)

conceptualization centered on face-to-face interactions. Even for online performances, the offline "back stage" is where authenticity may most readily lie while preparing an online "front stage" performance.

4 In addition to parents, potential employers were most frequently referenced as the reason why Facebook profiles were kept "lite" and used to present an idealized professional self. As we discuss above, such references were concentrated among senior high school and undergraduate students.

5 The discourse of "having nothing to hide" has relatively recently emerged as a broad response to Edward Snowden's revelations regarding U.S. governmental surveillance programs (see Daniel Sieradski's Twitter site https://twitter.com/_nothingtohide and critiqued by some observers; see also Shackford, June 12, 2013).

References

Bailey, J. (2015). A perfect storm: How the online environment, social norms, and law shape girls' lives. In J. Bailey & V. Steeves (Eds.), *eGirls, eCitizens* (pp. 22–46). Ottawa: University of Ottawa Press.

Bailey, J., & Steeves, V. (Eds.). (2015). *eGirls, eCitizens*. Ottawa: University of Ottawa Press.

Bailey, J., Steeves, V., Burkell, J., & Regan, P. (2013). Negotiating with gender stereotypes on social networking sites: From "bicycle face" to Facebook. *Journal of Communication Inquiry, 37*(2), 91–112.

Barnes, S. (2006). A privacy paradox: Social networking in the United States. *First Monday, 11*(9–4). Retrieved from http://firstmonday.org/article/view/1394/1312. Accessed February 2018.

Berger, M., Wallis, B., & Watson, S. (1995). *Constructing Masculinity*. New York and London: Routledge.

boyd, d. (2008). *Taken Out of Context: American Teen Sociality in Networked Publics*. Berkeley, CA: University of California.

boyd, d. (2014). *It's Complicated: The Social Lives of Networked Teens*. London: Yale University Press.

boyd, d., & Hargittai, E. (2010). Facebook privacy settings: Who cares? *First Monday, 15*(8), Retrieved from http://firstmonday.org/htbin/cgiwrap/bin/ojs/index.php/fm/article/viewArticle/3086/2589. Accessed February 2018.

Burkell, J., & Saginur, M. (2015). "She's just a small town girl, living in an online world": Differences and similarities between urban and rural girls' use of and views about online social networking. In J. Bailey & V. Steeves (Eds.), *eGirls, eCitizens* (pp. 129–152). Ottawa: University of Ottawa Press.

Cohen, J. (2012). *Configuring the Networked Self: Law, Code, and the Play of Everyday Practice*. New Haven, CT: Yale University Press.

Conrad, K. (2009). "Nothing to hide … nothing to fear": Discriminatory surveillance and queer visibility in Great Britain and Northern Ireland. In N. Giffney & M. O'Rourke (Eds.), *Ashgate Research Companion to Queer Theory* (pp. 329–346). Surrey, UK: Ashgate Publishing.

Doherty, T. (2017). *The Presentation of Self in "Online" Life: A Content Analysis of Instagram Profiles*. (Master of Arts), University of Calgary, Calgary.

Dommeyer, C., & Gross, B. (2003). What consumers know and what they do: An investigation of consumer knowledge, awareness, and use of privacy protection strategies. *Journal of Interactive Marketing, 17*(2), 34–51.

Emerson, T. (1970). *The System of Freedom of Expression*. Michigan: Random House.

Etzioni, A. (1999). *The Limits of Privacy*. New York: Basic Books.

Goffman, E. (1959). *The Presentation of Self in Everyday Life*. Garden City, NY: Doubleday.

Goffman, E. (1963). *Stigma*. New Jersey: Prentice-Hall.

Hargittai, E., & Marwick, A. (2016). "What can I really do?" Explaining the privacy paradox with online apathy. *International Journal of Communication, 10*, 3737–3757.

James, C. (2014). *Disconnected: Youth, New Media, and the Ethics Gap*. Cambridge: The MIT Press.

Johnson, M. (2015). Digital literacy and digital citizenship: Approaches to girls' online experiences. In J. Bailey & V. Steeves (Eds.), *eGirls, eCitizens* (pp. 339–360). Ottawa: University of Ottawa Press.

Karaian, L. (2012). Lolita speaks: "sexting," teenage girls and the law. *Crime Media Culture, 8*(1), 57–73.

Karaian, L. (2014). Policing 'sexting': Responsibilization, respectability and sexual subjectivity in child protection/crime prevention responses to teenagers' digital sexual expression. *Theoretical Criminology, 18*(3), 282–299.

Keeler, M. (2006). *Nothing to Hide: Privacy in the 21st Century*. Lincoln, NE: iUniverse.

Koskela, H. (2006). "The other side of surveillance": Webcams, power and agency. In D. Lyon (Ed.), *Theorizing Surveillance: The Panopticon and Beyond* (pp. 163–181). Collumpton, UK: Willan Publishing.

Lang, N. (February 21, 2015). Why teens are leaving Facebook: It's "meaningless." *Washington Post*. Retrieved from www.washingtonpost.com/news/the-intersect/wp/2015/02/21/why-teens-are-leaving-facebook-its-meaningless/?utm_term=.4e93fc7dd067. Accessed February 2018.

Lenhart, A. (April 2015). *Teens, Social Media & Technology Overview 2015*. Pwe Research Center. Retrieved from www.pewinternet.org/2015/04/09/teens-social-media-technology-2015/.

Livingstone, S. (2008). Taking risky opportunities in youthful content creation: Teenagers' use of social networking sites for intimacy, privacy and self-expression. *New Media & Society, 10*(3), 393–411.

Lyng, S., & Matthews, R. (2007). Risk, edgework, and masculinities. In K. Hannah-Moffat & P. O'Malley (Eds.), *Gendered Risks*. Oxon: Routledge-Cavendish.

Marker, B. (2011). *Sexting as Moral Panic: An Exploratory Study into the Media's Construction of Sexting*. (Masters of Science), Eastern Kentucky University, Richmond, Kentucky.

Marwick, A., & boyd, d. (2011). I tweet honestly, I tweet passionately: Twitter users, context collapse, and the imagined audience. *New Media & Society, 13*(1), 114–133.

Marwick, A., & boyd, d. (2014). "It's just drama": Teen perspectives on conflict and aggression in a networked era. *Journal of Youth Studies, 17*(9), 1187–1204.

Marx, G. (2003). A tack in the shoe: Neutralizing and resisting the new surveillance. *Journal of Social Issues, 59*(2), 369–390.

Marx, G., & Steeves, V. (2010). From the beginning: Children as subjects and agents of surveillance. *Surveillance & Society, 7*(3/4), 192–230.

Milford, T. (2015). Revisiting cyberfeminism: Theory as a tool for understanding young women's experiences. In J. Bailey & V. Steeves (Eds.), *eGirls, eCitizens* (pp. 55–81). Ottawa: University of Ottawa Press.

Monaghan, L. (2001). *Body Building, Drugs and Risk*. London: Routledge.

Murumaa-Mengel, M., Laas-Mikko, K., & Pruulmann-Vengerfeldt, P. (2015). "I have nothing to hide." A coping strategy in a risk society. In L. Kramp, N. Carpentier, A. Hepp, I. T. Trivundža, H. Nieminen, R. Kunelius, T. Olsson, E. Sundin, & R. Kilborn (Eds.), *Journalism, Representation and the Public Sphere* (pp. 195–207). Bremen: edition lumière.

Nau, J. (2014). *"Why protest? I've got nothing to hide." Collective Action against and Chilling Effects of Internet Mass Surveillance.* (Master of Arts in Peace and Conflict Studies), University of Kent, Marburg.

Nussbaum, E. (February 12, 2007). Kids, the internet, and the end of privacy: The greatest generation gap since rock and roll. *New York Magazine.* Retrieved from http://nymag.com/news/features/27341/. Accessed February 2018.

Paine, C., Reips, U.-D., Stieger, S., Joinson, A., & Buchanan, T. (2007). Internet users' perceptions of "privacy concerns" and "privacy actions." *International Journal of Human-Computer Studies, 65*(6), 526–536.

Pedersen, S. (2013). UK young adults' safety awareness online – is it a "girl thing"? *Journal of Youth Studies, 16*(3), 404–419.

Phelps, J., Nowak, G., & Ferrell, E. (2000). Privacy concerns and consumer willingness to provide personal information. *Journal of Public Policy & Marketing, 19*(1), 27–41.

Prensky, M. (2001). Digital natives, digital immigrants Part 1. *On the Horizon, 9*(5), 1–6. Retrieved from http://dx.doi.org/10.1108/10748120110424816. Accessed February 2018.

Raynes-Goldie, K. (2010). Aliases, creeping, and wall cleaning: Understanding privacy in the age of Facebook. *First Monday, 15*(1–4). Retrieved from http://firstmonday.org/ojs/index.php/fm/article/viewArticle/2775/2432. Accessed February 2018.

Regan, P., & Steeves, V. (2010). Kids R Us: Online social networking and the potential for empowerment. *Surveillance & Society, 8*(2), 151–165.

Roessler, B., & Mokrosinska, D. (Eds.). (2015). *Social Dimensions of Privacy: Interdisciplinary Perspectives.* Cambridge: Cambridge University Press.

Shackford, S. (June 12, 2013). 3 Reasons the "nothing to hide" crowd should be worried about government surveillance. Retrieved from http://reason.com/archives/2013/06/12/three-reasons-the-nothing-to-hide-crowd. Accessed February 2018.

Solove, D. (2007). "I've got nothing to hide" and other misunderstandings of privacy. *San Diego Law Review, 44,* 745–772.

Solove, D. (2011). *Nothing to Hide: The False Tradeoff Between Privacy and Security.* New Haven: Yale University Press.

Steeves, V. (2012). Hide and seek: surveillance of young people on the internet. In D. Lyon, K. Haggerty, & K. Ball (Eds.), *The Routledge Handbook of Surveillance Studies* (pp. 352–359). New York: Routledge.

Steeves, V., Milford, T., & Butts, A. (March 2010). *Summary of Research on Youth Online Privacy.* Ottawa: Office of the Privacy Commissioner Canada.

Stroud, S. (2014). The dark side of the online self: a pragmatist critique of the growing plague of revenge porn. *Journal of Mass Media Ethics, 29*(3), 168–183.

Sundén, J. (2003). *Material Virtualities: Approaching Online Textual Embodiment.* New York: Peter Lang.

Tufekci, Z. (2008). Can you see me now? Audience and disclosure regulation in online social network sites. *Bulletin of Science, Technology & Society, 28*(1), 20–36.

Tynes, B. (2007). Internet safety gone wild? Sacrificing the educational and psycho-social benefits of online social environments. *Journal of Adolescent Research, 22*(6), 575–584.

Utz, S., Muscanell, N., & Khalid, C. (2015). Snapchat elicits more jealousy than Facebook: a comparison of Snapchat and Facebook use. *Cyberpsychology, Behavior, and Social Networking, 18*(3), 141–146.

Vickery, J. (2015). "I don't have anything to hide, but…": The challenges and nego-tiations of social and mobile media privacy for non-dominant youth. *Information, Communication & Society, 18*(3), 281–294.

Westin, A. (1968). *Privacy and Freedom.* New York: Atheneum.

Wilson, B., & Hayhurst, L. (2009). Digital activism: Neoliberalism, the internet, and sport for youth development. *Sociology of Sport Journal, 26*(1), 155–181.

Youn, S. (2005). Teenagers' perceptions of online privacy and coping behaviors: A risk–benefit appraisal approach. *Journal of Broadcasting & Electronic Media, 49*(1), 86–110.

Chapter 7

Gender, sexting, and the teenaged years

Introduction

The social landscape of youth includes a virtually endless online space where relationships, including friendships and romantic partnerships, are established and reinforced as well as broken (Lenhart, Smith, & Anderson, 2015; boyd, 2014). Digital spaces, however, are too often permeated by misogyny and patriarchy, and structured by dominant and often archaic or repressive gender norms (Angrove, 2015; Bailey & Hanna, 2011; Bailey, Steeves, Burkell, & Regan, 2013; boyd, 2014). Bailey and Steeves' (2015) interviews with female teens in Canada further illustrates how such spaces fail to challenge sexism and the oppression of women, as apparent in the age old double standard though which the actions of males versus females online are interpreted. Online, for example, male behaviors are constructed as "pranks" and normalized, while females' as "dramatic" and "slutty," particularly when the behavior takes the form of digital sexual expression known as "sexting" (Marwick & boyd, 2014; Ringrose, Harvey, Gill, & Livingstone, 2013).

Lee and Crofts' (2015) define sexting as "the digital production of sexually suggestive or explicit images and distribution by mobile phone messaging or through the internet on social network sites ... extending it to the sending of sexually suggestive texts" (454). Practices that fall within the broad category of sexting include words and prompting that range in sexual suggestiveness as well as the sharing of digital nude or semi-nude images referred to as "nudes" or, if of male genitals, "dick pics." Sexting, in all its forms, is common among youth and adults. In the United States, scholars studying the prevalence of sexting among youth suggest that anywhere between four and 19 to 40% of teens have sexted (Bailey & Hanna, 2011; Lenhart, 2009; Ringrose et al., 2013), with upwards of 30% of youth having sent a "nude," and 45% having received a "nude" (Englander, 2012). Similar statistics are not available in Canada, instead there is an "absence of reported Canadian cases in which sexting between minors has been prosecuted" (Bailey & Hanna, 2011: 408). Nevertheless, our current study supports that sexting is even more common than the four to 40% purported in the United States.

How gender ideals or conceptualizations are internalized, performed offline, or function to define the self remains understudied; specifically in the largely unpredictable online context of sexual explorations. In this chapter, we show that sexting and discourses around sexting are gendered, interlaced in gendered norms with patriarchal undertones, and are thus repressive for both male and female youth, albeit, arguably, to differing degrees. Yet, we also recognize that the sensations youth derive from sexting (e.g., anxiety, freedom) suggest sexting represents a form of gendered self-presentation and risk taking during processes of identity negotiation.

Here we explore the attitudes and perceptions of youth related to cyber-risks involved with digital sexual expression. Specifically, we examine how perceptions and experiences are shaped by wider gender expectations reinforcing differential consequences for female and male teens. While our findings reinforce existing qualitative research findings focused on both female teens views of cyber-risk and sexting (e.g., Bailey & Steeves, 2015) and deconstructions of cyber-safety campaigns directed at largely white, heterosexual, and middle-class females (Karaian, 2014), our sample also includes the voices of male teens. As such we offer a widened epistemological lens that seeks to advance knowledge about the gendered positionality of sexting, especially in the area of distribution of "dick pics."

Gender, hegemonic masculinity, and risk

Although some youth engage in sexting, online landscapes continue to embody the "age-old double standard, where sexually active boys are admired and 'rated,' while sexually active girls are denigrated, shamed and despised as 'sluts'" (Ringrose, Livingstone, & Harvey, 2012: 12; see also Ringrose et al., 2013). The "double standard" being that, traditionally, the behaviors of men are governed by different "rules" than those of women (Crawford & Popp, 2003). The experiences and perceptions of teens involving sexting relate to this double standard and the concept of hegemonic masculinity. Although hegemonic masculinity remains a debated concept (see Connell, 1992, 1995; Connell & Messerschmidt, 2005; Hall, 2002; Jefferson, 2002; Messerschmidt, 2012), using the term as conceptualized first by Connell (1995; see also Carrigan, Connell, & Lee, 1985) and then by Connell with Messerschmidt (2005), reveals the oppressive nature of gender constructs within the hierarchical (and oppressive) structure of gender relations. Ricciardelli, Maier, and Hannah-Moffat (2015: 494) explain that:

> according to this definition, hegemonic masculinity is constructed in relation to, and occupies a position of superiority over, femininities and all other masculinities (see also Connell, 2002), legitimizing the hierarchical structure of gender relations by ensuring that subordinate masculinities are positioned at the bottom of the gender hierarchy.

Scholars focused on the gendered-risk nexus, particularly concerning females, show that "gendered understandings of risk produce new responsibilities and patterns of action, as well as new strategies for the definition, control and neutralisation of risk" (Hannah-Moffat & O'Malley, 2007: 2; see also Stanko, 1997). Perhaps it is in this context, again reflecting the gendered double standard and seeming female oppressiveness in online spaces, that females online, not males, are thought to require greater surveillance and protection from sexual exploitation as they are positioned as "something innocent, pure and at risk of contamination through active desire" (Ringrose et al., 2013, p. 307; see also Egan, 2013; Jackson & Cram, 2003; Tolman, 2012). As Milford (2015) argues, "too often, popular discourses neoliberally and patriarchally responsibilize girls and young women to self-protect against potential online risk, or recommend that they be protected through legislative initiatives, accepting online risk and gendered constraints as inevitable" (64). In these contexts, risks and opportunities are tethered to each other online, but also feature as significant for negotiation during adolescence in general (Livingstone, 2008).

Gendered risk and identity negotiating across private and public spaces

Research on adolescents has long targeted identity development, particularly as shaped through the formation of relationships with peers both on and offline (Harter, Stocker, & Robinson, 1996; Lerner & Steinberg, 2009). Given the two goals, of (1) developing a unique identity and (2) garnering acceptance from peers, permeate the everyday lives of adolescents, it is not surprising that online social network sites are particularly attractive for teens. Youthful self-exposure to cyberspace through webcams and video blogs highlight the agentic and active ways youth are approaching risk through information and communications technologies; indeed "exposing oneself can be connected to identity formation" and can be seen as "fun" (Koskela, 2006: 172). Despite the vie for agency and self-determination, particularly in teens' pursuit of self-discovery and intimacy, the lens of gender helps to illuminate structured inequalities between the experiences of males and females. Understandings of gender, masculinities, and femininities both inform and are shaped by online spaces. For instance, Bailey and Hanna (2011) report what they referred to as "certain gendered patterns" (11) across extant literature on sexting. They found that more females are likely to send sexts and report feeling pressured by a male to send nude or semi-nude images in comparison to males (see also Englander, 2012; Ringrose et al., 2012).

With or without such pressures, for some youth sexting takes on a seductive quality that is rooted in the potentialities of experience and thrill of sexual exploration and attraction (Koskela, 2004). Traditional gender understandings, however, relegate explicit sexuality to the space of "masculinities," which further informs the "double standard" and may have repercussions for youth online. Nonetheless, sexting, between willing consenting individuals, is exciting; the thrill being embedded in the emotional sensations underlying sexual attraction, possible intimacy, and sexual expression, as well as the processes of learning how to express sexual interest while achieving the desired gendered self-presentation (Hasinoff, 2012; Koskela, 2004; Lamb & Peterson, 2012). Yet the inevitable element of chance in sexting, the risk tied to not knowing how a sext will be received (i.e., if it will be kept, disclosed, or how the recipient will respond) are all part of navigating private and public spaces online. There is thus an inevitable element of identity formation for all persons of any gender.

Youth are undeniably aware of the public versus private aspect of being online and the ability for the private to transcend into the public even within boundary work around sexting (boyd, 2008; Lenhart, 2009). Englander (2012), in her study of 617 college freshmen from a state university in Massachusetts, showed that 13% of those who sexted reported problems because their photo was shown to their school peers. Moreover, despite youth being repeatedly taught that what happens with digital images once sent is outside of their control, nearly 75% of her participants who sexted believed their photograph was never seen by anyone other than the intended recipient. Youth, then, navigate sexual exploration and identity development as they choose to share "risky" images with a specific recipient – a thrilling and sensation seeking behaviour – that is even more risky because of the potentiality for the private to become public and the trust and emotionality in relationship seeking and intimacy building eschewed in such actions. As such we turn to explore how gendered expectations and the gendered double standard online shape experiences of sexting, especially in relation to gendered assumptions within public virtual (i.e., online) and physical (e.g., school) spaces, and the degree of deterrence versus enticement youth report towards sexting.

It must be noted that in most U.S. states and all of Canada, youth less than 18 years old can lawfully engage in consensual sex or sexual acts. Yet, despite a Supreme Court "personal use exemption" permitting consensual distribution of sexts in certain contexts in Canada (Sealy-Harrington & Menuz, June 2015), it remains a criminal offense (e.g., child pornography) for youth to photograph their sexual acts and possess, share, or distribute said photographs. Hasinoff (2012), speaking to legislation in the United States, explains: "all parties involved in explicit teen sexting are potentially child pornography offenders, whether they are victims, perpetrators, or consensual participants" (450; see also Poltash, 2013). Thus, it is in the content of digital sexual images that "innocent" behaviors can become "criminal" and feelings of vulnerabilities can become dominant despite the intentions and the conditions under which such photos were first created. Bailey and Hanna (2011) advise that "in their own long-term self-interest, it would probably be prudent for teens to avoid capturing and sharing with their partners widely distributable digital memorializations of their sexualized self-representations and sexual activities" (441).

Sexting and the salient double standard

Today, whether or not youth choose to engage in sexting, there exists gendered dimensions underpinning the norms governing perspectives, actions, and interpretations in online digital spaces – particularly in relation to sexting (Bailey & Hanna, 2011; Ringrose et al., 2013). Such norms include the aforementioned double standard associated with free expression of sexuality, where girls are labeled and stigmatized as promiscuous while boys are emboldened and rewarded as "studs" (Bailey & Hanna, 2011; Crawford & Popp, 2003; Handyside & Ringrose, 2017). From a co-ed group of four teens from Cyber City, ages 17 and 18, Victoria explains that for female youth the consequences of sending nudes are concerning:

> I think it's more of a reputation type thing, I mean breasts themselves aren't going to affect anything but it's more of the reputation that they receive from like, "oh my tits are all over Snapchat, what do I do now."

From the same group Frederick, a male age 18, further clarifies:

> I think with girls usually, if a girl is known for sending out nude pictures, then people are going to think that she's a slut or something like that, but if a guy sends it out, other people are going to think he's weird, if he's randomly sending it to somebody then people might think he's weird, but if say a girl asks the guy for it and he sends it to her, then maybe his buddies are like "nice man," that kind of thing.

These excerpts reveal the double standard and the associated slandering sexting can have on female youth. Of course, the negative stigma attached to being called a 'slut' greatly overshadows the neutered designation "weird" (see below for further discussion of the gendered use of "weird"). Our findings here are consistent with those of a PEW Internet survey (Lenhart, 2009), for example, which also reveals that images of girls can result in the person depicted being judged, labeled, and her reputation slandered.

In contrast to females sending nudes (often breasts), males are rarely chastised for sending "dick pics"; rather, the response to such behavior often projects the axiom "boys will be boys." For example, three 13-year-old females from Cyberville, describe receiving random "dick pics" from males:

VALERIE: I feel guys just persuade the girls; that's what I feel.
KIMBERLY: Girls they won't even ask for any pictures to guys or anything and [boys]'ll just send you a picture one day.
INTERVIEWER: Do you guys ever get pictures?
JULIA: I got one once.
KIMBERLY: Once.
VALERIE: Me too I got it once.

A group of five males, ages 15 and 17 from Cyber City, were asked their views about female peers' experiences with sexting. Asked if sexting is "a regular thing girls your age are expecting or dealing with?" Shaun replies "some, it kind of depends on your reputation." Deshawn agrees "yeah"; Bodie adds "if you're going to send an image back, then probably." The gendered discourses here are striking. Our female groups describe male teens sending digital nudes as "random" occurrences, normalized and common place. However, both male and female teens speak about the reputation of females as determining if they receive nudes randomly or due to presumed promiscuity. Rather than laying claims of hegemonic or traditional notions of masculinity to the sending of "dick pics," it must be recognized that there is nothing agentic or stoic about sending such images, thus such acts cannot be thought suggestive of hegemonic or traditional masculinities (Berger, Wallis, & Watson, 1995; Carrigan, Connell, & Lee, 1985; Connell, 1995; Nixon, 2001). Although they do fall in line with notions of laddist masculinities (e.g., boyish variations of masculinities that favor types of risk taking, pranks, violence, the sexual objectification of women, and sport; see Nichols, 2016; Ricciardelli, Clow, & White, 2010). Reflecting the gender double standard and seeming female oppressiveness, males who send "dick pics" are viewed as simply "boys being boys" – in essence "lads" – dealing with the hormonal changes of adolescence and the associated identity development that normalizes their sexual exploration (Chambers, Loon, & Tincknell, 2004; Deaton, 2013; Weiss, 2009). Females, however, receive no such absolution. Instead, they are framed in wider societal responses to cyber-risk as requiring surveillance and protection (Egan, 2013; Griffin, 1985; Jackson & Cram, 2003; Ringrose et al., 2013; Tolman, 2012). This discourse is also prevalent among our participants, such as one exchange between four females from Cyber City, ages 18 and 19:

FIONA: I've heard the phrase a lot that "guys will [be] guys," so if a guy sends a dick pic, "boys will be boys," but if a girl sends a nude, like everyone will …

SERENA: She's slut shamed.

FIONA: Yeah she's slut shamed, everyone is like how can you put your body out like that, your body is like a holy temple and all of these things, but if a guy shows any sort of genital parts, then it's like, they're just like "oh but he's just a boy."

SERENA: And if anything happens, say if that picture gets sent around, I don't think the guy would really even care much almost, if they would, they would care, but *if a girl's photo gets sent around, that's a way bigger deal* than if a guy's photo gets sent around. (added emphasis)

It is thus clear that well established offline norms regarding the gendered sexual double standard retain saliency online for teens today. What aggrandizes the impact of this hegemonic notion is the public permeability of online spaces; i.e., it acts to reinforce neoliberal notions of self-regulation and responsibilization online, but does so at a higher social valence level for females than males.

Gendered spaces: public versus private?

Although youth know that any texted or online communication intended as private has the potential to become public, this knowledge does not always impact their actions. Sexting is a form of risk taking with undefined but undeniable "riskiness." For example, even among individuals in committed and trusting relationships, the temporality of relationships makes sexting risky due to potentially harmful consequences. Serena, aged 19 from Cyber City, articulates a dimension of this risk:

> Personally what I've experienced, is with ex-boyfriends, it's usually them asking you, begging you to send pictures of yourself, it's never a voluntary, I've said "no" because of what I know now that they're my ex-boyfriends and I hate them, they could do anything … if it [end]'s on a bad note, something terrible can happen and I've had that, I didn't send this guy anything but he, but when I was breaking him with him, he was like "don't break up with me or I'm going to exploit you" and stuff like that, this guy [who] apparently loved me yesterday is saying these things today and had I sent him a bunch of things, I'd be scared to death that he was going to do something.

Serena's words reflect the coercive and exploitative aspects of pressure (here a form of blackmail) on females to send nudes, even within "consensual" relationships. The threat is emboldened by the gendered understanding that public exposure has potentially serious stigmatizing consequences for females.

The threat of the potential for such images to be circulated extends beyond what is searchable online, as suggested by Ava, age 15 from Cyber City: "just because you Google your name and naked pictures don't show up, doesn't mean that there's not stuff going around; anyone could have it." This problem is rendered further complex when threats are made to "Photoshop" faces onto nude bodies and post these publicly, if a female does not "heed" the directive to send nude images of herself (Powell & Henry, 2017). The sharing of images intended to be private is difficult to manage for all youth, but the pressure on females to regulate their online activities is often higher. This pressure relates not only to immediate parties involved (e.g., a "dating couple"), but can readily transcend from the private to the public sphere, both online and offline. For instance, Valerie, age 13 from Cyberville, provides an example of how sexting was used for blackmailing and the widespread offline impacts:

I know one of my closest friends, a couple, just before Christmas actually got caught up with the police because, someone called and they told the police that one of my good friends is being blackmailed by a guy with pictures and then so the police here went in that guy's phone and swiped all the pictures and there was a lot, there was a lot of pictures, cuz I just he was just blackmailing her, she just didn't really think of anything, but then he was sending to his friends, so he [the police] went around six houses and erased all of it on their phones.

In the situation Valerie describes, not only did the blackmailed youth's peer group see the digital images she sent, but likely also their parents, the police, and perhaps others during the investigative processes. Another permutation and added pressure on female teens comes from the affordances of the social network sites they use (i.e., the technological features that structure the limits of how users interact with online mediums; see Lanier, 2010). For instance, one such affordance, the "block" feature, can be used aggressively by males as a projection of power. A group of three 13-year-old females from Cyberville discussed this:

IRENE: Sometimes girls send photos and then the guys saves them and then when they break up, they kind of just....
AMELIE: Send them.
IRENE: They float around ... people get mean and start calling each other names.
INTERVIEWER: Oh, about the pictures?
IRENE: About the people.
AMELIE: They want you to do it, and then the boys want you to do it and then after they ask you for it, and soon as you're done, they block you.
GRETA: They block you.
AMELIE: And then you can just delete them and then send it around, and then the boyfriend will be like "gross" and all that, but he's the one who wanted it done.

That teens as young as 13 speak of such experiences, detailing the specific features and context of relational aggression, is striking. It suggests that the pressures male peers place on female teens today starts at very young ages (perhaps younger than previous generations) and is engendered by all the complexities of social connection online (boyd, 2014; Livingstone, 2008).

Consistent with Koskela's (2006) situating of online youth perceptions and practices within the context of neoliberal self-governance and surveillance, our female participants repeatedly referred to responsibility lying with themselves to regulate their sexual expressions online. In response, some go so far to purport a form of what we refer to as "cyber-abstinence," perhaps reflecting the influence of school-based messages. For example, in response to questions about how to handle the risks involved with sexting and using apps such as Snapchat, female participants responded "don't send nudes" (Patricia, 15, Cyberville), while others suggest "keep[ing] to yourself more" and to remember "you can't trust people" (Mary, 16, Cyberville). The discourse these youth engage in resonates with broader societal messages directed at female teens to abstain from sexting or, more generally, posting anything that could brand them a 'slut' or deviant (Hasinoff, 2012; Karaian, 2012, 2014). Thus, there is much pressure on teens to monitor online presentations of self and to present a carefully crafted self, both in their interactions with peers online and if engaged in sexting. A crafted self refers to an online self-impression management strategy that requires both emotional management and balancing between disclosing too little or too much information online. Focus group discussions reveal a line between over and under-sharing and the timing of sharing that, although rarely clearly marked, has potentially detrimental repercussions for youth who cross the line – including social alienation and hurt. Oversharing or sharing with poor timing can be as simple as sending an otherwise desired digital sexual image at an inappropriate time, "but if it's 2 pm, I'm at a lecture, it's a Wednesday, 'what are you doing?'" (Janiya, age 18, Cyber City).

What is also pronounced is the gendered nature in which the consequences facing female youth who "overshared" appear extensively grave. We see this in the example of males "blocking" the female sender after a nude is sent; but second, and arguably with wider impact, the non-consensual dissemination of one's nude images online.

What also comes across from our discussions is the unfortunate reality that personal self-management online, including whether one is successful in presenting a well-crafted self, is only part of the picture. For instance, Lina, age 17 from Cyberville, recalled a difficult situation with her boyfriend, who had much difficulty accepting that a "random" male sent her a photograph of his penis:

> Having a boyfriend is way worse, you have a boyfriend, there's this other guy trying to hit you up, and then you'll open this in front of boyfriend, they're like "why would they send you that out of the blue," and then you're in trouble, like "oh my god, it's really bad, it's actually really bad."

Lina confirms that not all nudes received are welcomed, and each can be a source of interpersonal or relationship challenges. However, what determines who is humiliated by being the subject of a nude digital image, despite their gender or if they are the sender or receiver, is difficult to determine. Unarguably however, a lack of control over the influence and impact of engaging with social media online is perhaps the overarching theme that runs across all of our focus group discussions. Indeed, 30 of our groups made 131 references to not feeling in control of content they post, and how it is responded to and taken up. Of these references, 87 were made in all female groups, with only 17 made in all male groups – the remaining 27 came from co-ed groups. However, the manner in which online spaces help to engender a collapse of social contexts (boyd, 2008) by obfuscating the boundaries of public and private is especially underscored for female teens, for whom public spaces are still largely hostile. The differentially gendered stakes of having a public online life are also raised in debates over the male distribution of "dick pics." In this final substantive section, we explore these debates in further detail, examining the particular question of the "awareness contexts" of males when sending "dick pics," and once again reinforcing the notion of lower stakes involved for males than females.

Debating "dick pics": gendered conceptions and consequences

Hegemonic gender norms permeated the discussions around sexting in general, evident in the afore-described "double standards." This became acutely evident in discussions over males distributing images of their penis to other females, including partners but also others networked socially online. The responses among females to questions about what motivates males to send "dick pics" is striking, as evidenced during one discussion among 17-year-old female youths from Cyberville:

INTERVIEWER: And do you think it's the same though for boys and girls, cuz you said boys send the pictures and they don't care, but girls obviously send them too (Rebecca and Carolyn reply affirmatively). But do you think it's a different context, like they think something different is going to come of it?

TAMARA: Well I think when a girl sends a picture, she'll like, "oh I like this dude, I think he likes me back, I'm going to send him a picture of my boobs, hopefully he'll like me more," but a dude is like, "oh I like my penis, I'm going to send it to this girl, hopefully she'll like it too, and hop on it."

REBECCA: And send it to 20 girls at once and hope they don't notice.

This excerpt shows a variety of the gendered components that underpin the sharing of digital images, including how some female teens report getting frequently asked to send nudes in return for an unsolicited nude they received or friends that had all received the same "dick pic" from some male youth hopeful that someone would respond with a nude in-kind. The notion that a seemingly intimate message is sent to multiple people at once in an effort to increase their odds of a reply hampers the sentiment that nude digital images represent a precursor for increased attraction and intimacy in relationships.

Here too males are represented from our female groups as rather unconcerned about the public dissemination of their nudes. In contrast, such public dissemination has potentially serious psychosocial consequences for females. It is thus telling that cyber-safety programs directed at responsibilizing teens about sexting are primarily pitched to females (Bailey & Steeves, 2013; Hasinoff, 2012; Karaian, 2014).

The sending and receiving of "dick pics," moreover, is rather normalized and is not thought damaging to a male youth's reputation, scandalous, nor indicative of moral inaptitude. Instead, male photographs of their "junk" are readily laughed at by some of our female teens, once received, because they are indifferent to the imagery. Janiya reflects:

> I mean me and my friends, this sounds so terrible, but, me and my friends we were, we had a carpool crew, and there was me and my five best friends throughout all of high school. We joked that we were, cuz *it was just a frequent thing*, where at the end of grade 12, as a grad gift, I'm making a scrapbook and the covers gonna be a collage of all the dick pics we got in the last three years, and we did it, this beautiful, bound collaged dick pic collection. So it becomes a funny thing, *I found no one takes it seriously*. When people do that, no one's like, "oh look at you," it's more like you show your friends and you laugh about it, which is kind of terrible, but it's like "you shouldn't have sent me that."
>
> (Added emphases)

In a different group, 19-year-old Carmen from Cyber City also explains that a lot of her female friends:

> have got dick pics and stuff, and every single time they do, they gather together as a group as girls and they laugh at that shit … so I can honestly say, if you get a dick pic from some random person, zero out of 10 times, is that girl saying "oh shit, I'm going to go have sex with that guy."

The idea of creating a scrapbook of "dick pics" evidences just how normalized and commonplace the sexting of male penises has become for many female teens – a fact resonating with the predominant patriarchal undertones in online and offline society.

Few of our female participants openly admitted to sending nudes but nearly all females discussed receiving "dick pics" (or knowing friends who have received them) – often unwanted – and other sexually suggestive messages. In Cyberville, a group of three females, age 17 from Cyberville, responded casually when asked if they received "dick pics and all that kind of stuff too?"

LINA: *Unwanted ones*, random ones.
ALLY: I get them all the time …

ZOEY: You don't even want it.

ALLY: I don't like it … not even a hello, just a picture.

LINA: Just send it, you'll open it and it'll be oh, "we're eating supper with my mom or something."

ALLY: They don't care where you are.

ZOEY: It doesn't make sense, *it's way more boys than girls sending nudes.* (added emphases)

The encroachment into public space (here a family meal) is evident as well, emboldening the argument that public spaces are safer for males. This exchange also raises the important question of whether females are experiencing unacknowledged trauma, to one degree or another, when they dismiss receiving images of male penises with shared laughter. Making a scrapbook of unsolicited "dick pics" is surely a form of "shallow resistance," but this does not temper the wider onslaught that occurs whereby each unsolicited nude received is not only a chargeable offence but an assault in the literal sense.

It is very clear that male teens engage in such activity since they may fear no long-term consequences. Unlike female youth (see Ringrose et al., 2013), male youth do not seem to be attacked morally for sending a nude picture. This is reinforced when groups are asked whether or not males are taking any of this seriously. In response this question, Janiya recalls "I've had guys that are like, 'what do you mean you showed your friends?' I'm like 'well you sent it to me, it's public property, once its online you can't control it anymore.'" Anna, age 19 in the same group as Janiya, agrees, elaborating:

> I always think, if I didn't ask for it, anyone's allowed to see it. If I was struck one evening, like man "that's what I want right now," then I'm not going to show it to anyone, but it's again, if it's afternoon on the Thursday, the weekday and someone sends me that, I'm going to show it to everyone, we're going to laugh about it, it's so stupid.

These female teens' response to the idea of a male not appreciating the sharing of his digital image, dismissing male authority over control of public space, seems to be direct resistance to the gendering of public space we have thus far highlighted. It suggests that when a male youth chooses to send a nude self-image that is not solicited, it is "fair game" to share the image without concern. This resistance may also be characterized as shallow: unlikely to change the wider discursive dynamics around public spaces and responsibilization. These responses also reveal both a stance forged in opposition to wider contexts experienced as obdurate and a new interpretation of the "double standard."

Also problematic is that such a response is, in essence, emotionally cold, insensitive, and reduces male youth to be unable to share their feelings about these experiences. Thus, not only is how female youth reacted to receiving "dick pics" thought problematic – a form of victim blaming where a female is held responsible for her own violated reaction to receiving an unsolicited image – but the fact that males too can be affected by pressures to sext is discounted. Because emotional responses are culturally read as emasculating, male youth may feel unable to express reactions that are not consistent with gendered norms. Victoria, age 17 from Cyber City explained that with "guys there's also a humiliation factor [when he sends a picture of his penis]." Experiencing shame or disinterest in sexting may leave a male youth potentially vulnerable in their identity negotiation, as they are thought to stray from gender norms. In consequence, a seeming necessity to pressure female youth to sext is artificially heightened, even endorsed, because of this traditional barrier to forthright sexual expression that informs gendered processes of socialization. Perhaps, then, the persisting gendered double standard and patriarchal contexts mediating sexual-risk experiences online encourages researchers to focus on the "digital citizenship" of female teens in particular (e.g., Bailey & Steeves, 2015). Although the double standard persists, and it may be normalized and commonplace for males to send "dick pics," researchers in the area have yet to unpack how male teens actually feel about the sending and sharing of such images. Without knowledge of males' standpoints, it may be assumed that they are indifferent to and collude with wider hegemonically reinforced behaviors.

Assuming all males are uniformly indifferent furthers traditional, largely stereotypical, understandings of males as emotionally indifferent and aggressively sexualized individuals (Connell, 1992, 1995). Our research provides a glimpse of male perspectives through responses to particular questions asked during focus group discussions, though our findings here remain necessarily tentative. Still, some males in our sample did express some regret over sending "dick pics." Ironically, their statements evidenced the relatively lighter penalty attached for such transgression. Admitting to having sent "dick pics" to females in the past, Frederick offers:

> I know personally me, some of my friends have bugged me about it, for doing that, cuz they found out about it, and they started bugging me about it, cuz they think it's weird for guys to do it, but not for girls to do it, right so, I think there's that part to it.

Although Frederick reports that his friends "bugged" him about sending the photograph, unlike females, he did not confess to feeling shamed or having his reputation deeply affected because of his actions; nor did he report concern about the image being shared widely. Frederick's use of the less overtly gendered descriptor "weird" may seem an odd word choice to refer to the male distribution of "dick pics" – it suggests the male is straying from gendered norms. The adjective recalls the gender double standard, where females who sext must endure much harsher adjectives describing their actions and their identities. Overall, his experiences are more focused on being teased than wider, caustic and degrading consequences. Our discussions with females corroborated the idea that males find it easier to 'brush off' shame related to sending "dick pics." Rebecca discloses:

> I feel when you're one of the guys it's easier to brush stuff off. That's not saying guys don't put up a front and they actually take it to heart, cuz they probably do, but girls I find take it a lot; they'll actually cry about it, guys probably just be upset obviously, but brush it in front of other people. Girls would probably cry if something happened to them.

The overwhelming pressure on female teens, the regularity of being assaulted with unsolicited "dick pics," and the dismissal of their right to consensual digital sexual expression is obviated from our focus group discussions. What is also apparent is that male teens seem to be completely unaware (the more reflective comments came from older teens on the cusp of young adulthood) of how females are experiencing receiving unwanted images. Combined with the reported threats of "revenge porn," the contexts of impunity within which males engage seem self-evident. To this end, we now turn to consider the various sources, such as school cyber-safety programs, that may be helping, albeit unintentionally, to reinforce this hegemonic, gendered landscape.

Gendered online "safety" messages

When asked questions about the types of messages they have received about sexting and cyber-safety, participants discussed experiences related to their schools. Discussions here reveal that messages about cyber-risk and safety, including sexting, are largely concentrated in middle school and junior high school. Programs delivered, however, were described as reactive (e.g., in response to an incident) efforts – rather than proactive. Notable, however, the messages they received are gendered, in that participants reflected on more time and emphasis being spent speaking to female youth rather than male youth about the repercussions of "sexting." For example, a group of three 17-year-old female students from Cyberville recalled a "big sexting" presentation that occurred the previous year. The presentation was related to an incident with male students sending "nudes to each other" (Lina). In response, the school issued talks, Zoey recalls, involving the separation of male and female students. Zoey argues that the school "waited for it to happen, to have the information when it was too late." Lina agrees: "they gotta wait for something to happen, then [they] can do something about it." By high school, the group reports, relatively serious incidents involving rela-tional aggression may "trigger" mandatory talks, but these are perceived to be largely ad hoc reactive responses and directed at females. "It's not very balanced," concludes Ally. Another group of female students, aged 15 and 17 from the same high school, raised the same issue. Naya: "it's like someone takes a [nude] picture and sends it and that goes around the school and then two days later there's a presentation." Patricia adds, significantly: "Yeah like *every girl gets a talking* to or like, and then it's just a presentation for the whole school" (emphasis added). Like Karaian's (2014) research examining the various cyber-based campaigns directed at teens, our participants provide evidence for a gendered underpinning to online risk, as females and not males are "talked to" about being responsible online.

Reflecting on received messages about online safety, Cyber City teens also consider the cyber-safety programming offered in their schools to be frequently gender biased; in essence perpetuating patriarchal and oppressive gender discourses and dichotomies. For instance, from a group of five females who have attended school together for a number of years, Judy (aged 15) recalls "one time in junior high school, they split up girls and guys and they gave separate conversations." Janelle (aged 16) jumps in, adding

> but *the girls' conversations were a lot longer than the boys*. The girls' was maybe two and a half periods and the boys was one period long, and … it's basically the same things but they just gave a longer speech to the girls of like, "well you better act like this and that."
>
> (Added emphasis)

Underpinning the patriarchal assumption that female youth require more "talking to" than male, Janelle's words also indicate the emphasis placed on female responsibilization, which is problematic for two central reasons: it (1) forces females to be embedded in discourses that promote powerlessness and suggests that female youth lack agency (and decision making capacities) due to their innate "innocence," and (2) trivializes male experiences thus forcing males to suffer in silence or risk violating the norms of socialized masculinities (Connell 1995). To this end, another example comes from Yasmin, an 18-year-old undergraduate student from Cyber City. Reflecting on cyber-safety talks in junior high school, she recalls "it was just generally presented to the class, but you could tell it was directed more to the female students." This applied especially regarding messages about sexting:

> Well in my experience, whenever you hear don't take nudes, it would also be the example of the girl sending the nude to the guy and he was sharing it with his friends, it was never talked about with girls getting dick pics.

Pedersen (2013) argues that if the focus is on the safety of females online, the underlying message is that the behaviors of males online do "not need safeguards" (404). However, despite this message, she found "boys are at least as at risk of cyberbullying than girls" (416). The gendered ways in which sexting is approached is notable in the prior excerpts, especially in terms of how incidences of sexting are handled in high schools.

Our participants reveal the importance of not partitioning messages by gender, but also addressed an issue that to our knowledge is not on the radar of educational programs in junior high or other grade levels: the ethics, impact and potential criminal charges that may apply for males distributing 'dick picks' to female students. Yasmin elaborates: "when I was in junior high we never, it was never talked about with girls receiving nudes, it was always the other way around." The youth in our sample referred to cases of school-based sexting incidents and school administration's very gendered responses to sexting scandals. Ironically, based on our discussions, the sending of male nudes is both common place and normalized, yet ignored in programming and talks. Such talks have the potential to have a greater impact if these gendered dynamics are given greater consideration, as well as what is often in the blind spot: male practices of sending and receiving nudes.

Discussion

Englander (2012), echoing the general public, posited "what on Earth are they thinking?" (5) in reference to youth sending sexually suggestive messages or images. She quite fittingly suggests youth engage in sexting because "what they often seem to be thinking about is their relationships" (5) − and, we would add, the associated thrill of growing intimacy and closeness. Consistent with the privacy mindsets frequently held by teens (see Chapter 6), not participating in sexting may leave a teen feeling left out, disengaged from peers or vulnerable in a relationship, which creates pressures to sext. boyd (2014) argues that teens are not so much addicted to social media as they are to each other, particularly given parental restrictions and highly scheduled lives that limit their time spent together. Teens, she suggests, seek opportunities to connect with peers without being subject to adult surveillance, and to create spaces in which they have the agency to employ identity and authenticity work free from adult intervention (boyd, 2014). She considers teens to be in a desperate grab for access to the social world that adults have readily available to them and frequently take for granted.

Overall, our findings indicate that, rather than empowering female youth through self-expression, gender inequities underpin the double standard that permeates online sexual expression and functions on multiple levels. Likewise, online sexual expression appears infused in shaming, and reputation slandering (see also Milford, 2015). Much of the progress made, then, with second-wave feminism, such as the movement of reclaiming the self-objectification of women to signify their sexual liberation and self-value as persons (see Gill, 2007), is unraveling in the online world, or has never applied there at all.

Consistent with our findings, researchers who have conducted focus group on teen interpretations document that discussions of sexting reveal a range of responses, from those who consider it promiscuous or too risky to "no big deal" (e.g., Lenhart, 2009). Suggestively, our participants' remarks reinforce long term sexual and gender norms disincentivizing any sexual expression among girls and young women (though see Crofts, Lee, McGovern, & Milivojevic, 2015). In this context, we also advance existing studies of female teenagers' experiences of sexting, by including the voices of young males – whose voices are sometimes neglected in such inquiries – as we explored their own responses to sexting, its gendered nature, and their own ostensible culpability in perpetuating the victimization of their female peers. While there is some evidence of older male teens offering reflections and a degree of empathy regarding the negative impact of sending unsolicited sexts to females, it is telling that we find no evidence of serious cogitation among our male participants regarding the long-lasting and caustic impact upon females in their peer group.

From our focus group discussions, it is clear that sexting is normalized, particularly "dick pics" sent non-consensually to female teens, and that female teens face much greater pressure to regulate their public spheres than males, based on starker consequences: a gendered double standard rooted in patriarchy and potential serious stigmatization. Moreover, it is significant to note that the more extreme outcomes of criminal acts such as "revenge porn" have resulted in teen suicidal ideation and death by suicide (e.g., Gillis, April 10, 2013; Grenoble, November 10, 2012). Although few circumstances become this grave, everyday online activities are overshadowed with misogyny and sexualized pressures. That some female participants "laugh at" the sexts they receive from males is, we argue, a form of resistance against this structured and iniquitous context. Yet this resistance remains shallow or delimited, as it indicates individualized responses which bear little impact on the wider "rape culture" still apparent in society and online (Rentschler, 2014). Moreover it suggests that there is something abnormal about any male who is negatively affected by such responses. A number of participants pointed to a lack of support in their school environment – where they often grapple most with such issues. Messages about sexting, we found, must be directed just as wholly to males as females within schools in order to reinforce that males too can feel shamed or harmed by the realities of sending and receiving of nude digital images. Discourses that emerged organically during focus group discussions placed responsibility to not sext almost exclusively on the female youth. The underlying naïve trust among youth may explain why some sext in the first place, albeit giving in to pressures from soliciting peers or romantic interests or for other personal reasons (e.g., relationship building). Of course, female youth are thought to require "protection" and "surveillance," but not from receiving dick pics from a male friend, acquaintance, peer, or romantic partner which is normalized, but instead from their potential to share personal "nudes."

Perhaps it is within processes of socialization informing self-discovery and identity construction that youth may engage in risky online acts of sexual exploration (i.e., sexting), virtual sexual experimentation, seek sensations, or act in ways thought to encourage peer group acceptance or intimacy with select persons. Yet, with or without pressures to sext, the moral and legal repercussions that follow such behaviors and the fact that male engagement in digital sexual expression tends to be normalized and "acceptable" cannot be denied (Albury, Funnell, & Noonan, July 2010; Ringrose et al., 2013).

Overall among youth sexting, either direct participation in or indirect exposure to sexting or its consequences forces engagement in gendered identity negotiation in the public or private sphere and lessons in self-presentation. Neoliberal responses to sexting are insufficient as they present solutions based on individual responses to atomistic circumstances, instead of a broader sociological topography of digital sexual expression that includes considerations of its enticements and gendered consequences. Our research begins to highlight the voices of both male and female teens in hopes their lived experiences can inform policy development. We confirm that gendered expectations and a double standard shape experiences of sexting, especially in relation to gendered assumptions within public spaces and the relatively little deterrence given the 'low stakes' for male youth who send non-consensual sexual content to female youth.

References

Albury, K., Funnell, N., & Noonan, E. (July 2010). *The politics of sexting: Young people, self-representation and citizenship.* Published in *Proceedings of the Australian and New Zealand Communication Association Conference: Media, Democracy and Change*, Old Parliament House.

Angrove, G. (2015). "She's such a slut!": The sexualized cyberbullying of teen girls and the education law response. In J. Bailey and V. Steeves (Eds.), *eGirls, eCitizens* (pp. 307–336). Ottawa: University of Ottawa Press.

Bailey, J., & Hanna, M. (2011). The gendered dimensions of sexting: Assessing the applicability of Canada's child pornography provision. *Canadian Journal of Women and the Law, 23*, 405–441.

Bailey, J., & Steeves, V. (2013). Will the real digital girl please stand up? Examining the gap between policy dialogue and girls' accounts of their digital existence. In J. M. Wise & H. Koskela (Eds.), *New Visualities, New Technologies: The New Ecstasy of Communication* (pp. 41–66). Farnham, Surrey: Ashgate.

Bailey, J., & Steeves, V. (Eds.). (2015). *eGirls, eCitizens*. Ottawa: University of Ottawa Press.

Bailey, J., Steeves, V., Burkell, J., & Regan, P. (2013). Negotiating with gender stereotypes on social networking sites: From "bicycle face" to Facebook. *Journal of Communication Inquiry, 37*, 91–112.

Berger, M., Wallis, B., & Watson, S. (1995). *Constructing Masculinity*. New York and London: Routledge.

boyd, d. (2008). *Taken Out of Context: American Teen Sociality in Networked Publics*. PhD Thesis, University of California, Berkeley.

boyd, d. (2014). *It's Complicated: The Social Lives of Networked Teens*. London: Yale University Press.

Card, Stucky, N.B., Sawalani, G. & Little, T. (2008). Direct and indirect aggression during childhood and adolescence: A metaa-nalytic review of gender differences, intercorrelations, and relations to maladjustment. *Child Development, 79*, 1185–1229.

Carrigan, T., Connell, R. W., & Lee, J. (1985). Towards a new sociology of masculinity. *Theory and Society, 14*, 551–604.

Chambers, D., Loon, J. V., & Tincknell, E. (2004). Teachers' views of teenage sexual morality. *British Journal of Sociology of Education, 25*, 563–576.

Connell, R. W. (1992). A very straight gay: Masculinity, homosexual experience, and the dynamics of gender. *American Sociological Review, 57*, 735–751.

Connell, R. W. (1995). *Masculinities*. Cambridge: Polity Press.

Connell, R. W. (2002) On hegemonic masculinity and violence: Response to Jefferson and Hall. *Theoretical Criminology, 6*(1), 89–99.

Connell, R. W., & Messerschmidt, J. W. (2005). Hegemonic masculinity: Rethinking the concept. *Gender & Society, 19*, 829–859.

Crawford, M., & Popp, D. (2003). Sexual double standards: A review and methodological critique of two decades of research. *The Journal of Sex Research, 40*, 13–26.

Crawford, M., & Ungar, R. (2000). *A Feminist Psychology*. Boston: McGraw Hill.

Crofts, T., Lee, M., McGovern, A., & Milivojevic, S. (2015). Making sense of sexting. In Crofts, T., M. Lee, A. McGovern and S. Milivojevic (Eds.). *Sexting and Young People* (pp. 161–178). New York: Palgrave Macmillan.

Deaton, D. L. (2013). Amy T. Schalet: Not under my roof: Parents, teens, and the culture of sex. *Journal of Youth and Adolescence, 42*, 157–163.

Egan, R. D. (2013). *Becoming Sexual: A Critical Appraisal of the Sexualization of girls*. Cambridge: John Wiley & Sons.

Englander, E. (2012). *Low Risk Associated with Most Teenage Sexting: A Study of 617 18-Year-Olds, MARC Research Reports Paper 6*. Bridgewater, MA: Massachusetts Aggression Reduction Center.

Gill, R. (2007). *Gender and the Media*. Cambridge: Polity.

Gillis, W. (April 12, 2013). Rehtaeh Parsons: A family's tragedy and a town's shame. *Toronto Star*. Retrieved from www.thestar.com/news/canada/2013/04/12/rehtaeh_parsons_a_familys_tragedy_and_a_towns_shame.html. Accessed February 2018.

Grenoble, R. (November 10, 2012). Amanda Todd: Bullied Canadian teen commits suicide after prolonged battle online and in school. *Huffington Post*. Retrieved from www.huffingtonpost.ca/entry/amanda-todd-suicide-bullying_n_1959909. Accessed February 2018.

Hall, S. (2002). Daubing the drudges of fury: Men, violence and the piety of the "hegemonic masculinity" thesis. *Theoretical Criminology, 6*(1), 35–61.

Handyside, S., & Ringrose, J. (2017). Snapchat Memory and Youth Digital Sexual Cultures: Mediated temporality, duration, and affect. *Journal of Gender Studies, 26*, 347–360.

Hannah-Moffat, K., & O'Malley, P. (Eds.). 2007. *Gendered Risks*. New York: Routledge.

Harter, S., Stocker, C., & Robinson, N. (1996). The perceived directionality of the link between approval and self-worth: The liabilities of a looking glass self-orientation among young adolescents. *Journal of Research on Adolescence, 6*, 285–308.

Hasinoff, A. (2012). Sexting as media production: Rethinking social media and sexuality. *New Media & Society, 15*, 449–465.

Jackson, S., & Cram, F. (2003). Disrupting the sexual double standard: Young women's talk about heterosexuality. *British Journal of Social Psychology, 42*, 113–127.

Jefferson, T. (2002). Subordinating hegemonic masculinity. *Theoretical Criminology, 6*(1), 63–88.

Karaian, L. (2012). Lolita speaks: "Sexting." teenage girls and the law. *Crime Media Culture, 8*, 57–73.

Karaian, L. (2014). Policing "sexting": Responsibilization, respectability and sexual subjectivity in child protection/crime prevention responses to teenagers' digital sexual expression. *Theoretical Criminology, 18*, 282–299.

Koskela, H. (2004). Webcams, TV shows and mobile phones: Empowering exhibitionism. *Surveillance & Society, 2*, 199–215.

Koskela, H. (2006). "The other side of surveillance": Webcams, power and agency. In D. Lyon (Ed.), *Theorizing Surveillance: The Panopticon and Beyond* (pp. 163–181). Collumpton, UK: Willan Publishing.

Lamb, S., & Peterson, Z. (2012). Adolescent girls' sexual empowerment: Two feminists explore the concept. *Sex Roles: A Journal of Research, 66*, 703–712.

Lanier, J. (2010). *You Are Not a Gadget: A Manifesto*. New York: Alfred A. Knopf.

Lee, M., & Crofts, T. (2015). Gender, pressure, coercion and pleasure: Untangling motivations for sexting between young people. *British Journal of Criminology, 55*, 454–473.

Lenhart, A. (2009). *Teens and sexting: How and why minor teens are sending sexually suggestive nude or nearly nude images via text messaging*. Washington, DC: Pew Research Center. Retrieved from www.pewinternet.org/Reports/2009/Teens-and-Sexting.aspx. Accessed February 2018.

Lenhart, A., Smith, A., & Anderson, M. (October 2015). *Teens, Technology and Romantic Relationships*. Washington, DC: PEW Research Center. Retrieved from www.pewinternet.org/2015/10/01/teens-technology-and-romantic-relationships/. Accessed February 2018.

Lerner, R., & Steinberg, L. (2009). *Handbook of Adolescent Psychology, Volume 1: Individual Bases of Adolescent Development*. Hoboken, NJ: John Wiley & Sons.

Livingstone, S. (2008). Taking risky opportunities in youthful content creation: Teenagers' use of social networking sites for intimacy, privacy and self-expression. *New Media & Society, 10*, 393–411.

Marwick, A. & boyd, d. (2014). "It's just drama": Teen perspectives on conflict and aggression in a networked era. *Journal of Youth Studies, 17*, 1187–1204.

Messerschmidt, J. (2012). Engendering gendered knowledge: Assessing the academic appropriation of hegemonic masculinity. *Men and Masculinities, 15*, 56–76.

Milford, T. (2015). Revisiting cyberfeminism: Theory as a tool for understanding young women's experiences. In J. Bailey and V. Steeves (Eds.), *eGirls, eCitizens* (pp. 55–81). Ottawa: University of Ottawa Press.

Nichols, K. (2016). Moving beyond ideas of laddism: Conceptualising "mischievous masculinities" as a new way of understanding everyday sexism and gender relations. *Journal of Gender Studies, 27*(1), 73–85.

Nixon, S. (2001). Resignifying masculinity: From "new man" to "new lad." In D. Morley & K. Robins (Eds.), *British Cultural Studies: Geography, Nationality, and Identity* (pp. 373–385). Oxford: Oxford University Press.

Poltash, N. (2013). Snapchat and sexting: A snapshot of baring your bare essentials. *Richmond Journal of Law & Technology*, *XIX*, 1–24.

Powell, A., & Henry, N. (2017). *Sexual Violence in a Digital Age*. Basingstoke: Palgrave Macmillan.

Rentschler, C. (2014). Rape culture and the feminist politics of social media. *Girlhood Studies*, *7*, 65–82.

Ricciardelli, R., Clow, K. A., & White, P. (2010). Masculinity portrayals in men's lifestyle magazines. *Sex Roles: A Journal of Research*, *63*, 64–78. doi:10.1007/s11199–010–9764–8.

Ricciardelli, R., Maier, K., & Hannah-Moffat, K. (2015). Strategic masculinities: Vulnerabilities, risk and the production of prison masculinities. *Theoretical Criminology*, *19*, 491–513.

Ringrose, J., Gill, R., Livingstone, S., & Harvey, L. (2012). *Qualitative Study of Children, Young People and "Sexting": A Report Prepared for the NSPCC*. National Society for the Prevention of Cruelty to Children. London.

Ringrose, J., Harvey, L., Gill, R., & Livingstone, S. (2013). Teen girls, sexual double standards and "sexting": Gendered value in digital image exchange. *Feminist Theory*, *14*, 305–323.

Sealy-Harrington, J., & Menuz, A. (June 23, 2015). *Keep It to Yourself: The Private Use Exception for Child Pornography Offences*. Calgary: Faculty of Law, University of Calgary. Retrieved from: ABlawg.ca.

Stanko, E. (1997). Safety talk: Conceptualizing women's risk assessment as a technology of the soul. *Theoretical Criminology*, *1*, 479–499.

Tolman, D. (2012). Female adolescents, sexual empowerment and desire: A missing discourse of gender inequity. *Sex Roles: A Journal of Research*, *66*, 746–757.

Weiss, K. G. (2009). "Boys will be boys" and other gendered accounts: An exploration of victims' excuses and justifications for unwanted sexual contact and coercion. *Violence Against Women*, *15*, 810–834.

West, C., & Zimmerman, D. (1987). Doing gender. *Gender & Society*, *1*, 125–151.

Chapter 8

Policies, practices, and concluding thoughts

In this book, we have addressed an array of topics related to youth and cyber-risk that range from the anxieties tied to the fear of missing out (FOMO), cyberbullying, hacking, and sexting, to discussions centered on attitudes towards and experiences of privacy and surveillance. Our qualitative research – focus group discussions with teens about their attitudes and experiences online, dealing with cyber-risks, and how they respond to the messages they receive from authorities regarding how to manage cyber-risk – contributes to knowledge from the perspective of teens, in their own words. Too often assumptions of cyber-risk are mapped on and projected towards teens – assumptions that often miss the mark. Yes, cyberbullying continues to be an issue, and yes, sexting, connected to wider concerns over privacy management, continues to bring focus to the anxieties teens grapple with on a daily basis. Here we illuminate the various ways teens are *interpreting* such risks. Doing so reveals a patterning of responses influenced by key sociological variables such as gender, age, and whether one lives in an urban or rural region.

In this concluding chapter, we aim to fulfill two interrelated objectives: first, we review key findings and theoretical implications explicated in this book based on our 35 focus groups with 115 Canadian teens. Second, reflecting on our findings and the general themes highlighted in the previous chapters, we examine the various policy implications of our findings which bear relevance for parents, educators, and the non-profit sector, as well as teens themselves for recognizing and managing online realities. Here, we turn anew to the words of our participants during focus group discussions, especially as our groups were all asked if they had any advice to offer other youth and adults. We draw from their responses, as well as our own theoretical and sociological framing of our findings, to inform those interested in addressing youth safety online and how to best approach areas of risk which are often perceived as sensitive and volatile. Our aim here is to set aside academic debates – although they will continue to inform our arguments – and bring to the fore practical outcomes of our study that can help foster trusting relationships and open lines of communication between teens and concerned adults. Finally, we turn to suggested areas for future researchers to continue to examine; putting forth areas of study that are only emerging, such as "digital self-harm" among teens and restorative justice in schools in relation to cyber-bullying, as well the need to accumulate the standpoints of parents, educators, and other stakeholders in the wider project of online safety governance.

Social connection, addiction, and the fear of missing out

There are clearly many enticements and positive features of going online, especially on social network sites (SNS). Social connection is a prevalent theme across all of our discussions with teens. Online is the *primary medium of interaction* for teens. It is where they discover who they are; explore their emerging identities, seek friendship, and, especially, reinforce established offline friendship networks. Online is also where contestation, discord and more aggressive and illicit interactions take place. In this book, we have highlighted both the opportunities and benefits of going online, namely social connection, as well as some of the risks associated with these opportunities (see Chapter 3).

Sensationalistic media coverage of the more serious – and exceptional – cases of online abuse, assault, criminal stalking, and harassment, resulting in self-harm and suicide in some cases, helps to fuel existing anxieties (e.g., over technology, youth, sexuality) that promote moral panics and, linked to these panics, disproportionate regulatory responses (boyd, 2014; Cassell & Cramer, 2008; Goode & Ben-Yehuda, 2009; Marker, 2011). Some youth, perhaps somewhat in consequence, are at relatively higher levels of risk than others regarding their online activities. A 2008 survey highlighted by boyd (2014) of a representative sample of U.S. teens found a minority (15%) of youth experienced sexual or physical abuse or parental conflict. This minority had significantly more problems both online and offline than others in the sample. Those facing serious problems in their offline lives are more likely to go online to seek attention from people met online, and in so doing their problems may be rendered more visible and subject to the permanency and searchability accorded to content posted to SNS (boyd, 2014; see Chapter 1). Teens who are at greater overall risk compared to their peers, for a myriad of reasons, are likely already facing other problems in their lives such as drug and alcohol abuse and problems with their families and/or at school. In other words, teens who are most at-risk offline tend to be those who face more serious problems when they go online.

In Chapter 3 we explicated the "flip side" of going online for social connection, including the constant negative social comparison and search for social acceptance, which leads to a fear of missing out. These risks are far more ubiquitous and impactful for teens than the risks often highlighted in sensationalistic media reports (e.g., rather rare occurrences attributable to stranger danger from sexual predators online). However, these risks seem to be relatively unacknowledged by teens, at least directly. Moral panics sometimes draw from the argument that teens are addicted to the various technologies they use. Our discussions revealed that the FOMO, searching for social acceptance and constant negative social comparison online are drivers of what appears to be addiction to technology per se. Our findings highlighted how the FOMO and the search for social acceptance plays into a constant negative comparison that may potentially lead to elevated levels of anxiety experienced in everyday life. Moreover, the identification of these risks rests with our own thematic analysis of focus group discussions – they are conclusions drawn by researchers – rather than identified explicitly by teens themselves.

Our discussions revealed certain demographic patterns regarding social connection. Females in Cyber City made the most references to social connection. This may indicate pressure on female teens to seek social connection – and thus approval and comparison – online, with female teens living in rural regions having "smaller, more interconnected offline networks," facilitating the "primary importance" of "offline relationships" (Burkell & Saginur, 2015: 145). However, as our research is qualitative in nature, geared to honing details of focus group discussions, we would caution against concluding that social connection 'matters more' to female teens than males. As we show throughout this book, male and female standpoints are heavily influenced by gender norms (West & Zimmerman, 1987). As we note in Chapter 3, when pressed some male groups admitted to being concerned over things like having "drunk party pics" posted about them online and losing their privacy, and potentially their reputation, in the process. This suggests a persistent influence of hegemonic masculinities on how cyber-risk is both experienced and interpreted (Connell & Messerschmidt, 2005; Messerschmidt, 2012; see especially Chapter 7 on sexting).

Being online has been tied to both positive and negative outcomes. Some scholars have shown, through their research, the positive side to technology usage and being online which includes increased feelings of social support that create a sense of connectedness with others, improve social group affiliation and self-concept clarity, or even a feeling of civil responsibility (Bannon, McGlynn, McKenzie, & Quayle, 2015; Davis, 2013; Thurlow & Bell, 2009). Yet it is debatable whether being online increases, decreases or has created a new form of loneliness. On one side, for example, Sherry Turkle (2017) suggested that "we are increasingly connected to each other but oddly more alone" "np," while Livingstone and Sefton-Green (2016) instead argued that young people and their parents do "have time for each other" despite the time spent online (165).[1] The teens in our sample also offered insight into the negative and positive aspects of what it means to be online, here offering advice to other youth regarding online addiction and social connection:

I'd say minimize your use.... Social media does help you stay connected, make friends and stuff ... and then sometimes you really do need it to like, not be out of the loop I guess and then maintain contact with your friends; but the internet is filled with highs and lows, and you don't need to be 13, in puberty with your raging hormones and then you see one bad thing on the internet, that just takes you a minute to read but it ruins the next eight hours of your day ... so especially when you're emotionally developing, you don't need to be going through all that as well.

(Carmen, age 19, Cyber City)

Carmen's advice is twofold: spend less time online and, especially for younger teens, not to internalize negative encounters with peers to the extent that it starts to negatively impact everyday life, both offline and online.

Related to wider concerns about internet "addiction," researchers have also drawn attention to how the use of social media has changed lifestyle behaviors and, in some cases, may impact young people's well-being (Smahel, Wright, & Cernikova, 2015). Researchers concerned with how being online has impacted youth health around the world have confirmed that the internet has brought about negative effects on youth's physical, psychological, emotional, and social health and well-being, including changes in morality (Abbasi & Manawar, 2011). From an international perspective, and with participants ranging in age from children to university students, researchers have associated the overuse of the internet, including social media use, with sleep deprivation, obesity, anxiety, and decreased physical activity. In terms of physical health, for example, Chahal, Fung, Kuhle, and Veugelers (2013) found that increased social media usage and internet overuse is associated with shortened sleep duration, while Kim and colleagues (2010) associated it with decreased physical activities. Other negative physical effects from being online include headaches and eyestrain (Smahel et al., 2015). Discussing outcomes of social media on mental health and well-being, researchers have tied SNS use to aggression, depression, addiction to the internet, emotional instability, identity challenges, being violated, bullied or victimized online, self-harming behaviour, and even suicidal ideation (Aboujaoude, 2010; Cheung & Wong, 2011; Ko, Yen, Liu, Huang, & Yen, 2009; Marchant et al., 2017; Smahel et al., 2015).

Some scholars, however, have tied SNS use – among both adults and teens – to positive psychological outcomes, including enhanced self-esteem and well-being (given positive feedback from friendship networks), sense of social support, community, and life-satisfaction, and increased social capital (Ellison, Steinfield, & Lampe, 2007; Oh, Ozkaya, & LaRose, 2014; Valkenburg, Peter, & Schouten, 2006). boyd (2014) helps to contextualize wider concerns for youth internet addiction, arguing that "there is no doubt that some youth develop an unhealthy relationship with technology. For some, an obsession with gaming or social media can wreak havoc on their lives, affecting school performance and stunting emotional development" (78). However, boyd also recognizes that the language of "pathology" and "addiction" suggests that youth have no agency, no control over their impulses, and cannot manage their priories; instead, only technologies determine outcomes – not the person (see also Chapter 3). As became evident across our focus groups, all youth will at some point and likely repeatedly struggle at different times with how to respond to unwelcome or unsolicited texts or posts – particularly if they are the subject of the postings – alongside the need to manage their emotional and personal reactions, both on and offline. Also evident from our research, is the fact that much of the driving force behind the FOMO, need for social approval and "addictive" behavior online is based on the projected audience of offline peer networks. Understanding this context is critical to informing policies and practices based on productive conversations, trusting relationships, and open communication with parents and others in positions of authority, who are most likely to be approached by youth and are thus well positioned to guide youth in how best to navigate the online world in a safe and comfortable way. The challenge, of course, remains how to instill a strong sense of agency to explore and establish social connection while mediating the risks inherent to being online. Understanding that youth are most concerned about other youth in their immediate peer networks (usually at school) is essential in properly situating appropriate responses. We turn next to an area which complicates this response: the appropriateness of monitoring teens' activities online.

"Tough love"? Monitoring and surveillance of teens in cyberspace

In Chapter 4, we highlighted two trends regarding teens' attitudes towards the surveillance of their activities online. First, they expressed a general acceptance for school-based surveillance of students' online activities, which we argue indicates an emerging acquiescence and internalization of *panoptic hegemony*, as part of a wider neoliberal framework of self-responsibilization and self-governance. We define panoptic hegemony as both the ubiquitous presence and, more significantly, the wider *expectation for surveillance*. While using social media we expect to be watched and, in many respects, expect to be able to watch others (Calvert, 2000). Second, while generally accepting of the pragmatics of school-based surveillance to help instill an environment of safety and security, our participants were far more critical of the approach parents take when it comes to mediating their online activities.

Our participants often supported active surveillance in schools; some expressing great confidence in the widespread surveillance powers of educators. When asked for advice about how schools can better manage online risk, some suggested ramping up efforts at surveillance to reinforce licit behavior of students on and offline, at least while on school grounds.

Christine, age 19 from Cyber City, makes this point, alluding to a "zero tolerance" approach to issues such as cyberbullying:

> I would like to see schools implementing a very strict no tolerance and maybe monitoring … like full scale perimeter, but if there's computers on, the school computers, monitoring what is being sent on the school computers, because there are privacy issues with them monitoring your cell phone, but the minute that you're on a school computer, you're technically complying to [the school] accessing your information. And so I think that's the same that should happen … be like, if you're on Wi-Fi, you're following our rules, and they have a right to search you in that sense. So I think, they just really need to step up in the sense, it's not one of the things you brush off to the side, and you don't get police to come when it's already an issue; so I think like for schools, they need to create a policy and then, law enforcement needs to like figure out a better system of how to check like, maybe hire trackers.

Christine's statement is certainly one of the more forcefully put endorsements of surveillance, but it is also important to note how she pitches surveillance as a preventative measure – a deterrent – against illicit online activities and relational aggression; one that would help remove the need for reactive law enforcement responses. As we discuss in Chapter 4, it is highly unlikely that most schools have the sort of panoptic power that Christine suggests in place. However, some researchers have found that some Canadian schools do place efforts into tracking student activities outside of the classroom, such as what they post online (Steeves, 2010). Steeves (2010) also found some schools have punished students for posting illicit content online, such as one case where a student posted anti-Semitic remarks, even though this was done after school hours and through an online platform not related to the school.

Whether or not schools are investing heavily on surveillance technologies, for our participants the *expectation* of being watched – of panoptic hegemony – is notable and may help inform best practices for schools aiming to gear policies regarding technology use in the classroom. This is not to suggest that our participants felt teachers could always effectively monitor students in the classroom. A we highlight in Chapter 4, many of our participants verged on mocking teachers' efforts to restrict technology in the classroom, pointing to variable application of policies at the level of the school board and/or the classroom. Evident from our discussions, teens are active in their consideration of these issues and do often "push back" against dominant narratives regarding cyber-risk and cyber-safety. Some expressed ingenuity in terms of hiding their use of cell phones and other devices in the class. Similarly, Hope (2005) found "that students hide their online activities from teachers by physically shielding the screen and deleting histories; *they also use the computer to put the teacher under surveillance*" (quoted in Steeves, Milford, & Butts, March 2010: 15; emphasis added).

This agency was also evident during discussions centered on parental mediation of children's online activities. Steeves and Webster (2008) observed that "as parental supervision increases, children's willingness to divulge private information decreases" (9). However, we draw from the distinction between 'monitoring' and 'surveillance' (Kerr & Stattin, 2000; Racz & McMahon, 2011; Stattin, 2001); the former is more accepted than the latter. As youth express sympathy for parental roles (e.g., they should monitor they children), where the monitoring is fully disclosed and practiced with open communication. The latter, however, is often perceived to be done covertly and intrusively, as such, surveillance debases trust and is relatively easily circumvented where detected. If anything, drawing from comparable findings in criminology, surveillance acts not to eradicate risk but to displace the observable online spaces where teens go and to where risk is similarly, and, ironically, more covertly displaced (cf. Cornish & Clarke, 1987).

In line with prior research on parental monitoring (e.g., Stattin & Kerr 2000), our focus group discussions reveal more sympathy – sometimes laced with reservation – for parental monitoring that is fully disclosed and "understood" to occur given parental concern for child safety and security. Research on parental monitoring is unequivocal: high parental knowledge of children's activities is consistently linked to measures of good adjustment. The question becomes how such knowledge is acquired. Trust is maintained through ongoing communication and children's spontaneous disclosures of information rather than parental tracking and surveillance (Kerr & Stattin 2000; Racz & McMahon 2011; Stattin 2001). As we highlight in Chapter 4, teens often welcome, even seek, transparent parent monitoring such as sharing passwords that are understood as only to be used in emergencies. Unfortunately, many "spyware" applications are marketed to (rightly or wrongly) concerned parents who may or may not disclose their surveillance practices (Anderson, January 2016; Fisk, 2016; Marx & Steeves, 2010). Research with teens, however, consistently finds that "teens rely most heavily on parents and peers for advice about online behavior and coping with challenging experiences.... For general advice and influence, parents are still the top source for teen internet and cell phone users" (Lenhart, Madden, Smith, Purcell, Zickuhr, & Rainie, November 2011: 6). Lenhart and colleague's (November 2011: 6) research also tellingly finds, from a representative sample of U.S. teens, that "86% of online and cell phone-using teens say they have received general advice about how to use the internet responsibly and safely from their parents," "70% of online and cell-using teens say they have gotten advice about internet safety from teachers or another adult at school," and that "58% of teen internet and cell phone users say their parents have been the biggest influence on what they think is appropriate or inappropriate when using the internet or a cell phone."

While some parents may worry that their teenaged children would likely reject their efforts to offer advice (in some cases such efforts may well be met by dismissive body language), these findings suggest that *consistent* interactions which, over time, sediment a mutual sense of trust and perhaps even respect, can and should be a goal to work towards. Here we draw a connection between how teens receive messages of cyber-safety from parents to the degree of communication and monitoring to further mitigate against risky encounters online. Of course, teens who may be more "at risk" and engaged in higher risk practices may lead some parents to feel justified in engaging in surveillance out of a "tough love" drive for protection of their children. While this may be a natural impulse, Stattin and Kerr (2000: 1082) remind us that "children with externalizing problems hide their norm-breaking behavior from their parents more than other children, which results in their parents knowing less." They advise parents that "in addition to controlling the child's whereabouts, parents should try to optimize conditions for the child to disclose information about his or her everyday experiences" (2000: 1084).

Again, our results are telling, particularly when accounting for gender and location. In the former, gender, females in Cyber City more frequently than those in Cyberville reported antagonistic feelings towards parental surveillance. Females, who are often more directly targeted with messages of managing cyber-safety online than males, may be here evidencing resistance to what they perceive to be excessively intrusive mediation by parents (Bailey & Steeves, 2013; Hasinoff, 2012; Karaian, 2014). In the latter, location, rural environments may help build up higher levels of social capital which are undercut in more individualistically-oriented urban regions (Burkell & Saginur, 2015; Putnam, 2000). Researchers have also suggested, based on empirical findings, that some parents focus their surveillance energies more on daughters than sons (Bailey & Steeves, 2013; Johnson, 2015; Lenhart & Madden, 2007; Shin, Schriner, & Cho, 2009). Indeed, it also is entirely possible that males may have reservations about surveillance but brush these off and/or do not recognize these given the influence of prevailing gender norms related to hegemonic interpretations of masculinities (Connell & Messerschmidt, 2005; Ricciardelli, Clow, & White, 2010).

Relational aggression, school programs, and gendered realities

As one of the leading scholars researching youth and the internet, dana boyd has argued – and we strongly agree – that in some nations bullying and, more recently, cyberbullying have "become a national obsession" (boyd, 2014: 130). In the United States, as of 2012, 48 states and the federal government had implemented laws designed to address bullying, with many referring specifically to interactions online (boyd, 2014). As of 2017, all 50 states have passed laws against school-based bullying, with Georgia being the first in 1999, and Montana being the last and most recent state (see www.bully police.org). In Canada, serious cases of online harassment, stalking, and invasion of privacy have been legally dealt with using existing Criminal Code statutes. Several Canadian Criminal Code offences deal with bullying regardless of the medium through which the bullying occurs. Depending on the exact nature of the behavior, individuals could acquire a variety of charges, including criminal harassment, uttering threats, intimidation, mischief in relation to data, unauthorized use of computer, identity fraud, extortion, false messages, indecent or harassing telephone calls, counselling suicide, incitement of hatred, and defamatory libel (see www.getcybersafe.gc.ca/cnt/cbrbllng/prnts/lgl-cnsqncs-en.aspx). Some Canadian provinces have attempted to add further legal "teeth" through provincial legislation. For instance, Alberta's *Education Act* was revised in 2012 to define bullying as:

> repeated and hostile or demeaning behaviour by an individual in the school community where the behaviour is intended to cause harm, fear or distress to one or more other individuals in the school community, including psychological harm or harm to an individual's reputation.
>
> (www.mediasmarts.ca)

This definition is in line with a frequently cited academic definition of bullying which emphasizes an imbalance in power between the victimizer and victim, involving deliberate and repeated aggression among peers (Olweus, 1978, 1993; but see also Olweus, 2012).

Alberta's law requires students to report cyberbullying if they witness it; those who do not face possible suspension or expulsion – of course, enforcing such legislation is near impossible. In May 2013, Nova Scotia passed their *Cyber-safety Act*, inspired by the death of Rehtaeh Parsons, who committed suicide at 17 after being sexually assaulted offline and subsequently criminally harassed online (Gillis, April 12, 2013; Ruskin, December 11, 2015). However, the Cyber-safety Act was struck down in December 2015 on constitutional grounds. Critics argued that it infringed upon rights to freedom of expression and had an overly broad and vague definition of cyberbullying, and failed to require proof of intention to harm (Ruskin, December 11, 2015). Privacy lawyer David Fraser expressed these criticisms in response to the constitutional challenge:

> Anything that hurts anybody's feelings, if it's done online, it's cyberbullying. You can be liable, you can sue somebody for cyberbullying, you can be subject to an order that can cut you off from the internet, confiscate your electronic devices. It's absolutely Draconian.
>
> (Ruskin, December 11, 2015)

As of this writing, new anti-cyberbullying legislation is being proposed in Nova Scotia, with some arguing that since striking down the legislation incidents of cyberbullying have increased, with organizations' abilities for monitoring and prevention undercut by the repeal (Corfu, April 15, 2017). On the federal level and in response to several serious cases of cyberbullying, in March 2015 the Canadian government implemented a new law, Bill C-13, *Protecting Canadians Against Online Crime Act*, which criminalizes harassing or annoying behavior conducted online, and also sanctions the posting of non-consensual intimate images (Coburn, Connolly, & Roesch, 2015). The law has come under criticism for not addressing cyberbullying but, inadvertently, stymying the privacy rights of Canadians through emboldened governmental surveillance powers (Shariff & DeMartini, 2015). Coburn and her colleagues (2015) also argue this law will not be effective given many youth are not likely to understand it, that it may create additional problems regarding youth non-disclosure (especially regarding "sexting"), and may bring in a disproportionate amount of marginalized youth into the criminal justice system. The problem lies in the ambiguity of the behaviors associated with cyberbullying, and drawing from wider criminological critiques, the unlikely ability of criminal justice legislation alone to ameliorate social problems (Christie, 2004, 2017 [1993]; Roberts, Stalans, Indermaur, & Hough, 2003). Indeed, criminalizing "bullying" and "cyberbullying" suggests that there are just two clear sides to bullying: that of the victim and of the perpetrator – the innocent versus the guilty. As boyd (2014: 136) argues, "by focusing on blaming the perpetrator and protecting the victim, well-intended adults often fail to recognize the complexity of most conflicts." Furthermore, zero tolerance and punishment initiatives may create greater and new harms that inadvertently "create the bullies that they're intended to stop" (136).

Not surprisingly then, interviews with students also reveal that those who engage in cyberbullying sometime consider their actions to be justified reactions to the aggressions of another cyberbully; in other words, they do not *perceive* their own reactions as cyberbullying but a defensive response (Law, Shapka, Domene, & Gagné, 2012). In this context, behaviors that get subsumed under the rubric of cyberbullying will not be ameliorated unless such conflicts are unpacked and understood – both in personal, social, and school spaces. Our own discussions with teens about cyberbullying and online conflict suggest that a broader and more inclusive term, relational aggression, is useful to help highlight how such interpersonal conflicts are experienced. The discussions also reveal gendered patterns which raise questions about whether there are distinct features between males and females regarding relational aggression, or whether hermeneutic issues regarding how such conflicts are defined and experienced.

In Chapter 5, we argue that relational aggression (defined as the manipulation of relationships with the explicit intention to hurt others; see Coyne, Linder, Nelson, & Gentile, 2012), more accurately pinpoints specifically gendered aspects of conflict. We suggest that while both male and female participants associated "drama" with conflict amongst females, it is also likely that males may also experience the same stresses but not identify these or dismiss them as they fall outside the remit of "cyberbullying" and "drama" (Connell, 2005; Connell & Messerschmidt, 2005). Of interest, references to drama were found fairly equally between Cyber City and Cyberville participants. As we highlight in Chapter 5, societal conceptions of drama often adhere to a "mean girl" discourse, which acts to "pathologize feminine social aggression and implicitly treat male aggression as neutral" (Bailey & Steeves, 2015a: 10). Alongside references to drama and sexting (discussed below), many participants brought up hacking as a primary concern. This concern does not relate to the broader popular imagery around "hacktivists" that often targets large organizations, governments, and corporations, but rather relates specifically to offline peer networks. Relational aggression extends to concerns over hacking where (often school-based) peers may threaten to hack into a student's device as part of a wider conflict. Chapter 5 thus reinforces our broader finding that the more emotionally and interpersonally consequential concerns about going online are most often related to immediate peer groups – especially those in school. In Chapter 5, we also mined an under-explored area in cyberbullying research: that of "digital self-harm," which refers to instances, deemed a form of attention seeking, where a young person posts content online and responds to this content themselves (often both the original post and subsequent replies are anonymous) (Englander, June 2012b). Interestingly, some of our participants recognized digital self-harm as a familiar if not relatively rare behavior. We thus capture a spectrum of behaviors that may seem relatively trivial, such as "trolling" oneself anonymously online, to more serious cases of relational aggression. However, the connections between these phenomena is the ongoing and often negative social comparison and social acceptance that leads to a FOMO and anxiety about how one is being perceived by immediate peer groups.

Digital sexual expression and the persistence of the gendered double standard

Besides "drama" and cyberbullying, relational aggression was very strongly related to "sexting" among our participants. Parents and educators may well ask "what are they thinking" by engaging in digital sexual expression, though Englander (2012a) reminds us that they are often thinking primarily of their (again, offline) relationships, and, we would add, those which are consensual when nudes are distributed. It is important to acknowledge that sexting can be thrilling as teens explore new experiences and encounters with intimacy and sexual expression. Such expression can be a form of "empowering exhibitionism," leading to greater self-confidence and a sense of identity in relation to others (Koskela, 2004). We examine our participants' experiences not only with sexting, but the wider societal responses to sexting through school-based cyber-safety programs. Overall, our discussions reveal that sexting, far from being empowering for female teens, reinforces gender inequities linked to a persistent double standard that applies now to online behaviors (Ringrose & Barajas, 2011; Ringrose, Harvey, Gill, & Livingstone, 2013). The double standard acts to reinforce shaming (specifically, "slut shaming" of females) and reputation slandering (Angrove, 2015; Milford, 2015). Particularly revealing among our discussions is the relatively ubiquitous experience among female teens of receiving pictures of male penises, commonly referred to as "dick pics." In Chapter 7 we explored how the gender double standard applies, specifically how males are held to a lower standard of judgement when they distribute – with or without consent – a nude self-picture to one or, in some cases, many females among their peer group. Among our male participants there is not much evidence of reflective thinking about the impact of sending nudes. Even male participants in their later teen years described the sending and receiving of nudes among their male peers as "weird," but seemed to lack active reflection about the impact for others, especially female peers, and the implications for unsolicited and non-consensual distribution.

During our discussions on sexting, it became apparent that a large factor influencing a lack of male responsibility relates to both the lack of programming about sexting (and other cyber-risks) in high school, as well as the gendered nature of the programs our participants experienced. As we highlight in Chapter 7, some students experienced having both separate sessions according to gender (one for males, another for females) as well as longer sessions for female students than male. These are, of course, the experiences of a small number of teens, and we do not suggest schools structure these programs in this way with poor intentions or even, at times, consciously. However, our research is consistent with others. In Bailey's (2015) research with young females, for instance, some participants found school curricula to implement "individually oriented responses typically aimed exclusively at girls" (42). One participant, 20-year-old Mackenzie, advocated the implementation of mandatory women's studies courses for both male and female students. "That's the kind of activities that are going to challenge … sexism and oppression of women," she argues (42). As Johnson (2015: 344) also argues,

> it is also important that boys not be left out of discussions of "girls" issues' in order to shift the narrative away from "girls" need to protect themselves' to all youth need to be responsible, ethical, and active digital citizens.

It is more likely that gender norms which are by their nature *hegemonic* are structured given relatively unacknowledged assumptions regarding who are victims and victimizers when it comes to risky behaviors such as sexting (Connell & Messerschmidt, 2005; Ringrose et al., 2013). Female youth appear more at risk for experiencing negative repercussions than males, which helps justify the extra focus they receive through cyber-safety messages. Discourses that emerged organically during focus group discussions placed responsibility to not sext almost exclusively on the female youth. Some of our female participants recalled literally laughing, as a group, with "dick pics" shared by male peers (one group recalled collecting these images in a scrap-book). Such laughter could be interpreted to suggest some females do not take such images seriously. Females showing each other these images and laughing at them indicates, we argue, a form of resistance against a wider, patriarchal context. Yet this resistance remains shallow or delimited, as it indi-cates individualized responses which bear little impact on the wider "rape culture" still apparent in society and online (Rentschler, 2014). With a measure of irony, some of our older male participants revealed a sense of betrayal over the non-consensual distribution of their own "dick pics." Yet here it became apparent that the "stakes" involved for male teens are relat-ively low compared with females.

It is clear that, if not already implemented, messages about sexting in schools must be directed just as wholly to males as females in order to reinforce that males too can feel shamed or harmed by the realities of sending and receiving of nude digital images. Males need to be made more aware about not only the legal and potential criminal implications (i.e., potential child pornography charges), but the caustic and misogynistic environment sending non-consensual nudes engenders. If school-based cyber-safety pro-grams addressing cyberbullying and especially sexting are catered more to female teens than males, this serves to reinforce well established gender norms that are subsequently internalized and reproduced through future generations. Again, related to relational aggression, there may be a blind spot regarding male victimization and/or anxiety, with the assumption that they are more often the victimizers than victims involved in online conflict. There seems to be an assumption among educators that by high school students "should know better." While we would not necessarily disagree, it is apparent that much more support is needed, even after junior high school, where most of the cyber-risk messages related to cyberbullying and sexting are received. Our participants did experience "talks" related to sexting in high school, but often in response to a particular incident of sexting in schools. Ringrose, Gill, Liv-ingstone, and Harvey (2012) conducted focus groups in London, England, found older teens to be "more mature in their resilience and ability to cope" than younger teens who "were more worried, confused and, in some cases, upset by the sexual and sexting pressures they face" (18). Significantly, "their age meant that parents, teachers and others did not support them sufficiently, even though sexual pressures are experienced at younger ages" (Ringroseet al., 2012: 18). Relatively recent studies, like Marwick and boyd's (2014) interviews with U.S. teens, show that there appears to be a decline of cyber-bullying by high school but not necessarily a decline in "drama." Programs and ongoing communication with teens about cyber-risk are still clearly needed in high school, perhaps pitched at wider issues related to digital citizenship.

Privacy mindsets: neoliberalism and having nothing to hide

Youth anxieties centered on relational aggression, including cyberbullying, drama, hacking, and sexting, are often linked more broadly to a felt sense of *lacking control*, especially as it relates to issues of privacy management on and offline. In Chapter 6, we critique assumptions, often generated through media accounts, of teens not caring about privacy online. Since the advent of SNS and "web 2.0" multimedia and participatory culture (e.g., YouTube, Facebook, Twitter, etc.), researchers have consistently demonstrated that teens do, in fact, care about privacy and take active steps to manage the (often invisible) audiences and contexts they project to online (Bailey & Steeves, 2015b; boyd & Hargittai, 2010; James, 2014; Jenkins, 2006; Livingstone, 2008; Tufekci, 2008). We advanced knowledge in Chapter 6 about the life course of privacy concerns by showing how youth adapt to the gravitation away from Facebook towards newer and at present more popular alternative SNS. While we briefly review some of teens' more popular privacy management strategies, the more prescient theme from our discussions relates to the privacy *mindsets* that teens hold, and the emergence of what appears to be a new, or establishing, mindset that can be related to the acquiescence to panoptic hegemony. We first highlight three mindsets established in the literature: "privacy as social, privacy as 'in your hands' and privacy as forsaken online" (James, 2014: 27). We show that all three of these mindsets retains purchase among our participants. However, we also highlight the emergence of a "nothing to hide" mindset as teens grow older, which is buttressed by the mindsets of privacy being "in your own hands" and "forsaken." The "nothing to hide" mindset, however, differs since it shuns the notion that privacy is only relevant if one is not "doing anything wrong." The application of the "nothing to hide" mindset to online sociality is a relatively new development, only starting to receive academic attention (Cannataci, 2015; Crossman, 2008; Nau, 2014; Solove, 2011). Here we extend this literature to address how this mindset is gaining traction among teens, especially as they mature into young adults.

Steeves and Webster (2008: 8) also found that as teens grow older, "they become increasingly more willing to disclose private information online ... 17-year-olds were more likely to display the least privacy-protective behavior (38.0%) than any other age reported in [their] survey." They also find males to be more likely than females to disclose private information. Alongside trends related to age (i.e., the salience of the "nothing to hide" mindset among older teens), feelings of lacking control online and having "nothing to hide" were concentrated among female teens in Cyber City. Research has consistently indicated that young girls and women are far more safety conscious about their activities online than males given that public discourses and official programs regarding privacy usually target females (boyd & Hargittai,

2010; Karaian, 2014; Pedersen, 2013). Youn (2005: 105) similarly argues that "girls perceived more risk from information disclosure, whereas boys perceived more benefits from information disclosure and were willing to provide more information to a Web site." Such gendered initiatives may also be of greater relevance to females living in urban regions. It is possible that teens in rural areas, due to less consistent Wi-Fi and cellular access, have to rely more on close-knit offline community connections which undercut the emphasis on the individual to rely on him or herself. While research comparing urban versus rural teen SNS use finds similarities regarding what SNS are being used and for what purposes (Burkell & Saginur, 2015), further exploration of privacy mindsets, the messages teens receive in terms of cyber-safety, and the possible impact of differential community practices and dynamics is worth exploring in future research (see also below).

Greater initiatives in school to reinforce digital citizenship among teens directly relates to the "nothing to hide" mindset. Declaring indifference to surveillance and privacy is a highly individualistic self-governing mentality; one that neglects scenarios in which young people may wish to secure privacy in order to take advantage of being fully active digital citizens. Teens may wish, for example, to engage in digital activism (Wilson & Hayhurst, 2009), consenting digital sexual expression (Koskela, 2006), and manage discreditable stigma (Goffman, 1963). Individualistic privacy mindsets also blinds against concern over corporate surveillance and consumerism (e.g., targeted advertising; Marx & Steeves, 2010; Steeves, 2012).

The "nothing to hide" mindset also reinforces the idea that those peers who are concerned for privacy may well be engaging in illicit activities (O'Reilly, Karim, Taylor, & Dogra, 2011; Solove, 2007); that is, the mindset reinforces divisions among teens and likely generates pressure among early adopters of this mindset to follow suit. Here too school initiatives can center on building a sense of community and mutual empathy among younger as well as older teens to help ameliorate the divisive impacts of such mindsets. What is fundamentally absent is a sociological imagination regarding the personal trouble of privacy management (Mills, 1959). Framing privacy as a public issue would help teens consider more explicitly the value of social conceptualizations of privacy, linked to mutual respect and shared responsibility.

Future research

Several important areas of exploration are suggested here to extend our knowledge regarding youth and both cyber-risk and societal responses. While this book centers on the experiences of youth, who make numerous references to parents and educators, further research exploring the perspectives, experiences, and attitudes of parents and educators (i.e., teachers, counselors, principals, trustees) is crucial to help provide a more comprehensive view of how cyber-risks are perceived and responded to as well as the potential for more *restorative* responses to online experiences.

Research with parents exploring their own experiences and reactions to cyber-risk and the utility of surveillance, for example, would benefit from a comprehensive sampling of different populations of parents. To what extent are parents relying on "spyware" technology to keep tabs on their children? Are some parents rejecting such practices? What influences parents to use such technologies; is it the influence of other parents, targeted advertisements, or both? Do parenting practices change according to birth order; i.e., do parents treat their first-born child differently than their second, third, etc. in terms of when they are allowed to access technology, the extent they are monitored, and/or surveilled? Are daughters under greater scrutiny than sons? To what extent does age mediate these dynamics? Are experiences of parents who are recent immigrants different from those who are second or third generation, or more established in their country? These questions – and those raised below – are not exhaustive but present important areas for further research.

Through the book, we also highlighted teen experiences with particular teachers and school responses to cyber-risk. Students seemed assured, for instance, that teachers and other educators in their school could monitor their activities in real time. There were also a range of experiences regarding class-room technology policies and practices. Further research exploring "best practices" related to cyber-risk from the perspective of educators would offer significant insights, as there are only a handful of studies in this area (e.g., Fisk, 2016; Livingstone & Sefton-Green, 2016). We were told by our participants that programs and talks offered in schools are focused on female students, with the implication that male students "get a pass" for sexting or cyberbullying. To what extent is this the experience of educators? Are there official policies governing technology in the classroom, and policies in place regarding the types of programming offered to teens? Both authors, during their visits to schools to conduct focus groups, and during dissemination activities with participating schools, were informed of 'incidents' going on at the time, including serious threats involving police response and non-consensual distribution of nudes. That cyber-risks are ongoing and persistent problems in the school raise questions about how schools are responding given the atemporal and placeless nature of cyberspace.

This leads us to suggest a further area for research involving schools: the potential of restorative justice to combat cyber-risk. While the literature on the connections between cyberbullying and offline bullying is voluminous (e.g., Hinduja & Patchin, 2014; Li, 2007), there are relatively few peer reviewed publications exploring the connections between restorative justice and cyberbullying (e.g., Duncan, 2015). Unlike the formal criminal justice system which rests on a "zero sum game" adversarial model of justice, restorative justice is an alternative system based on notions of restitution (Bazemore,

2001; Braithwaite, 2002; Dignan, 2004). At heart restorative justice involves a direct encounter between victims and offenders of crime, with the aim that the offender considers in a deep sense (opposed to the shallow iteration of responsibility proffered through formal criminal justice responses) their impact not only on the victim, but the wider community, and is therefore shamed, but in a way that reintegrates them back into inclusive social networks (Bazemore, 1998; Bazemore, Dicker, & Nyhan, 1994; Braithwaite, 1989).

Although the connections between cyberbullying and restorative justice remain a new area, Coburn and her colleagues (2015) suggest that "the use of quality circles in schools has been shown to encourage youth to share their cyberbullying experiences" insofar as such "circles" or conferences help to establish "a safe environment for young people might help encourage disclosure of serious issues" (573; see also Paul, Smith, & Blumberg, 2012). At first restorative justice may not seem appropriate to address transgressions in cyberspace, given the often-anonymous encounters and low possibility of securing a "victim-offender mediation" offline. Needless to say, even if securing the participation of a "cyberbully" were possible, effective mediations are not likely to occur over web-based communications applications like Skype. However, as we have demonstrated in this book, the more serious cases of cyber-risk are often those linked back to offline peer groups in school. These are often not as anonymous as media-reported stories often suggest. There are many challenges here, such as securing participation, and having parties involved recognize their responsibility. Yet given the gendered aspects impacting experiences of teens with cyber-risk, restorative justice sessions have the potential to instill a greater sense of responsibility for both victims and victimizers (and moreover, the processes through which victimization may lead to offending behaviors). To what extent is restorative justice being used to address cyberbullying in schools? What are the challenged involved, or at least perceptions of its potential? Where it has been tried, is there evidence of success in terms of victim satisfaction and victimizer responsibility, as well as evidence of desistance or efforts to desist from illicit behavior?

Such questions are also highly pertinent for male students. While our sample includes male teens whose discussions helped raise questions about whether males are experiencing cyber-risks the same way (e.g., with cyberbullying but especially with regards to sexting and "dick pics"), further research should unpack in more detail. In particular, we would ask what motivates males to send "dick pics" versus females to send "nudes." Are there different motivations when sending to a partner in a "consensual" relationship versus a wider array of random recipients? What emotions are experienced after sending such images, especially after the responses they receive? Are there (gendered) pressures from other peers acting to help perpetuate such behaviors? Questions regarding effects of age also complement those of gender. To what extent is the "aging out" of cyber-risk we have illustrated in this book a fundamental experience of growing up today?

Relatedly, to what extent is the "nothing to hide" privacy mindset ubiquitous among older teens? Is this mindset – evidently, an internalization of a wider neoliberal ethos of self-management, prudentialism, and responsibility (Rose, 1996) – evident also for younger teens? At what point does it become salient, under what influences, and what are the processes affecting its internalization or possible rejection? Are "tweens" and younger children growing up today more adept at navigating the social media landscape than older "millennial" teens, or less so? What are the influences on their dispositions? Finally, further rural and urban comparisons would offer significant advances in knowledge, helping to tease out environmental factors and help better fashion policies and practices geared to teens growing up in these different settings.

The "nothing to hide" and "privacy in your hands" mindsets may be linked to a "broader ethos of individualism" which James (2014: 37) found "prevalent in American culture" alongside associated discourses of self-responsibilization. Our discussions with teens find evidence for the salience of this mindset among Canadian teens as well. A recent study of attitudes toward privacy in Estonia (Murumaa-Mengel, Laas-Mikko, & Pruulmann-Vengerfeldt, 2015) found the majority of participants express fatalistic attitudes – i.e., expressing they have no control over data collected from governments and corporations, especially information collected over mobile phones and tablets. Moreover, the "nothing to hide" argument was most salient among adults 25–34 years of age and older respondents aged 65–74 (the sample of 1,000 Estonians ranged in age from 15 to 74). Although sociocultural context certainly bears an impact – the authors suggest this may be due to Estonia's totalitarian history where private life was annexed by the state – further cross-cultural research would help to unpack cultural influence on attitudes towards privacy. It may well be that the "nothing to hide" mindset is a coping strategy in response to neoliberal influences; one impacting societies on a more global scale.

As with much qualitative research, the insights gained from a focused exploration of lived experiences and attitudes undercuts complementary knowledge regarding the extent and severity of the cyber-risks explored in this book, i.e., from representative and statistically significant samples. Our focus groups revealed that wider and more inclusive concepts such as relational aggression may be better suited in quantitative surveys to capture etiological factors. In addition, mixed method studies which include both quantitative and qualitative components, or mixing various qualitative approaches, is warranted. Livingstone's (2009, 2016) research, for instance, benefits from both interviews and participant observation, helping to tease out potential differences between "what they say" and "what they do." Paralleling this perspective in discussions of study participants, research that focuses on parents *or* educators exclusively may also miss the opportunity to address overlaps between these populations (e.g., parent-teacher associations), as well as ask questions about how educators perceive parents in their efforts to regulate their teens' online lives, and vice versa. Research is needed, in sum, which "triangulates" methods to widen the epistemological impact of generated knowledge.

Finally, further exploration on the effects of legislative responses with the aim of regulating teens' online activities and mitigating risk and harm is warranted. Some have critiqued legal responses to sexting and cyberbullying (e.g., Coburn et al., 2015; Karaian, 2012). Coburn and her colleagues (2015) argue that laws targeting cyberbullying, for instance encouraging students to report experiences of harassment or victimization to authorities, might have the opposite of their intended effect. Students will likely worry about 'snitching' on others and will be *less* likely to seek help. They argue

> it makes sense to develop and implement better conflict resolution strategies to teach youth rather than use punitive measures that may only serve to further alienate those who are likely to have a myriad of social and behavioural problems.... Services that seek to support young people with mental health issues should be increased.
>
> (Coburn *et al.*, 2015: 572, 573)

Such research nicely dovetails with our suggestions of researcher focusing on schools, with questions about the efficacy of certain laws governing education or code of conduct and standards of practice.

While knowledge regarding the cyber-risks youth are facing and effective responses to these risks is increasing, there remains large gaps in our understandings about relevant etiology as well as social processes. Our aim in this book has been to raise awareness that attending to risks simultaneously affects how teens engage positively online, for connection and validation. Ignoring this dialectical relationship risks the amplification of social problems rather than their de-escalation.

Note

1 Notions of "screen time" and the associated restrictions in how much time youth, particularly children, are permitted to spend on their "screens" are frequent points of discussion and commentary in contemporary society. Such discussions, however are less pronounced among our sample, which is likely because our participants are teens rather than children.

References

Abbasi, S., & Manawar, M. (2011). Multi-dimensional challenges facing digital youth and their consequences. *Cybersecurity Summit (WCS), 2011 Second Worldwide* (pp. 1–5): IEEE. Retrieved from https://ieeexplore.ieee.org/iel5/5963768/5978775/05978784.pdf.

Aboujaoude, E. (2010). Problematic Internet use: An overview. *World Psychiatry, 9*(2), 85–90.

Anderson, M. (January 2016). *Parents, teens and digital monitoring.* Pew Research Center. Retrieved from www.pewinternet.org/2016/01/07/parents-teens-and-digital-monitoring/.

Angrove, G. (2015). "She's such a slut!": The sexualized cyberbullying of teen girls and the education law response. In J. Bailey & V. Steeves (Eds.), *eGirls, eCitizens* (pp. 307–336). Ottawa: University of Ottawa Press.

Bailey, J. (2015). A perfect storm: How the online environment, social norms, and law shape girls' lives. In J. Bailey & V. Steeves (Eds.), *eGirls, eCitizens* (pp. 22–46). Ottawa: University of Ottawa Press.

Bailey, J., & Steeves, V. (2013). Will the real digital girl please stand up? Examining the gap between policy dialogue and girls' accounts of their digital existence. In J. M. Wise & H. Koskela (Eds.), *New Visualities, New Technologies: The New Ecstasy of Communication* (pp. 41–66). Farnham, Surrey: Ashgate.

Bailey, J., & Steeves, V. (2015a). Introduction: Cyber-Utopia? Getting beyond the binary notion of technology as good or bad for girls. In J. Bailey & V. Steeves (Eds.), *eGirls, eCitizens* (pp. 1–17). Ottawa: University of Ottawa Press.

Bailey, J., & Steeves, V. (Eds.). (2015b). *eGirls, eCitizens.* Ottawa: University of Ottawa Press.

Bannon, S., McGlynn, T., McKenzie, K., & Quayle, E. (2015). The positive role of Internet use for young people with additional support needs: Identity and connectedness. *Computers in Human Behavior,* (53), 504–514.

Bazemore, G. (1998). Restorative justice and earned redemption: Communities, victims, and offender reintegration. *The American Behavioral Scientist, 41*(6), 768–813.

Bazemore, G. (2001). Young people, trouble, and crime: restorative justice as a normative theory of informal social control and social support. *Youth & Society, 33*(2), 199–226.

Bazemore, G., Dicker, T., & Nyhan, R. (1994). Juvenile justice reform and the difference it makes: An exploratory study of the impact of policy change on detention worker attitudes. *Crime & Delinquency, 40*(1), 37–53.

boyd, d. (2014). *It's Complicated: The Social Lives of Networked Teens.* London: Yale University Press.

boyd, d., & Hargittai, E. (2010). Facebook privacy settings: Who cares? *First Monday, 15*(8). Retrieved from http://firstmonday.org/htbin/cgiwrap/bin/ojs/index.php/fm/article/viewArticle/3086/2589. (accessed November 2014).

Braithwaite, J. (1989). *Crime, Shame and Reintegration.* Cambridge: Cambridge University Press.

Braithwaite, J. (2002). *Restorative Justice & Responsive Regulation.* Oxford: Oxford University Press.

Burkell, J., & Saginur, M. (2015). "She's just a small town girl, living in an online world": Differences and similarities between urban and rural girls' use of and views about online social networking. In J. Bailey & V. Steeves (Eds.), *eGirls, eCitizens* (pp. 129–152). Ottawa: University of Ottawa Press.

Calvert, C. (2000). *Voyeur Nation: Media, Privacy, and Peering in Modern Culture.* Boulder: Westview Press.

Cannataci, J. A. (2015). *The Individual and Privacy.* Farnham, UK: Ashgate Publishing Limited.

Cassell, J., & Cramer, M. (2008). High tech or high risk: Moral panics about girls online. In T. McPherson (Ed.), *Digital Youth, Innovation, and the Unexpected* (pp. 53–76). Cambridge, MA: The MIT Press.

Chahal, H., Fung, C., Kuhle, S., & Veugelers, P. J. (2013). Availability and night-time use of electronic entertainment and communication devices are associated with short sleep duration and obesity among Canadian children. *Pediatric obesity, 8*(1), 42–51.

Cheung, L., & Wong, W. (2011). The effects of insomnia and internet addiction on depression in Hong Kong Chinese adolescents: An exploratory cross-sectional analysis. *Journal of Sleep Research, 20*(2), 311–317.

Christie, N. (2004). *A Suitable Amount of Crime.* London: Routledge.

Christie, N. (2017 [1993]). *Crime Control as Industry: Towards Gulags, Western Style.* London: Routledge.

Coburn, P., Connolly, D., & Roesch, R. (2015). Cyberbullying: Is federal criminal legislation the solution? *Canadian Journal of Criminology and Criminal Justice, 57*(4), 566–579.

Connell, R. (2005). *Masculinities (2nd Ed.).* Berkeley, CA: University of California Press.

Connell, R., & Messerschmidt, J. (2005). Hegemonic masculinity: Rethinking the concept. *Gender & Society, 19*(6), 829–859.

Corfu, N. (April 15, 2017). With no law to stop them, some cyberbullies resume their old ways. *CBC News.* Retrieved from www.cbc.ca/news/canada/nova-scotia/cyberbullying-legislation-cyber-safety-act-cyberscan-unit-roger-merrick-1.4084409.

Cornish, D., & Clarke, R. V. (1987). Understanding crime displacement: An application of rational choice theory. *Criminology, 25*(4), 933–948.

Coyne, S., Linder, J., Nelson, D., & Gentile, D. (2012). "Frenemies, fraitors, and mean-em-aitors": Priming effects of viewing physical and relational aggression in the media on women. *Aggressive Behavior, 38*(2), 141–149.

Crossman, G. (2008). Nothing to hide, nothing to fear? *International Review of Law, Computers & Technology, 22*(1–2), 115–118.

Davis, K. (2013). Young people's digital lives: The impact of interpersonal relationships and digital media use on adolescents' sense of identity. *Computers in Human Behavior, 29*(6), 2281–2293.

Dignan, J. (2004). *Understanding Victims and Restorative Justice.* Maidenhead, UK: Open University Press.

Duncan, S. (2015). Cyberbulling and restorative justice. In R. Navarro, S. Yubero, & E. Larranaga (Eds.), *Cyberbullying Across the Globe: Gender, Family and Mental Health* (pp. 239–257). Switzerland: Springer.

Ellison, N., Steinfield, C., & Lampe, C. (2007). The benefits of Facebook "friends": Social capital and college students' use of online social network sites. *Journal of Computer-Mediated Communication, 12*(4), 1143–1168.

Englander, E. (June 2012a). *Digital self-harm: Frequency, type, motivations, and outcomes.* Bridgewater, MA: Massachusetts Agression Reduction Center.

Englander, E. (2012b). *Low risk associated with most teenage sexting: A study of 617 18-year-olds. MARC Research Reports Paper 6.* Bridgewater, MA: Massachusetts Agression Reduction Center.

Fisk, N. (2016). *Framing Internet Safety: The Governance of Youth Online.* Cambridge: The MIT Press.

Gillis, W. (April 12, 2013). Rehtaeh Parsons: A family's tragedy and a town's shame. *The Toronto Star*. Retrieved from www.thestar.com/news/canada/2013/04/12/rehtaeh_parsons_a_familys_tragedy_and_a_towns_shame.html.

Goffman, E. (1963). *Stigma*. New Jersey: Prentice-Hall.

Goode, E., & Ben-Yehuda, N. (2009). *Moral Panics: The Social Construction of Deviance (2nd Ed.)*. Malden: Wiley-Blackwell.

Hasinoff, A. (2012). Sexting as media production: Rethinking social media and sexuality. *New Media & Society, 15*(4), 449–465.

Hinduja, S., & Patchin, J. (2014). *Bullying Beyond the Schoolyard: Preventing and Responding to Cyberbullying (2nd Ed.)*. Thousand Oaks, CA: Corwin.

Hope, A. (2005). Panopticism, play and the resistance of surveillance: Case studies of the observation of student Internet use in UK schools. *British Journal of Sociology of Education, 26*(3), 359–373.

James, C. (2014). *Disconnected: Youth, New Media, and the Ethics Gap*. Cambridge: The MIT Press.

Jenkins, H. (2006). *Fans, Bloggers, and Gamers: Exploring Participatory Culture*. New York: New York University Press.

Johnson, M. (2015). Digital literacy and digital citizenship: Approaches to girls' online experiences. In J. Bailey & V. Steeves (Eds.), *eGirls, eCitizens* (pp. 339–360). Ottawa: University of Ottawa Press.

Karaian, L. (2012). Lolita speaks: 'Sexting', teenage girls and the law. *Crime Media Culture, 8*(1), 57–73.

Karaian, L. (2014). Policing 'sexting': Responsibilization, respectability and sexual subjectivity in child protection/crime prevention responses to teenagers' digital sexual expression. *Theoretical Criminology, 18*(3), 282–299.

Kerr, M., & Stattin, H. (2000). What parents know, how they know it, and several forms of adolescent adjustment: Further support for a reinterpretation of monitoring. *Developmental Psychology, 36*(3), 366–380.

Kim, Y., Park, J. Y., Kim, S. B., Jung, I.-K., Lim, Y. S., & Kim, J.-H. (2010). The effects of Internet addiction on the lifestyle and dietary behavior of Korean adolescents. *Nutrition Research and Practice, 4*(1), 51–57.

Ko, C.-H., Yen, J.-Y., Liu, S.-C., Huang, C.-F., & Yen, C.-F. (2009). The associations between aggressive behaviors and Internet addiction and online activities in adolescents. *Journal of Adolescent Health, 44*(6), 598–605.

Koskela, H. (2004). Webcams, TV shows and mobile phones: Empowering exhibitionism. *Surveillance & Society, 2*(2/3), 199–215.

Koskela, H. (2006). 'The other side of surveillance': Webcams, power and agency. In D. Lyon (Ed.), *Theorizing Surveillance: The Panopticon and Beyond* (pp. 163–181). Collumpton, UK: Willan Publishing.

Law, D., Shapka, J., Domene, J., & Gagné, M. (2012). Are cyberbullies really bullies? An investigation of reactive and proactive online aggression. *Computers in Human Behavior, 28*, 664–672.

Lenhart, A., & Madden, M. (2007). *Teens, privacy & online social networks: How teens manage their online identities and personal information in the age of MySpace*. Washington, DC: PEW Internet and American Life Project.

Lenhart, A., Madden, M., Smith, A., Purcell, K., Zickuhr, K., & Rainie, L. (November 2011). *Teens, kindness and cruelty on social network sites: How American teens navigate the new world of "digital citizenship"*. Washington, DC: PEW Research

Center. Retrieved from www.pewinternet.org/2011/11/09/teens-kindness-and-cruelty-on-social-network-sites/.

Li, Q. (2007). New bottle but old wine: A research of cyberbullying in schools. *Computers in Human Behavior, 23*, 1777–1791.

Livingstone, S. (2008). Taking risky opportunities in youthful content creation: Teenagers' use of social networking sites for intimacy, privacy and self-expression. *New Media & Society, 10*(3), 393–411.

Livingstone, S. (2009). *Children and the Internet: Great Expectations, Challenging Realities*. Malden, MA: Polity Press.

Livingstone, S., & Sefton-Green, J. (2016). *The Class: Living and Learning in the Digital Age*. New York: New York University Press.

Marchant, A., Hawton, K., Stewart, A., Montgomery, P., Singaravelu, V., Lloyd, K., … & John, A. (2017). A systematic review of the relationship between internet use, self-harm and suicidal behaviour in young people: The good, the bad and the unknown. *PLoS One, 12*(8). Retrieved from https://doi.org/10.1371/journal.pone.0181722. (Accessed December 2017).

Marker, B. (2011). *Sexting as Moral Panic: An Exploratory Study into the Media's Construction of Sexting*. (Masters of Science), Eastern Kentucky University, Richmond, Kentucky.

Marwick, A., & boyd, d. (2014). 'It's just drama': Teen perspectives on conflict and aggression in a networked era. *Journal of Youth Studies, 17*(9), 1187–1204.

Marx, G., & Steeves, V. (2010). From the beginning: Children as subjects and agents of surveillance. *Surveillance & Society, 7*(3/4), 192–230.

Messerschmidt, J. (2012). Engendering gendered knowledge: Assessing the academic appropriation of hegemonic masculinity. *Men and Masculinities, 15*(1), 56–76.

Milford, T. (2015). Revisiting cyberfeminism: Theory as a tool for understanding young women's experiences. In J. Bailey & V. Steeves (Eds.), *eGirls, eCitizens* (pp. 55–81). Ottawa: University of Ottawa Press.

Mills, C. W. (1959). *The Sociological Imagination*. Harmondsworth: Penguin.

Murumaa-Mengel, M., Laas-Mikko, K., & Pruulmann-Vengerfeldt, P. (2015). "I have nothing to hide". A coping strategy in a risk society. In L. Kramp, N. Carpentier, A. Hepp, I. T. Trivundža, H. Nieminen, R. Kunelius, T. Olsson, E. Sundin, & R. Kilborn (Eds.), *Journalism, Representation and the Public Sphere* (pp. 195–207). Bremen: edition lumière.

Nau, J. (2014). *"Why Protest? I've Got Nothing to Hide." Collective Action Against and Chilling Effects of Internet Mass Surveillance*. (Master of Arts in Peace and Conflict Studies), University of Kent, Marburg.

Oh, H. J., Ozkaya, E., & LaRose, R. (2014). How does online social networking enhance life satisfaction? The relationships among online supportive interaction, affect, perceived social support, sense of community, and life satisfaction. *Computers in Human Behavior, 30*, 69–78.

Olweus, D. (1978). *Aggression in the Schools: Bullies and Whipping Boys*. Oxford, UK: Hemisphere.

Olweus, D. (1993). Victimization by peers: Antecedents and long-term outcomes. In K. Rubin & J. Asendorpf (Eds.), *Social Withdrawal, Inhibition, and Shyness in Childhood* (pp. 315–341). New York: Psychology Press.

Olweus, D. (2012). Cyberbullying: An overrated phenomenon? *European Journal of Developmental Psychology, 9*(5), 520–538.

O'Reilly, M., Karim, K., Taylor, H., & Dogra, N. (2011). Parent and child views on anonymity: "I've got nothing to hide."' *International Journal of Social Research Methodology, 15*(3), 211–223.

Paul, S., Smith, P., & Blumberg, H. (2012). Revisiting cyberbullying in schools using the quality circle approach. *School Psychology International, 33*(5), 492–504.

Pedersen, S. (2013). UK young adults' safety awareness online – is it a "girl thing"? *Journal of Youth Studies, 16*(3), 404–419.

Putnam, R. (2000). *Bowling Alone: The Collapse and Revival of American Community.* New York: Simon and Schuster.

Racz, S., & McMahon, R. (2011). The relationship between parental knowledge and monitoring and child and adolescent conduct problems: A 10-year update. *Clinical Child and Family Psychology Review, 14*(4), 377–398.

Rentschler, C. (2014). Rape culture and the feminist politics of social media. *Girlhood Studies, 7*(1), 65–82.

Ringrose, J., & Barajas, K. (2011). Gendered risks and opportunities? Exploring teen girls' digitized sexual identities in postfeminist media contexts. *International Journal of Media and Cultural Politics, 7*(2), 121–138.

Ringrose, J., Gill, R., Livingstone, S., & Harvey, L. (2012). *Qualitative study of children, young people and "sexting": A report prepared for the NSPCC* London: National Society for the Prevention of Cruelty to Children.

Ringrose, J., Harvey, L., Gill, R., & Livingstone, S. (2013). Teen girls, sexual double standards and "sexting": Gendered value in digital image exchange. *Feminist Theory, 14*(3), 305–323.

Roberts, J., Stalans, L., Indermaur, D., & Hough, M. (2003). *Penal Populism and Public Opinion: Lessons from Five Countries.* Oxford, New York: Oxford University Press.

Rose, N. (1996). The death of the social? Re-figuring the territory of government. *Economy and Society, 25*(3), 327–356.

Ruskin, B. (December 11, 2015). Court strikes down anti-cyberbullying law created after Rehtaeh Parsons's death. *CBC News.* Retrieved from www.cbc.ca/news/canada/nova-scotia/cyberbullying-law-struck-down-1.3360612.

Shariff, S., & DeMartini, A. (2015). Defining the legal lines: eGirls and intimate images. In J. Bailey & V. Steeves (Eds.), *eGirls, eCitizens* (pp. 281–305). Ottawa: University of Ottawa Press.

Shin, W., Schriner, M., & Cho, S. (2009). *Teen online privacy and POS (Parent Over Shoulder): Effects of parental mediation on online teen disclose of personal information.* Paper presented at the International Communication Association, Chicago, IL.

Smahel, D., Wright, M., & Cernikova, M. (2015). The impact of digital media on health: Children's perspectives. *International Journal of Public Health, 60*(2), 131–137.

Solove, D. (2007). "I've got nothing to hide" and other misunderstandings of privacy. *San Diego Law Review, 44,* 745–772.

Solove, D. (2011). *Nothing to Hide: The False Tradeoff Between Privacy and Security.* New Haven: Yale University Press.

Stattin, H. (2001). Candid, not monitored, children run less risk of becoming delinquent. *Lakartidningen, 98*(25), 3009–3013.

Stattin, H., & Kerr, M. (2000). Parental monitoring: A reinterpretation. *Child Development, 71*(4), 1072–1085.

Steeves, V. (2010). Online surveillance in Canadian schools. In T. Monahan & R. Torres (Eds.), *Schools Under Surveillance: Cultures of Control in Public Education* (n.p. (Kindle Ed.)). New Brunswick: Rutgers University Press.

Steeves, V. (2012). Hide and seek: Surveillance of young people on the Internet. In D. Lyon, K. Haggerty, & K. Ball (Eds.), *The Routledge Handbook of Surveillance Studies* (pp. 352–359). New York: Routledge.

Steeves, V., Milford, T., & Butts, A. (March 2010). *Summary of research on youth online privacy*. Ottawa: Office of the Privacy Commissioner of Canada.

Steeves, V., & Webster, C. (2008). Closing the barn door: The effect of parental supervision on canadian children's online privacy. *Bulletin of Science, Technology & Society, 28*(1), 4–19.

Thurlow, C., & Bell, K. (2009). Against technologization: Young people's new media discourse as creative cultural practice. *Journal of Computer-Mediated Communication, 14*(4), 1038–1049.

Tufekci, Z. (2008). Can you see me now? Audience and disclosure regulation in online social network sites. *Bulletin of Science, Technology & Society, 28*(1), 20–36.

Turkle, S. (2017). *Alone Together: Why We Expect More from Technology and Less From Each Other (2nd Ed.)*. New York: Basic Books.

Valkenburg, P., Peter, J., & Schouten, A. (2006). Friend networking sites and their relationship to adolescents' well-being and social self-esteem. *CyberPsychology & Behavior, 9*(5), 584–590.

West, C., & Zimmerman, D. (1987). Doing gender. *Gender & Society, 1*(2), 125–151.

Wilson, B., & Hayhurst, L. (2009). Digital activism: Neoliberalism, the Internet, and sport for youth development. *Sociology of Sport Journal, 26*(1), 155–181.

Youn, S. (2005). Teenagers' perceptions of online privacy and coping behaviors: A risk–benefit appraisal approach. *Journal of Broadcasting & Electronic Media, 49*(1), 86–110.

Index

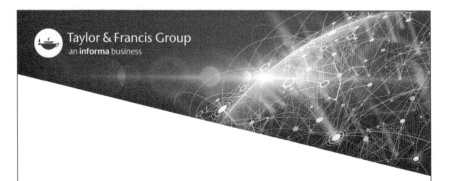